SHIVAJI THE FOUNDER

OF

MARATHA SWARAJ

SHIVAJI THE FOUNDER

OF

MARATHA SWARAJ

C. V. VAIDYA

GYAN

Published by

Gyan Publishing House
5, Ansari Road
Daryaganj, New Delhi-110002
Phone: 011-47034999, 9811692060
E-mail: books@gyanbooks.com

Distribution Network
gyanbooks.com
India, USA, Canada, UK, Australia

ISBN: 978-93-6780-179-6 (HB)

First Published, 1931

2nd Impression 2024

Printed at: Gyan Press, Delhi.

SHIVAJI THE FOUNDER OF MARATHA SWARAJ
Author: C.V. VAIDYA

B. I. S. M. Puraskrita Grantha Mālā, No. 26

SHIVAJI THE FOUNDER
OF
MARATHA SWARAJ

BY

C. V. VAIDYA, M. A., LL. B.

Honorary Fellow, University of Bombay,
Vice-Chancellor, Tilak University,
President, Bharat-Itihasa-Shamshodhak Mandal, Poona.

POONA

1931

INSCRIBED WITH PERMISSION

TO

SHRI. BHAWANRAO SHINIVASRAO

ALIAS

BALASAHEB PANT PRATINIDHI, B.A.,

Chief of Aundh

In respectful appreciation of his deep study of Maratha history and his ardent admiration of Shivaji Maharaj,

THE FOUNDER OF

MARATHA SWARAJ

PREFACE

The records in Maharashtra and other places bearing on Shivaji's life are still being searched out and collected in the Shiva-Charitra-Karyalaya founded by the Bharata-Itihasa-Samshodhak Mandal of Poona and important papers bearing on Shivaji's doings are being discovered from day to day. It is, therefore, not yet time, according to many, to write an authentic life of this great hero of Maharashtra and I hesitated for some time to undertake this work suggested to me by Shrimant Balasaheb Pant Pratinidhi, Chief of Aundh. I have now, however, accepted this suggestion, as the materials already discovered are plentiful enough and throw new light on many incidents in Shivaji's life. They deserve to be described afresh with the help of this new light and many wrong ideas about Shivaji require to be corrected or eradicated at once.

First among these new records of Shivaji is the *Shiva-Bharata*, a poetical life of Shivaji, written by Paramanand, his court-poet and by his order. Though a poem, especially one called Bharata, exaggerates many things, there are some facts which can never be exaggerated or invented. Thus *Shiva-Bharata* may exaggerate the beauty of Shivaji's mother or the prowess of Shivaji in battle. But it cannot invent a new date or a new name or even a new incident. Especially we may bear in mind that Paramanand was a contemporary poet writing at Shivaji's suggestion and had thus at command the assistance of reliable papers and persons. Those who seek to minimise the value of this work because it is a poem are really mistaken in their view and may be said to be inexpert in the appreciation of evidence. And when they compare it to Prithviraj-Rasa for this view, they forget that the latter poem is of little historical value, not because it is a poem, but because it was written 300 years after Prithviraj, when people had forgotten many facts about him and had necessarily to invent them to fill up gaps. They should rather compare *Shiva-Bharata* with Prithviraj-Vijaya, a poem composed in his time and by his order. It has been corroborated by many inscriptions recently found (as shown in my History of Mediæval Hindu India, Vol. III). Indeed like the former only a portion of this poem has been found and probably like it again it was half-finished by the poet himself.

The next material to be noticed is a heap of papers found in recent research such as letters, sanads, kaifiyats, mahjars (testimonials of persons present in court at the settlement of a dispute), etc. All this material hitherto found by Rajawade, Parasnis, Deva and other researchers has been collected and printed according to sequence of dates in a volume specially prepared and published by the Shiva-Charitra-Karyalaya called "Shivakalin-Patra-Sara-Sangraha."

Thirdly, we have the correspondence from English, Dutch, French and Portuguese settlements in India at the time, published already under their respective authority. Extracts from English letters referring to Shivaji have been put together and published by the Mandal in a separate volume (called English Records of Shivaji).

Of other papers, Jedhe S'akavali, which is a list of events by dates prepared in the family of Jedhes who were co-workers of Shivaji, is particularly important.

Finally, Mahomedan writings of the time have also been collected by the Shiva-Charitra-Karyalaya and extracts from them have been published, especially from Muhammadnama.

It goes without saying that statements in all these documents made by friends, foes and foreigners have to be tested in the crucible of probability and trustworthiness. The temptation to exaggerate or falsify is natural to many writers, as also the desire to record mere hearsay. But events, dates or names cannot be questioned when noted by contemporary writers. And generally the rule may be followed that when two documents contradict each other, the older document may be trusted for facts though not for motives or opinions. An attempt has been made in the following pages to give a detailed and connected account of Shivaji's life from these sources, as tested by these rules. Assistance has been taken from papers written on successive topics in Shivaji's life by noted persons and collected in a volume called "Shiva-Charitra-Nibandhavali." But on many points I have taken my own view of the matter.

It may lastly be noted that this life, though written by a Maratha and an admirer, tries to keep the balance of a judge's mind in apportioning blame or praise. I hold that a life should be written by an admirer and a countryman, who naturally takes a favourable view of his hero's motives, wherever possible. But I also hold that in ascertaining facts and in judging of moral and political justifications, the writer must maintain an impartial attitude. How far I have succeeded in this direction, I leave it to my readers to judge.

My thanks are due to Shrimant Balasaheb Pant Pratinidhi, Chief of Aundh, for strongly suggesting to me the writing of this book. Shrimant Balasaheb is a careful student of Maratha history and an ardent admirer of Shivaji. But for his encouragment this book could not have been written and consequently has been dedicated to him. He has been kind enough to supply the pictures inserted in this book. My thanks are also due to Sardar K. C. Mehendale for going over the book while in press and for suggesting corrections and additions where necessary.

Poona,
September 1931. } C. V. Vaidya.

ABBREVIATIONS

PS = Patrasarasangraha.
J = Jedhe S'akavali.
S = Sabhasad.
SB = Shiva-Bharata.
SNS = S'ukranītisāra.
ER = English Records on Shivaji.

TABLE OF CONTENTS

APPENDIX

SHIVAJI THE FOUNDER OF MARATHA SWARAJ.

Shivaji.

From an old painting in the British Museum, before 1707.

SHIVAJI THE FOUNDER
OF
MARATHA SWARAJ

INTRODUCTION

The greatest figure in the modern history of India is undoubtedly that of Shivaji, the founder of Maratha independence in the seventeenth century. Indeed he may be said to rank high among the highest men in the history of the world, both ancient and modern. He was, as is generally conceded, an undaunted soldier and a consummate commander like other heroes of the world. But what was more in him and what is not yet recognised is that he was a most virtuous, conscientious and god-fearing soldier and conqueror. Alexander and Cæsar may capture our imagination by their astounding careers of continuous conquest, but they do not strike us by their moral greatness. And they only conquered and enslaved hosts of foreign peoples, a feat which can never be morally defended. The great heroes of the world may be put into four classes. The lowest class is that of those conquerors who, like Alexander, enslave other people. Higher than these are those heroes who, in defence of their country, fight manfully but unsuccessfully like Hannibal or Anangpal. Higher still than these are those who fight in the cause of their country and are successful, like Pratapsinh or Wallace. But highest are those who, like Washington or Garibaldi, by their exploits secure independence to their own people and destroy foreign domination. Shivaji, like these two, delivered his people from the oppression of an alien rule and religion and he may be put on a par with these two unquestionably great men. But he seems to be greater than even these men, when we bear in mind that he had to fight against two powerful empires and with means neither sufficient nor efficient, at least in the beginning. The Americans and the Italians were as strong and civilized as the English and the Austrians who oppressed them and were further generally united. Shivaji, on the other hand, had the illiterate and unwarlike Mawlas as his soldiers and was opposed by many of his own Maratha compeers. Shivaji's success against the vast armies of Delhi and the large ones of Bijapur, composed of fierce Moguls and Pathans, Siddis and Arabs as also

Rajputs and Marathas, seems almost miraculous. He was thus a hero of whom any nation may be proud and of whom the Marathas and the Hindus generally are justly so.

Shivaji's greatness as a soldier and commander is no doubt accepted by all; but what is not generally conceded is that he was also morally great. He has been misrepresented by his enemies and even by his friends, namely the Bakharkars, so much that we usually hear it said that Shivaji was a murderer and a marauder. Recent research has, however, proved that these calumnies are unfounded and that Shivaji as a conqueror was a highly moral hero. In the following pages will be found a refutation of such charges as being unfounded and disproved from *contemporary* records. Such misconceptions have no doubt recently been cleared. When the Prince of Wales himself laid the foundation of Shivaji's statue at Poona in 1921, he spoke of Shivaji as one of India's greatest soldiers and statesmen, and as the founder of Maratha greatness.[1] The word 'greatness', we think, was used by His Royal Highness in its most extended sense, including also Shivaji's moral greatness. The fact that Shivaji respected the sanctity of mosques and the honour of women is accepted even by his enemies and this alone, in times when temples were constantly demolished

1. *The Times of India*, 21th November, 1921.

and Hindu women violated or carried away as slaves by Mahomedans, would suffice to place him in the rank of the greatest heroes of the world.

The life of Shivaji again is all the more charming by the fact that it is full of wonderful incidents in which he always successfully extricated himself from the dangerous positions into which his enemies placed him, with a resourcefulness and a courage which are unsurpassed in the history of the world and which excited the admiration of even his enemies. Such thrilling incidents as his duel with Afzalkhan, his march in a dark rainy night from the fort of Panhala pursued by the horsemen of Siddhi Johar, his surprising attack on Shaistekhan at midnight in his own camp when surrounded by thousands of soldiers, his escape from confinement at Agra under the very nose of Aurangjeb, his safe return after an incognito travel through Northern India, eluding the vigilance of all the officers of the Mogul empire, and finally his coronation by which he announced the foundation of an independent Maratha kingdom in Maharashtra by anointing and crowning himself as king with the Hindu religious Vedic ceremony of Rajyabhisheka, strike us like almost the incidents of a romance. Neither the most powerful Mogul empire nor the immediately neighbouring kingdom of Bijapur which both had strenuously tried to destroy him, could prevent this ceremony from being performed nor could they nullify it during Shivaji's life by conquering him. It is no wonder that his followers looked upon his life as charmed and as under the protection of Bhavani, the tutelary deity of Shivaji; nay they even looked upon him as an Avatara of Vishnu, as the *Shiva-Bharata* describes in detail.

Powerful centres of activity, physical, mental and moral, are created by the will of God from time to time and in all climes. As Carlyle has said, "Institutions may disappear and kingdoms and nations, but this will always remain, namely the certainty of heroes being sent us and their being worshipped when sent." One of such heroes, indeed, one of the few greatest heroes of the world, was Shivaji by his exploits, his intrepidity, his resourcefulness and undaunted courage in difficult positions, his continuous success and lastly his almost unique moral greatness as respecter of women and of places of religious worship.

We will give in this book a connected account of Shivaji's life and exploits from contemporaneous records, both Indian and foreign, rarely noticing the accounts given in later Bakhars which usually exaggerate events and often invent them in their attempt to show off Shivaji's ingenuity. We will notice controversial or unimportant matters in notes given in small type here and there, which the reader may, if he likes, pass over.

I. SHIVAJI'S ANCESTORS

A high ancestry is not a *sine qua non* of a hero's greatness and it matters little if Maloji, Shivaji's grand-father, was a cultivator or an ordinary 'bargir' (cavalry soldier). But it is now proved beyond doubt (1) that the Bhosale family to which Shivaji belonged was descended from the Sisodia kings of Mewar who are looked upon as of the bluest blood among Rajputs, and (2) that Maloji was the son of a mansabdar. It is usually supposed that this high ancestry was invented for Shivaji by Balaji Avaji Chitnis, when he was crowned as king by Gagabhat with Vedic rites. But we find that this same Rajput descent has been mentioned by Jayaram who, years before Shivaji's coronation, wrote a poem on Shahaji. Therein he says that Shahaji was descended from Dalip born in the family of the Rana who was the foremost among all kings of the earth.[1] This Dalip was, we find, a grandson of Lakshmanasen, Rana of Chitod, who came to the throne in 1303 A. D. (Gaurishankar Ojha). Maloji is given as 15th in descent

1. महीच्या महेन्द्रामधे मुख्य राणा । दलीपास त्याच्या कुळीं जन्म जाणा ॥
तयाच्या कुळीं माल भूपाळ झाला । जळानें जयें शंभु सम्पूर्ण केला ॥

Valipāsa was wrongly read for दलीपास which is the dative of दलीप.

from him and taking 20 years for each generation, we properly find Maloji flourishing about 1600 A.D. in the Deccan. It is not yet ascertained exactly who came first to the Deccan. But the genealogy given by Chitnis says that Devarajaji, son of Bhosaji, came to the Deccan about 1415 A. D. We know that Rajput families came to the Deccan from time to time to seek service under the Mahomedan kings of Bedar, and later of Ahmednagar and Bijapur. Indeed Maharashtra was settled originally by northern Kshatriyas of the Lunar race, Bhojas and Yadavas, in the 7th century B. C. (Bhandarkar); and from that time, northern Kshatriya families constantly came to the Deccan to seek fortune, even founding empires like the Chalukyas from Ayodhya in the sixth century A. D.[1], and the Rathods in the eleventh[2]. The present leading Maratha families in the Deccan claim descent from these, and also from other northern Rajput families, such as the Nimbalkars from Paramaras and the Jadhavas from Yadavas of Dwarka (Hemadri). It is thus not strange that the Bhosale family which came to the Deccan in the 15th century to seek service under Mahomedan kings, claims descent from the Sisodias of Udaipur. It is again possible that the Bhosales came to the Deccan and settled about Verul near Daulatabad, after the Durga Devi famine, which is

1. Our H. M. H. I., Vol. I. 2. See राष्ट्रौढवंशवर्णन-काव्य.

said to have lasted for twelve years from 1392 to 1404 A. D., and they easily got into several vacant Patelships of the district. The nature of the Kshatriyas is to rule[1] and not to cultivate, and we usually find northern Kshatriyas as Patels or Deshmukhs in the Deccan during Mahomedan rule.

These Maratha Kshatriya families were originally treated as on a par with northern families, and we find that marriage relations between them[2] were usual. This intercourse, however, ceased about the 13th century for several reasons, chiefly owing to the splitting up of castes into sub-castes at this time caused by new high notions of purity of blood. Brahmins, we find, also sub-divided about this time into two sections, northern (Pancha Gauda) and southern (Pancha Dravida). The Bhosales who came to the Deccan hereafter naturally contracted marriage relations with the leading Maratha families of the south, such as the Nimbalkars and the Jadhavas. These also constituted their sub-castes by counting 96 Maratha families as of high lineage, imitating the counting of the northern Kshatriya or Rajput families at 36. But this bifurcation did not exist before the 11th century A. D., as we actually find two families among the northern 36, namely the Senas of Bengal and the Gahadval Rathods of

1. दानमीश्वरभावश्च क्षात्रकर्म स्वभावजम् । (गीता).
2. Our H. M. H. I., Vol. III. p. 385.

Kanauj, stating in their inscriptions of that period that they came from the Deccan. On all these considerations, the claim of the Bhosale family that they are descended from Sisodias may be accepted as historically sound. In fact even Mahomedan writers admit this claim when they state that Dalipsing belonged to an illegitimate branch of the Sisodias of Mewad.

The name Bhosale has been explained in two ways. Devraj who came to the Deccan was a son of Bhosaji, and his descendants were called Bhosale, 'la' being a termination in Marathi meaning 'of' e. g. Desala. Others derive the name from Bhose, a village in the Verul district, where the family first settled and Bhosala, like Gokhala, means 'of the Bhose village.' Surnames arise in many ways and it is always difficult to correctly explain surnames.[1]

The oldest list of the 96 Maratha families (c. 1700 A. D.) which we have yet found, gives the name Bhosale, among the 96, as shown in our paper on them[2]. It would have been extremely interesting to know, if a list dating from before the 17th century

1. From enquiry of Pandit Sukhdeo Prasadji, Prime Minister of Udaipur, it appears that "the name Bhosaji does not occur in their genealogical tables nor is it common among Rajputs." It is probable that this name as usual was inserted by pedigree-writers to explain the surname.

2. *Shiv Charitra Nibandhawali*, Vol. 2, p. 52.

had been found, whether that list contains this name so that we could have assured ourselves of the Bhosales being already in the Deccan and included among the Marathas.

The gotra of this family in this oldest list is given as Kaushika, which is different from the gotra (Baijavāpa) of the Sisodias; but it is a maxim adopted in the Deccan, after Mitakshara, that Kshatriyas have no gotras of their own and have to take the gotras of their preceptors. When the Bhosales came to the Deccan and settled as Marathas, they must have chosen new preceptors from among Deccani Brahmins and thus taken the new gotra Kaushika. The present Rajagurus of the Bhosales of Kolhapur and Satara are of a different gotra (S'akalya) which shows that their family was selected as preceptors after Babaji. These new Rajagurus belong to Arvi on the Bhima higher up than Pedgaon, and appear to have been selected by Maloji.[1] Even in Rajaputana, the gotras of the Rajput families differ from those of their preceptors, though the maxim that Kshatriyas have no gotras of their own is accepted even there. It is, therefore, of no consequence that the gotra of the Bhosale family is Kaushika, and this does not prove that the Bhosales are not descended from the Sisodia royal family of Udaipur.

1. The first sanad of the Arvikars is from Maloji and Vithoji (PS 36).

II. BABAJI AND MALOJI

Shiva-Bharata properly enough commences its account of Shivaji with Maloji, his grand-father, the first powerful and prosperous prince of the Bhosale family; but it would be a mistake to suppose that power and prosperity began with him. The Bakharkars omit all mention of everything that happened before Maloji, it being probably forgotten; and they could only account for his fame and riches by supposing a treasure find. Grant Duff, disbelieving the story of the find, surmised that Maloji acquired riches by committing dacoities. Others think that Maloji and his brother Vithoji were poor cultivators and migrated with their wives from Deulgaon, their village, to Verul to seek maintenance. Finding agriculture unremunerative even there, they finally entered the service of Jadhavrao as common 'bargirs' or cavalry soldiers.[1] Recent research has shown that Maloji's father Babaji was a mansabdar and enjoyed the fief of Pande Pedgaon, an important town on the Bhima, now in the Nagar District. Formerly it

1. Both these statements are not correct, as Verul was the original habitat of the Bhosales and as the land about Verul is very fertile.

was a prosperous place, being on the route to Bedar and Bijapur from Konkan and the Western Ghats. A sanad issued from the court of Babaji Raje, dated December 1597 A. D.[1] shows this. The title 'Raje' was not bestowed on Babaji by any king but was one enjoyed by all Maratha higher families. Indeed the title was used even in the 8th century A. D., as Kumarila remarks in his commentary on the S'abara Bhashya that persons in the Deccan, even though they do not rule any town or country, call themselves Rajas. This title, therefore, was usually taken by Maratha higher families such as Bhosales, Shirkes &c. In Andhra they even now use the word Raju similarly. But the Bhosales were also Rajas or kings for all practical purposes in their fiefs, and Babaji Raje Bhosale was one such feudal lord under Nizamshahi. Strong mansabdars were usually posted on the frontiers of kingdoms and the Bhima was the dividing line between Ahmednagar and Bijapur kingdoms. *Shiva-Bharata* thus properly calls Maloji a king, *i. e.* a feudal lord and adds that he, with many such feudal lords, served the Nizamshah who ruled from Devagiri alias Daulatabad.[2]

1. No. 367 of Rajwade Khand XV, Margashirsha 1519.

2. This was the original capital of Nizamshahi. Ahmednagar was subsequently built by Ahmedshah on the Sina and treated as a second capital, Junnar being too far off from Daulatabad or Devagiri.

One can understand how the Bhosales, who first settled about Daulatabad or Devagiri were subsequently granted mansabs on the Bijapur frontier. We do not know as yet who first got this fief of Pedgaon.[1] But the document above referred to clearly proves that Babaji Raje was in the enjoyment of it in 1597 A. D.. *Shiva-Bharata*, though it does not refer to Babaji, appears to know him, as it states that Maloji first enjoyed a kingdom *inherited* from his ancestors and that when he subsequently got many other fiefs from the Nizamshah, he left it into the hands of his officers.[2]

Maloji and his brother Vithoji served the Nizamshah with distinction and got many 'mokasas' for maintenance of forces, as also many villages and lands in Inam. These were as follows :— (1) The three perganas of Elur (Verul), Derhadi and Kannarad[3] (all in the Nizam state now); Kannarad was given with 'kot' and 'kila' or fort and included Jategau and Vakadi[4]. (2) The towns

1. Pedgaon, now in ruins, is eight miles from Shrigonda, on the Bhima, with Hemadpanti temples of Shiva and Rameshwar. Moguls encamped here long when they fought against the Marathas in the 18th century (Ahmednagar Gazetteer). They even built a fort here which is also in ruins. There is a fine temple still intact, however, on the Bhima which is well worth a visit.

2. SB 1, 70. 3. PS 29, dated 1606 A. D.

4. Rajwade Khand XV, No. 370.

(Kasba) of Lasur pergana Gandapur, Adharsul pergana Ahmedabad and the villages of Porle (ditto), Pimpalvadi pergana Paithan and Gaudagau or Ahmedabad.[1] So far as we have ascertained, Jategaon is in Karmala (Sholapur), and Adharsul is near Yeola. We may be sure that the grantors took care that the mokasas granted should not form a continuous territory.

The position of these fief-holders was practically that of kings, inasmuch as they administered the territory assigned, maintained their own armies and could make grants of lands; but they were not hereditary owners of their fiefs, as fiefs appear constantly to have been resumed and granted to others. We actually find, from record PS 25, dated Kartika of S'. 1527 or Oct. 1605 A. D., that the fief of Pande Pedgaon was then in the enjoyment of Malik Amber.[2] We can thus understand how new deeds of gifts were constantly sought by grantees of lands on the ground that the fief was now in the possession of a new holder. Mansabs or mokasas and jagirs differed, we think, in this that the latter were hereditary and not resumable at will. The mansabdars or feudal lords kept troops of soldiers for service of the state. The state no doubt maintained its own army; but it also relied on

1. Khand XV, No. 371.

2. हल्लीं परगने मजकूर साहेबासी अर्जानी झाले.

the troops of its fief-holders for service when required. This system continued down to the days of the Peshwas.

Babaji Raje Bhosale then was the feudal lord of Pande Pedgaon and the same fief continued for a time in the possession of Maloji. Indeed Maloji was associated with Babaji in its possession, even in 1596 A. D., as a sanad is issued by him[1] in that year. Maloji thus was not a cultivator but a feudal lord from the first and had under his command an army. He afterwards obtained renown as a soldier; and consequently many more and more important mansabs were bestowed upon him. Maloji and his brother Vithoji are styled 'Sarguroh' or leaders of bands ('Guroh' means band) and some places given are described as 'Gurothal' or the head-quarter of a band.[2] Maloji not only thus became more powerful but also more prosperous owing to these fiefs. We may, however, still accept the story of a treasure find; for Maloji, who was deeply religious, built the temple of Ghrishneshvara Mahadeva at Verul (one of the well-known twelve Jyotirlingas in the whole of India)[3] and also excavated and built a tank on the

1. PS 10. 2. As Korle, Khand XV, No. 369.

3. This temple does not now exist; the present temple is said to have been built by Ahilyabai about the end of the 18th century A. D.

top of the Shambhu Mahadeva hill near Satara, another Shiva shrine of fame in Maharashtra. This latter fact is referred to in a document dated 1606 A. D.[1]

The Bhosales were worshippers of Shiva like their ancestors of Udaipur, and Maloji used his riches in building the shrine at his original habitat in Maharashtra, and provided water on the top of the Shambhu Mahadeva hill, as pilgrims were handicapped for want of water there. The story of the treasure find may be accepted, because, among Hindus, it is considered proper that treasure found should be expended on temples and other charitable works. The power of Maloji as a feudal lord was, however, clearly acquired by his bravery, though he already had the nucleus of an army which he had inherited from his father.

Maloji being a mansabdar by birth had properly enough for wife a daughter of the Nimbalkars who were a powerful fief-holder family established at Phaltan. The Nimbalkars are Paramaras and thus Maratha Rajputs of pure blood. Maloji had no son for a long time; and according to the beliefs of his time, he prayed both to his tutelary god Mahadeva and a Mahomedan saint named Shah-sharif. By their blessings, in later life, he got two sons and named them Shahaji and Sharifji

1. PS 35.

respectively, after the saint. Some doubt this origin of these names ; but as it is given in *Shiva-Bharata* itself,[1] we may accept the fact as true.

It is certain that Maloji died about the end of S'. 1528 or the middle of A. D. 1606, as in a sanad of S'ravan, S'. 1529, we have the mention of Maloji as deceased[2] and as subsequent documents mention Vithoji alone.[3] How old he was at the time of his death it is difficult to say. When it is stated that he had no son for a long time, it is not intended to convey, as might be under western social conditions, that he was more than 50. Marathas then married early, even as now, and had children naturally at an early age as compared with western people. It is stated in a letter of Shahaji that his mother Umabai was alive in S.' 1551 or A. D. 1629 and thus she survived her husband for about 23 years at least.[4]

Maloji is said to have been killed in the battle of Indapur fought by the Nizamshahi forces against Bijapur.[5] Indapur was beyond the Bhima and was consequently sometimes claimed by Adilshahi though to the north of Nira.

1. SB 1, 96. 2. मरहूम Khand XV, No. 372.
3. Khand XV, Nos. 375, 377 of S'. 1533.
4. PS 498. 5. SB 2, 5.

III. SHAHAJI

When Maloji was killed in 1606, Shahaji was five years old.[1] The birth of Shahaji, therefore, may be placed in 1601 A. D. He was brought up by his uncle Vithoji, who comforted his brother's widow, though separate, and promised her to bring up her two sons. Shahaji who was a capable boy soon showed signs of vigour and when taken to the Nizamshah (Burhan being then on the throne), he was installed in the fiefs of his father[2]. When Shahaji became major *i. e.* about 16 years old and " when he showed sings of youth on his face, "[3] Jadhavrao gave him his daughter Jija in marriage with great delight. Although we do not know the exact date of this marriage, we may place it in 1617 A. D. It is thus clear from this account of *Shiva-Bharata* that the fantastic story of a promise to Maloji by Jadhavrao on a Rangapanchami day, on seeing the two pretty children play with ochre, to give Shahaji his daughter in marriage, the subsequent refusal of Jadhavrao to carry out the promise on his wife's protest against marrying her daughter to the son of a ' bargir, ' and the disturbance created next by Maloji by throwing

1. SB 2, 1-5. 2. SB 2, 34. 3. SB 2, 39.

a dead pig into a masjid to attract the attention of Nizamshah towards this breach of promise, is all a myth created by the imagination of Bakharkars. The story is absurd on its face in more ways than one. Shahaji, we know, know, was not the son of a common 'bargir' but of a powerful mansabdar. He was the son of the rich Maloji Bhosale and Umabai, daughter of a Nimbalkar, both families being of the bluest blood. Secondly, no Mahomedan king of that time would have brooked the throwing of a dead pig into a masjid, nor would any Hindu of that time, especially of the religious temperament of Maloji, who had got sons through the blessings of a Mahomedan fakir, have committed such a sacrilege. Students of Shivaji's life must now scrap and forget this absurd story.

Vithoji dying some time hereafter, the leadership of the family came naturally to Shahaji, son of the elder Maloji, and he, with his brother Sarfoji and his eight cousins (sons of Vithoji), served the Nizamshah and pleased Malik Amber, the minister, by his bravery and astuteness[1]. He must have been about 18 years old at this time, an age at which almost all Indian princes begin their military career. An unfortunate incident about this time led to enmity between Shahaji and his father-in-law Jadhavrao. While Maratha sardars after

1. SB 3, 1-7.

attending a Durbar of the Nizamshah were departing from the palace, each one trying to crowd out the others, the elephant of a sardar named Khandagale became unruly and trampled some footmen to death. Dattaji, son of Jadhavrao, attacked the elephant. A skirmish thus began between him and Khandagale and the latter was assisted by the sons of Vithoji. A regular duel ensued between Dattaji and Sambhaji, son of Vithoji, in which Dattaji was killed. Lukhji Jadhavrao who had departed already heard the terrible news of his son's death, and, infuriated, returned to attack Sambhaji. Shahaji now went to the help of his cousin Sambhaji and a battle was fought wherein Sambhaji was killed. The Nizamshah himself, on hearing of this scuffle, came out, and, intervening, separated the combatants. Thus began that enmity between Jadhavrao and Shahaji, according to *Shiva-Bharata*, which the Bakharkars have wrongly carried back to the time of Shahaji's marriage with Jijabai.

One result of this scuffle was that Jadhavrao thought that the Nizamshah was unduly in favour of the Bhosales, and he left his service and went over to the Moguls. This desertion was taken advantage of by Adilshah, who invited the Moguls to attack Nizamshahi from the north while he attacked it from the south. A great battle was fought between the two sides at Bhatavadi in 1624 A. D.

Shiva-Bharata gives a detailed description of this battle and mentions by name the many captains in the three armies, namely of Delhi, Bijapur and Ahmednagar. Eventually Malik Amber obtained a signal victory over the two allies, Mulla Mahmad, Sar-Lashkar of Bijapur, being killed and many captains of the Mogul and Bijapur armies being taken prisoners. The Bhosales fought bravely on Malik Amber's side, Sharifji being among the slain in the army of Ahmednagar. This was Shahaji's first brilliant exploit on the battle-field. The battle is referred to in a letter of Pedro, an Italian traveller, dated 1624 October 31st[1], which supports the account of *Shiva-Bharata* and may thus be taken to have been fought some time in the middle of that year.

It is probable that Shahaji got at this time, as reward, the mokasas of Poona and Supa[2], which were beyond the Bhima and which were, as stated before, subjects of frequent conflicts between Ahmednagar and Bijapur. Malik Amber, who, as minister, had kept up the tottering kingdom of

1. PS 217.

2. PS 81 of Feb. 10, 1618 shows Poona in possession of a Mahomedan and PS 82 shows that Patas was in that of Sarjarao. See also PS 85, 87, 93 &c. The word पुण्य in SB 1, 45 means holy and not Poona as the clause ' on the bank of Bhima ' in the next line proves.

Nizamshahi, was favourably disposed towards Shahaji, who was also, it appears, appointed Sar-Lashkar or general in Ahmednagar army.

Shiva-Bharata relates that the sons of Vithoji became hereafter jealous of Shahaji's greatness and began to hate him, as is usual with Hindu cousins. Malik Amber seems to have supported Shahaji's cousins in the quarrel, as the ruling power, also as usual, keeps up disputes in powerful sardars' families. Shahaji was dissatisfied and he retired to Poona where he built a house for himself. From there he was invited by Ibrahim Adilshah to enter his service and Shahaji with his followers became an Adilshahi sardar.[1] This is supported by a document[2] dated 19th December 1625, in which Shahaji is contemptuously described as 'Shahaji Bhosala, Adilshahi'. Another document[3], a sanad dated 28th July, describes him, however, as 'Meherban Shahaji Raje Sarlashkar'. Both these documents relate to the Poona District and show that while in July 1625, Shahaji was a Sarlashkar or commander of forces in Nizamshahi and enjoyed the fief of Poona, in December 1625 he was in Adilshahi service and Poona had been taken away from him.

Shahaji rendered important services to Adilshah by conquering Mudhoji of Phaltan and some

1. SB 5, 9–12. 2. PS 225. 3. PS 222.

refractory chiefs in Karnatic and in Keral[1], He remained in Adilshahi service from about October 1625 to about the end of 1627. From a document[2] dated 10th January 1626, it appears that he was then a Sarlashkar in Adilshahi, and at his request the Adilshah granted the 'desagata' of Talebid and some rights on the fort of Panhala to Sambhaji and Dharoji Mohite. These were probably relatives of Shahaji's second wife who belonged to the Mohite family.

In May 1626 Malik Amber died and about a year or so after[3] Ibrahim Adilshah also died. The former was succeeded by his son Fattehkhan who was favourably disposed towards Shahaji, and the latter by Mahomed Adilshah who was a staunch Shia and an intolerant Mahomedan. About the change of policy the latter initiated we shall speak later ; but Shahaji now thought it safe to leave his service and go to Nizamshah, his old master. He again got his Poona mansab to which was added Patas apparently. It also seems that Nizamshahi was threatened at this time by Shahjahan and Shahaji being called by the Nizamshah thought it proper to join his old master. The Poona pergana with Patas was given him again and he was sent against the advancing Mogul force. Shahaji appears from a sanad issued by him in Poona per-

1. SB 5, 17-18. 2. PS 226. 3. May 1627 (J).

gana, dated 8th March 1628[1], to have come back to Nizamshahi in the beginning of 1628[2] while another sanad is issued by him on August 3, 1628, for Kasba Patas.[3] Shahaji remained in this service till the fall of Nizamshahi in 1636, with the exception of a short interval, when he had gone over to the Moguls, as will be presently related.

1. PS 262.

2. The words in PS 262 हल्ली साहेब ए तर्फेसी एऊनु पा मजकूर कबज केले need not be interpreted to mean that the possession was taken forcibly, as my friend V. G. Apte thinks. There is no mention of the possession being forcible. and " Shahaji came and took possession of the Pergana " may also mean that he came, being authorised by Nizamshah to take possession. We need not, therefore, hold that Shahaji was at this time in the service of Adilshah.

3. PS 275.

IV. BIRTH OF SHIVAJI

In this interval Shivaji was born to Shahaji on Phalgun Vadya 3 S'. 1551, corresponding to 18th February 1630 A. D., on the fort of Shivneri near Junnar. This date of Shivaji's birth was first found mentioned in Jedhe S'akavali by Lokamanya Tilak, who was surprised to find this new date as against that given by Grant Duff on the basis of statements in Bakhars *viz.* [illegible] May, 1627. The new date was, however, subsequently found in the stone inscription at Tanjore recorded in 1803 A. D. *Shiva-Bharata* also gave this new date; and lastly Gaurishankar Ojha found it in a horoscope of Shivaji recorded in the collection of horoscopes made by Shivram Jyotishi in Jaipur state about 1688. Sabhasad, the oldest Bakharkar of Shivaji, curiously enough, gives no date for the birth of Shivaji. The new date given in four such reliable documents found at such distant places as Poona, Kolhapur, Tanjore and Jaipur may be accepted now as the most probable date of Shivaji's birth for reasons which will appear from the following disquisition.

The birth-place of Shivaji is accepted by all as the fort of Shivneri. The great difficulty before the Bakharkars was to explain how Shivaji came to be born on the Shivneri fort. The account of *Shiva-Bharata* in this connection is simple and believable. Junnar was them under Nizamshahi. The keeper of its fort on the Shivneri hill near it, named Vishvasrao (Vijaya, son of Shidhoji[1]) gave his daughter in marriage to Sambhaji, eldest son of Shahaji; and for that marriage Jijabai went to the fort, though she was advanced in pregnancy, as a son's marriage is the happiest moment in a Maratha wife's life, generally one of continuous service. It was impossible that she would remain at home in Poona. This marriage was easily arranged as Shahaji was then in the service of the Nizamshah. After the marriage, Shahaji went against Daryakhan the Mogul, as stated before, leaving his pregnant wife on the fort for delivery.

As against this probable account, the Bakharkars relate that "Shahaji was fleeing from Mahuli with his pregnant wife, pursued by the Moguls and by Jadhavrao who was then in their service, that Shahaji saying to his wife 'I am pursued by your father' cruelly left her behind, that she was found by Jadhavrao weeping and crying, and that he, for her safety against seizure by Mahomedans, sent her to the fort of Shivneri. There Shivaji was born in May 1627." There are so many absurdities and incongruities of date in this account that it can

1. SB 7, 80.

only be explained on the supposition that the Bakharkars had no idea of either the dates or the sequence of these old events. Thus Shahaji's fleeing from Mahuli, we now know from Mahomedan history, took place in 1636 A.D. and not in 1627 and at that date Jadhavrao had already been murdered as will be related presently. Secondly, Shivneri was not then in the possession either of Jadhavrao or of Shahaji and Jadhavrao could not have sent Jijabai there for protection.

How a wrong date could be given by Bakharkars of such an important event as the birth of Shivaji, it is difficult to explain. Several conjectures have been made and it is suggested that the Bakharkars wrongly caught hold of the horoscope of one of the brothers of Shivaji, he having more than one, as will be stated later on. It is also suggested that astrologers in the days of the Bakharkars *viz.* the 18th century, concocted a horoscope for Shivaji with five planets in their 'uchcha' (ascendant), following the general belief that all heroes have such a conjunction at their birth. Even the poem *Shiva-Bharata* states, following the usual poetical description[1], that five planets were in their ascendant at Shivaji's birth. But the planets were not so in 1630 as we find from calculation, and they were roughly so in 1627. This controversy, there-

१. ततो ग्रहैः पञ्चभिरुच्चसंस्थैः —कालिदास

fore, cannot be finally settled, unless we have evidence of a contemporary character, alluding to the birth-day celebration of Shivaji in a particular year. Such celebrations must have taken place every year, especially after Shivaji's coronation, though some believe that the practice of holding celebrations of birth-days of kings began much later. We must, therefore, meanwhile accept the new date as the most probable one.

We would caution the reader, however, against attaching much importance to this controversy as the difference of age created by the new date is only of two years and nine months, and does not much change the aspect of the several incidents in Shivaji's life. Thus it does not matter whether Shivaji died at the age of 50 or 52 or began his career at the age of 15 or 17.

It is properly believed that the name 'Shivaji' was bestowed on the child because it was born on the Shivneri fort[1] under the protection of its goddess Shivai. The name of the fort is certainly older than Shivaji, and there is still pointed out a fallen house on the hill fort in which Shivaji was born. The temple of Shivai in the side of the hill may have been built subsequently; but the shrine itself, containing the 'Svayambhu' idol is very old.

1. SB 6, 63.

V. THE FALL OF NIZAMSHAHI

We are not concerned here with the exact details of this fall, but we will give a short account of it chiefly from *Shiva-Bharata*. The Nizamshahi kingdom was, no doubt, doomed to extinction before the gradual advance of the Mogul empire under the successive rule of four able emperors. That empire had already eaten up Khandesh and Berar which was one of the five Mahomedan kingdoms born out of the kingdom of Bedar. But the scene of the fall of Nizamshahi at this period is kaleidoscopic in its rapidity and change of colour. When Shahaji rejoined Nizamshahi in 1628, it gained strength for a time under the ministership of Fattehkhan, though he himself was an incapable successor of Malik Amber. Jadhavrao having also returned to Nizamshahi service at this time, Nizamshahi looked strong again. But the king on the throne, Murtiza, was vicious, being addicted to wine,[1] fickle-minded and cruel. When a kingdom is doomed cruel and incapable kings and faithless and corrupt ministers appear on the scene. Hamidkhan, an unprincipled man, acquired ascendancy at this time over Murtiza Nizam and induced him

1. SB 8, 25.

to imprison Fattehkhan for leaning inwardly towards the Moguls. Everyone was suspected as being in the employ of the enemy, especially Jadhavrao who had previously gone over to the Moguls. He was openly insulted one day by the king in Durbar, and he in disgust rose up and left the court. As he was passing through the portico of the palace, he was attacked by the hirelings of Hamidkhan and Jadhavrao and his two sons and one grandson were killed. This happened on 12th August 1630.[1] These murders which took place a few months after Shivaji's birth, sent a thrill throughout the kingdom, having been committed in the palace itself and by the king's order or at least connivance. Shahaji now thought it safe to leave Nizamshahi service ; but he could not go back to Adilshahi which had sent Muraripant to overrun his Poona jagir. Poona city had been plundered and even burnt[2] and the territory annexed to Bijapur, with a new fort called Daulat Mangal, built on the Bhuleshwar hill, treated as headquarters.[3] Shahaji, therefore, went over to the Moguls who received him with open arms and bestowed mansabs upon him and his son Sambhaji. Thus Nizamshahi lost two of its able sardars in 1630 and the Moguls advanced upon it ostensibly to punish it for giving shelter to the Mogul rebel, Khan Jahan

1. S'ravan Purnima, S'. 1552 (J). 2. PS 332. 3. PS 2093.

Lodi. Nature also added its hardships at this time as a dire famine overtook Maharashtra, in consequence of the failure of rains in 1630.

Nizamshahi was thus, at this time, in the clutches of foe and famine. The Nizam was invested in his chief fort of Daulatabad by the army of Shahajahan. Mahomed Adilshah, fearing that the Moguls might soon become his immediate neighbours, sent an army under Randullakhan and Muraripant to relieve the investment and tried to send supplies to Fattehkhan in the fort. The Bijapuris also fought with Mahabatkhan, the Mogul investor of the fort, but were defeated. Fattehkhan eventually surrendered the fort and handed over the Nizamshahi kingdom with all its treasure, its forts and its territory to the Moguls, receiving a jagir for himself. This event happened in June 1632[1]. *Shiva-Bharata* sheds a tear over the fall of the great kingdom which had 80 thousand cavalry, 80 and 4 more forts, a rich country and many powerful sardars who had defeated the armies of the haughty Delhi emperors, with their forces, "suddenly falling on the enemy like eagles".[2] It, however, attempts to explain the fall in a historical manner and states that Fattehkhan was an incapable successor of his great father, that Jadhavrao was murdered by the unscrupulous Hamidkhan and that God punished

1. Jyeshtha S'. 1554 (J). 2. SB 8, 44.

the kingdom for this atrocity with a famine. A graphic description of the famine is given in the poem and this famine is also mentioned in Jedhe S'akavali and in Mahomedan and other accounts.

A few further details of the fall of Nizamshahi may be given from other accounts. On the advance of the Moguls, Fattehkhan was released by Murtiza on 18th January 1631[1], probably under the belief that he would be able to assist the kingdom in its crisis. But he ungratefully murdered the Nizam himself and placed on the throne a scion of the family. He handed over this scion even to the Moguls when he surrendered the fort of Daulatabad; and the Moguls sent the young Nizam to the fort of Gwalior where he subsequently died or was murdered. *Badshahanama* and Orme papers mention Burhan as murdered by Fattehkhan, but this is probably a mistake and it was Murtiza who was murdered by him, as stated in the *Ahmednagar Gazetteer*, p. 397. The name of the prince handed over is given as Hussain by Orme and the date of handing him over as 19 Zehedge or 28th June, 1632.[2] Fattehkhan received a jagir from the Moguls for himself, a part of which consisted of places given by them to Shahaji.

1. Paush Vadya 11, S'. 1552 (J).
2. *Shivaji Nibandhavali*, I, 2. p. 90, 92.

Shahaji now found himself left in the lurch, losing the support of the Moguls on the one side and being already an enemy of Mahomed Adilshah on the other. He did not, however, sink, but boldly struck a new path. He formed the audacious plan of setting up, not a Maratha kingdom for himself, that was not thought feasible yet, but the Nizamshahi itself under a new king. He caught hold of a queen of the Nizamshah and her son and crowned him as king on the Pemgiri fort in September 1632.[1] This fort is built on an isolated hill at the end of a spur from the Baleshwar range.[2] Daulatabad and Nagar being in the hands of the enemy, Shahaji selected this fort properly, being in the centre of the kingdom set up by him. Every kingdom was then in need of a fort for its second capital and place of retirement. The present territory of Nagar and Nasik districts was in his possession at this time, he having been deputed, long before this, by the Moguls themselves to take that part of the country. He found it feasible to set up a new rule in this territory with the help of the many Maratha captains there who were favourably disposed towards him[3], even against two such powerful adversaries as Shahjahan and Mahomed Adilshah who now joined the Moguls

1. Bhadrapada S'. 1554 (J). 2. *Ahmednagar Gazetteer.*
3. SB gives names of these in 9, 5-7

to destroy Shahaji. Shahaji fought with them for three years and his final stand was at Mahuli, a fort in the Konkan below Junnar and Shivneri. But eventually finding the task hopeless, especially as the Nizamshahi Queen was suspected of an intention to go over to the Moguls, he, like Fattehkhan, ended the struggle amicably, by making over the puppet king to the Moguls ; and receiving a jagir for himself, he entered the service of Mahomed Adilshah. The Nizamshahi territory was divided between the two conquerors, the country to the south of the Bhima going to Adilshah. Shahaji retained his jagir of Poona and Supa as a sardar now under the Adilshah. He retained his own 'kingdom', as the *Shiva-Bharata* says, consisting of Poona, Supa and Indapur perganas which were between the Bhima and the Nira, the old boundary of the Bijapur kingdom. Shahaji handed the fort of Mahuli to the Moguls in the beginning of 1636 and finally entered the service of Mahomed Adilshah. J states that "Shahaji went to Mahuli and there he was besieged by Ranadullakhan and Khanjama, Suba of the Moguls. The Moguls took possession of the Nizamshah, and Shahaji Raje became a servant of Adilshah. in S'. 1557. Ranadullakhan had taken with him Kanoji Jedhe and Shahaji met him there."

VI. CHILDHOOD AND EDUCATION

Born in February 1630, Shivaji was six years old when Shahaji took him to Bijapur with his whole family in 1636, on his finally entering the service of Adilshah. These six years Shivaji must have spent at several places such as Shivneri, Junnar, Poona and lastly Mahuli. When he was born, Shahaji was absent on an expedition against Daryakhan. He returned about a year after and had the first sight of his son who was destined to be greater than himself. The usual auspicious ceremonies being performed, Shahaji again went against the Moguls and Shivaji remained on the Shivneri hill, as it was not usual with Maratha captains to take their families with them, when on active operations (a practice subsequently given up by the imperial Peshwas, who imitated the Moguls greatly to their ruin, as experienced on the field of Panipat). It appears that Shahaji's Poona territory had already been returned to him by Adilshah who changed his policy towards Nizamshahi constantly, now fighting against it, now aiding it. It is probable that when Shahaji for a time went over to the Moguls, Shivaji with his mother lived at Poona, and Sambhaji went with his father to

Mahabatkhan, the Mogul general, for getting a mansab for himself. Subsequently, when Shahaji returned to Nizamshahi service and when after the fall of Daulatabad, he set up Nizamshahi anew, Shivaji must have lived at Junnar, Shahaji's head-quarters in 1633.[1] Shahaji lived subsequently at Mahuli, where Shivaji, being then five or six years old, must have marked with his precocious faculties both the greatness and the fall of his father. Hereafter Shivaji must have lived for about two years both at Poona which was now in Shahaji's possession as jagir under Adilshahi and at Bijapur, the capital where every sardar had to pass some portion of his life. When Shahaji subsequently got the jagir of Bangalore and made that important city with its fort his head-quarters, Shivaji with his mother was taken from Poona to Bangalore by Dadaji Konddeo, Shahaji's agent at Poona (Sabhasad). There he lived for about four years *i.e.* from

1. Orme papers mention that during the siege of Daulatabad by the Moguls, the wife and daughter of Shahaji with part of his treasures were betrayed into the hands of Khan Khanan by the treachery of Burkhurdarkhan (S. Ni. 2, 1, p. 72). But there is no confirmation of this in any account. Shivaji was born in 1630 and thus he may have been with his mother in 1633. This report speaks of a daughter only. It must have been a false rumour but it supports the idea that Jijabai must have had a daughter born to her before Shivaji.

his 9th to the 12th, when he was sent to Poona finally as we shall presently relate.

It my be stated here that the story of Shivaji haughtily not making a salam to the Adilshah at Bijapur when taken to his Durbar by Shahaji is unbelievable. Having seen Durbars of the puppet Nizamshah at Mahuli, it is impossible to believe that Shivaji was so ignorant as to behave haughtily or absurdly or was not acute enough to disguise his inner motives, if he had any at that age. The story of his drawing his sword and cutting down a butcher who was slaughtering a cow openly in a street of Bijapur is still more unbelievable. Even in Mahomed Adilshah's time, cows could not have been slaughtered openly in streets, nor could Shivaji have escaped the consequences of such a folly in the capital of a Mahomedan king. Such stories are invented to adorn the tale of a hero's life, as indicating his future activities and we may safely set them aside as unbelievable.

A Hindu child's education begins usually at his sixth year, and we may be sure that at that age Shivaji's education began under good teachers, whether he was at Poona or at Bijapur or at Bangalore. In his childhood, on the various forts, Shivaji made elephants, horses, soldiers and forts of mud, as boys usually do even now in Divali days[1]. Later

1. SB 7, 21-27.

when he was fit to learn he was taught writing in company with the sons of ministers of his age[1]. Shivaji, we may also believe, heard conversations in Sanskrit in the court of Shahaji at Bangalore where, as described by Jayarama, there were many learned pandits with Shahaji and southern pandits usually speak fluently in Sanskrit even now, though the case is different in Maharashtra. We may believe Jayarama when he says that Shahaji took an intelligent part in the poetical disputations which were held before him among the learned pandits of his court. It is thus probable that Shivaji from his ninth to twelth year which were passed at Bangalore, not only learnt reading and writing but also listened to conversations in Sanskrit and got accustomed to its phraseology. This will explain how hereafter he listened intelligently to Mahabharata recited at Poona to his mother and grasped its lessons firmly. It is at least certain that Shivaji knew how to read and write, as is proved by several documents from the English factories themselves.[2] There are even found a few papers which have some words in Shivaji's hand-writing at the end as was usual in state documents of that time. The idea that Shivaji was so illiterate that he could not even sign his name, first started by Duff, is not correct and may hereafter be given up.

1. SB 9, 71, 74.
2. At the end of PS 848, Revington's letter from

(on next page)

VII. INVESTMENT WITH JAGIR AUTHORITY

When Shivaji was 12 years old or had entered on his 12th year[1], he was invested with the powers of a jagirdar by Shahaji and sent to Poona with his mother Jijabai. It may be stated here that Shahaji had six children from Jijabai, only two of whom were then alive, namely Sambhaji and Shivaji. Whether Shivaji was Jijabai's last son cannot be stated as the wording in *Shiva-Bharata* is not clear. It is indeed probable that during the twelve years from Shivaji's birth in 1630 to his being sent to Poona in 1642 A. D., Jijabai might have had children born to her but they all died in infancy. As her last living son, Shivaji must have been her darling and she gladly went to Poona to superintend his education as well as to act as regent during his minority. It is suggested

---

Surat (No. 26, English Records) we have the words " Deliver the letter into his (Shivaji's) own hands; for these Brahmins make letters to speak what they please." No. 60, English Records, is a letter by Gyfford in which he says, " Yesterday arrived a letter from the Rajah written by himself to Raoji." PS 3, 1640 and 1643, which are Surat letters, refer to traeties *signed* by Shivaji.

1. SB 9, 1.

by Bakharkars that Jijabai was disliked by her husband and was hence sent away. But there is nothing whatever to show that she was on bad terms with her husband. Moreover, in no Rajput prince's family do we find wives sent away either owing to being disliked or owing to quarrels between co-wives. Further Jijabai's eldest son Sambhaji who was now about 18 years old and already a captain, was retained by Shahaji at Bangalore. The sending of Jijabai with Shivaji to Poona cannot, therefore, suggest that she was disliked by Shahaji.

Two reasons may be assigned for this action. Shahaji was usually at a great distance from his jagir of Poona, being mostly on active service; and when he was finally settled at Bangalore, he was almost always far away from Poona. Jagir business consequently suffered, though entrusted to an able administrator like Dadaji Konddev. Absentee land-lordism is always troublesome and unprofitable and Dadaji Konddev must have asked for a master present at the head-quarters of the jagir. Document PS 493, dated February 1644, is no doubt issued in the name of Shahaji Raje, but this does not mean necessarily that Shahaji was then in Poona. Applicants might have gone as far as Bangalore to obtain fresh sanads of inam and letters might have been issued from there by Shahaji. Even supposing that the document was issued at Poona by Shahaji himself, we must admit that Shahaji had gone over to Poona from Bangalore with great trouble. To prevent such inconveniencc to both prince and subjects, Shahaji must have thought it proper to transfer the jagir of Poona to his son Shivaji who at twelve years of age must have shown signs of capacity and to keep him at Poona under an affectionate regent and an able guardian. Secondly as Sambhaji was kept with himself at Bangalore, he would not aspire to the Poona jagir, and he might be given that of Bangalore, the more important one of the two, he being his eldest representative. It was thus a kind of partition made by the father during his life-time. Shahaji had no doubt another son by his younger wife (supposed to be his favourite wife); but, as will be seen hereafter, Bangalore was intended by Shahaji to be given to Sambhaji and not to Vyankoji, his step-brother.

The transfer of jagir to Shivaji in the records of Bijapur with its consent must have taken some time and although Shivaji was sent to Poona as jagirdar in 1642, Shahaji continued to issue sanads fill 1644 and perhaps later still. We hence have a sanad issued from Shivaji's court[1] so late as 20th Jan. 1646, bearing the seal 'Pratipachchandrarekheva &c.' used throughout his life. We can

1. PS 510.

explain this document and this seal on the supposition that the Poona jagir now stood in Bijapur records in Shivaji's name. We must note that a jagirdar then was entitled to have a seal, to make grants, to administer territory and to have ministers, the chief of them being called Peshwa. *Shiva-Bharata* properly states that when Shahaji sent Shivaji to Poona, he gave him Amatyas (ministers) and Maulas (hereditary servants) as also elephants, horses, soldiers and birudas (titles, seals etc.), banners and treasure.[1] Thus Shivaji was practically an independent jagirdar under Bijapur with separate ministers, seal, banner etc. at the age of 12. He began to learn work under the supervision of his mother who, as regent, appears herself to hear complaints,[2] and Dadoji Konddev still issued orders on various subjects.[3]

We can thus understand how a Dutch letter from Vengurla, dated April 1660,[4] describing Shivaji's career says, " The late Sultan Mahomed Adilshah has taken into service a captain named Shivaji who was a son of the old Shahaji ... He is revolting against His Majesty for the last 10 or 12 years. "

1. SB 10, 25–26. 2. PS 513 of 2nd April, 1646.
3. *Ibid.* 4. PS 830. Trans. p. 74, S. N. I. 2, I.

NOTE :—Extent and Nature of Shivaji's Fief.

It would be interesting, though somewhat difficult, to determine the extent and nature of the fief which Shivaji got at this initial stage of his life We have several papers which give us information on this subject. Pergana Poona was the centre of this fief; it was in the possession of Shahaji from his early days (1628 A. D.). A pergana had 'tarafs' (sides) and 'karyats' (sub-divisions). Document No. 22, p. 42, Rajawade Khand 18 (PS 2093), is a sanad issued from the court of Shivaji dated S'. 1600 (1678 A. D.). It gives the purport of the application presented by Moro Vithal Honap, Desh-Kulkarni of Karyat Maval as follows :—

" I am the Desh-Kulkarni of pergana Poona for the villages of Taraf Haveli, Sandus, Kare Pathar, Nirthadi, Karyat Maval, Sandas Khurd (small) and Taraf Patas. When Nizamshahi conferred on Maharaja (Shahaji) the said pergana (Poona) and when Maharaja sent havaldars and karkuns to collect revenue, I sent my gumastas to every Taraf; for Karyat Maval, Gupchup was sent as my agent and he rendered accounts and presented papers to me; but on his acting harshly against the ryots, he was removed and Namaji Landa was sent as my gumasta from Poona. When Nizamshahi disappeared (for a time) and when Murar Jagdev, in behalf of Adilshahi, burnt Poona and annexing the pergana founded a new chief town at the foot of Daulat Mangal fort on Bhuleshwar hill, I went to reside there and Namaji worked in Karyat Maval, rendering accounts and presenting papers to me there. When finally Poona was given in mokasa to Maharajasaheb (Shahaji) by Adilshahi (in 1636 A. D.) and when he under him conferred on Saheb (Shivaji) the mokasa of Karyat

Maval and on Mambaji Raje Bhosale (Shahaji's nephew) of Sandas Khurd and when Havaldaras and Karkuns went to Karyat Maval on your (Shivaji's) behalf, Namaji dishonestly represented himself as Desh-Kulkarni and on my complaint, Saheb (Shivaji) ordered the rights of Desh-Kulkarni to be given to me." etc. etc.

It appears from this account that Shahaji had the idea of establishing Shivaji in Poona even from 1636 and that Shahaji's mokasa included the whole of Poona pergana with Patas. We have already stated that when Shahaji finally entered the service of Adilshah, all the territory between the Bhima and the Nira was conferred upon him and thus Indapur and Supa perganas must also have belonged to him ; and these must have been transferred to Shivaji at this time (1644) as jagir. We have the mention of Indapur being under Shivaji in another important paper dated 25th October 1646.[1] This is a sanad issued by Shivaji Raje to Kaji Sajju of Kari confirming his old inam for service in the masjid, "in spite of the fact that he did not take out a sanad when Shivaji obtained the mokasa in San seet (1645) June." This shows that Indapur had also been transferred to Shivaji's name in 1645. Pergana Supa similarly seems to be in Shivaji's possession as shown by document PS 518 which is a sanad issued by Shivaji in 1646 July for Loni in Supa and which mentions that the pergana was granted to Shivaji in San seet. Another document of 1646 clearly speaks of Shivaji being in possession of pergana Supa. PS 556, a sanad issued by Shivaji and dated July 1649, has the words हाली परगने सुपे साहेबास मुकासा अर्जानी जाला. हाली here means simply at present and not in that particular year. The word सनसीत are definite and show that

1. See also PS 520, 521 and 522, dated 30th October 1646.

that pergana was granted in 1645. That Supa and Baramati were in the possession of Shahaji in May 1639 is proved by document PS 453, though in 1636 they seem to be in possession of Kheloji Raje (PS 418). Shahaji must have got this pergana lying between the Bhima and the Nira at the end of 1636 when he got the other perganas in jagir.

The fief of Poona, Supa and Indapur which Shivaji now got was in its nature a jagir though it is spoken of as mokasa in several papers. We must state here that the difference between a jagir and a mokasa was that the former was enjoyed hereditarily for the upkeep of dignity while the latter was given temporarily for administration. If given for maintenance of troops, it was called saranjam. In the interesting petition to Adilshah PS 710 (in which Shahaji says, "We are Rajput"), Shahaji uses both the words jagir and saranjam with respect to territories solicited for maintenance of troops. Shahaji originally got this fief as mokasa and mokasas were resumable; indeed mokasas were constantly resumed. Thus PS 417, dated 25th March 1637, issued by Shahaji to Deshmukhs of Poona has the words " now this pergana has been assigned to Saheb as mokasa," while PS 244, dated 25 July 1628, states the same thing हाली मोकासा etc. and refers to the first acquisition by Shahaji of this pergana from Nizamshahi. Indeed another earlier document, PS 272, dated 17th May 1628, is issued by another authority for Pimpri in Poona and so is PS 246, dated 15th April 1627, issued by still another authority to Moroba Gosawi in the same village Pimpri. The mokasa, however, re-gifted by Adilshah to Shahaji after the fall and division of Nizamshahi was practically a jagir though described in documents as mokasa; for that the same perganas were transferred to Shivaji, son of Shahaji, shows that the mokasa was looked upon as hereditary.

Jagirdars had apparently no judicial powers and there was a subedar of the Prant, appointed by the central government. Suba means a division and subedar, a governor of that division who had authority over all the mahals in that division. Another precaution taken by the central authority was the keeping of important forts in jagir territory under the direct control of government, though lesser forts were allowed to remain in the possession of the mokasdar or jagirdar. Thus the forts of Kondana and Purandar in Poona district were under officers appointed (Nāmjād) by the central authority. Purandar was at that time in the hands of a Brahman killedar and Kondana, of Dadaji Konddeo who was also subedar of the district. He was no doubt the karbhari of Shahaji. But his position as subedar and killedar was derived from government. We have two documents, PS 456 and 457, in which Dadaji Konddev is called subedar and he settled disputes between litigants through panchayats of the caste (got). This position may have been conferred on him, after or before he was appointed agent by Shahaji. In any case it shows that the central government could not find a Mahomedan officer to hold the fort in such a distant and mountainous part and this weakness was taken advantage of by Shivaji as we shall presently relate.

The jagirdar or mokasdar had no right to dispossess Deshmukhs or Desh-Kulkarnis who, as hereditary officers of the karyats. continued to function as revenue officers even when governments were changed. Their services, however, were at the disposal of the mokasdar in all matters. They kept forces and with these they atteneded on the subedar also, whenever required to do so. The Deshmukhs of the twelve Poona mavals (or valleys of revulets issuing from Sahyadri and passing through gorges) were a turbulent people and were usually kept under powerful Maratha mansabdars for that reason.

The income of Shivaji's jagir is said by Sabhasad to be 40 thousand hons. It may be noted here that the coin then current in Maharashtra was hon (Sanskrit-suvarna) which was worth about Rs. 3. Rupee currency was introduced later by the Moguls. This income does not seem strange as the revenue of the Poona district at present is about sixteen lakhs of rupees. We must remember that the value of the rupee was then much greater than now and that Shivaji's jagir was about one-half of the present district of Poona. Sources of revenue then were also not many, consisting, as revenue did, chiefly of land-tax. The jagirdar had of course all this income to himself, but the mokasdar rendered account to the central authority, when paying the fixed revenue into the government treasury minus his dues. If the revenue fell short or if it increased by the extension of cultivation, the loss or profit belonged to the mokasdar. It was the duty, therefore, of a mokasdar and subedar where the mahals were khalsa (directly under government) to see that the territory was fully cultivated. The jagirdar for his own benefit naturally saw to the prosperity of the jagir by the extension of cultivation and also the protection of the territory. For the latter purpose, he had to maintain a force, and also to keep some forts well armed and provisioned. We can thus understand why Shahaji, when he sent Shivaji to Poona as jagirdar, sent with him forces, elephants, horses, and sufficient treasure. He also had a new seal prepared for him with the well-known inscription as already stated. PS 555, a letter from Shivaji's court addressed to Karkuns and Deshmukhs of pergana Poona, dated July 1649, has this seal on it and it confirms the Inam of Mahadaji Gosavi in Moreshwar village. Inam differed from jagir and mokasa, being the free grant of a village or lands for religious purposes or for meritorious service and was always inheritable.

Why Maharaj Shahaji Raje issues sanads and orders in Poona, Supa and Baramati perganas hereafter can be explained only on the supposition that he was still looked upon as the superior authority. If he had given the mokasa of the three perganas to Shivaji under himself, he had no power to interfere in their administration, and the more so, if he had got the perganas actually transferred to Shivaji in state records. But we have such letters as PS 649, dated 10th November 1653, addressed to Karkuns and Deshmukhs of pergana Poona about the Bidwai of the bazar at Charholi which was issued specially to confirm an old order by himself and there are others also issued similarly. We may grant that Shahaji's authority was respected by Shivaji even after he was made the jagirdar. Shivaji had, however, sometimes to assert his own authority as we shall presently see.

VII. PLAN FOR FOUNDING SWARAJ

Installed in Poona as a jagirdar who had to administer a territory, to maintain a force and even to take part in actual fighting, Shivaji was naturally taught subjects required to be learnt by a ruling chief. He was no doubt taught athletics, as was usual then with all Maratha boys, and the art of wrestling or Niyuddha. But he was also taught riding horses and elephants and to use the sword, the bow, the javelin and the patta (a long slender sword). The art of building forts and making them impregnable and also arithmetic, so essential for taking accounts, were further taught[1]. "He became a good archer and marksman, and skilled in the use of the various swords and daggers then used in the Deccan." (Duff). He also learnt examining and valuing jewels, an art necessary at all times for a prince[2].

At sixteen thus Shivaji was, with his precocious faculties, master in all the arts of governing. Even ordinary princes in those days were fully grown up at that age and it is no wonder that in 1646 A. D. Shivaji was fully equipped to take up the duties of a ruling jagirdar, being trained under the care of

1. SB 10, 35, 38. 2. SB 10, 39.

S. 4

an affectionate mother-regent and a successful administrator-minister. As stated before, this was also the age of majority, according to Hindu law, and Dadaji Konddev gradually gave him work in the various departments of administration as a matter of training.

More than all, however, Shivaji was instructed in politics as taught in the Smritis and the Nitis, and specially in that unique work of the ancient Hindus, the Mahabharata, which is both Smriti and Niti. This vast poem not only teaches Moksha (absolution) and Bhakti (devotion), but it also teaches the highest lessons in Dharma and Artha, *i. e.* morality and worldly affairs. Shivaji drank deep the lessons given in this wonderful work, lessons which he, in his future life, put to the test and followed. He was deeply religious also and a devout Hindu. But the lesson which *Bhagavadgita* taught him was to respect the religions of others and Shivaji throughout his life respected mosques and fakirs, not insulting them even in revenge. He confirmed their existing grants and even gave them new ones.

But a devout Hindu that he was, he could not brook to see Hindus trampled under foot as Hindus, Hindu temples and idols desecrated and cows slaughtered daily in all places. More painful was the sight of Hindu young women carried away not only in times of war but even in times of peace.[1] And he resolved to free Maharashtra from the curse of a foreign religion and a foreign yoke. "He resolved, even at the early age of 15, to acquire independence for this." (Amatya). He realised the difficulties that confronted him and he knew that he was incurring the danger of losing his all. This was the thought which had kept back many brave Maratha captains, like his own father Shahaji, from attempting the task. Their short-sighted selfishness induced them to keep what they had and serve even a foreign oppressive master. This was the very caution which Dadaji Konddev gave Shivaji when he came to know of his resolve. But Shivaji was, we think, too deeply imbued with the political maxim of the Mahabharata to be moved from his purpose :—

"No man beholds good things with't danger braved.
He sees them only if through danger saved."[2]

Dangers must be braved if one has to achieve great things. One may perish in the attempt but without encountering such dangers one cannot achieve the highest goal.

The means Shivaji had at hand were also quite insufficient to cope with two such powerful enemies as Delhi and Bijapur. But the Maha-

1. किती गुज्रिणी ब्राह्मणी भ्रष्टवीती । (Ramadas).
2. न संशयमनारुह्य नरो भद्राणि पश्यति ।
संशयं पुनरारुह्य यदि जीवति, पश्यति ॥ महा. भा.

bharata story of Vidula and her despairing son must also have, we think, strengthened his purpose. Vidula's son had been defeated by his enemy and coming back to her he wept in despair. "Go back," said the heroic Rajput mother, "to fight again with the enemy. I would rather see you die on the battle-field, than live a beggar." "How can I fight and get success?" whined the boy. The mother gave the immortal advice[1],

"Arise, awake and yoke yourself,
To th'noble work of your up-lift,
Believing that it will be so.
With minds unfaltering and unpained."

"Where are the means?" again said the boy and Vidula replied, "Take these ornaments and make a beginning, and if you put your heart into it, you will collect men by thousands." It seems to us that Shivaji was full of the story of Vidula and her son, when he resolved to establish Swaraj for the Hindus, with the small nucleus of the jagir he had and to stake all and even his life in the attempt; for the Mahabharata says in Rajadharma Shantiparva :—"One thousand horsemen of one mind are enough to conquer the whole world." The great bane of the Hindus was that they never were of one mind. Manuchi has observed, "If only the

1. उत्थातव्यं जागृतव्यं योक्तव्यं भूतिकर्मसु ।
भविष्यतीत्येव मनः कृत्वा सततमव्यथैः ॥ (म. म. उ.)

Rajputs combined, they would drive away the Mogul." The Kshatriyas always fought among themselves throughout Indian history like the Greeks; it was only once that, like the Greeks again, they formed a confederacy against the common enemy; but it did not long subsist. The Mogul emperors knew how to pitch one Rajput king against another and thus to use the bravery of both against their own enemies. Maratha captains, similarly, in the Deccan fought with one another and were employed by Mahomedan kings similarly for their own benefit. Shivaji had marked even in childhood how Shahaji had almost succeeded in holding his own against both Delhi and Bijapur with the help of Maratha captains. If Shahaji had taken the advantage of the name of the puppet Nizamshah for combining Marathas, Shivaji could combine them in the name of religion, of Brahmins and cows, of idols and the safety of the honour of Hindu women. The Hindus from ancient times had no doubt no idea of nationality and patriotism was a sentiment unknown to them; nor did Shivaji work under patriotic motives; but the cry of religion in danger always appealed to the Hindus and Shivaji resolved to combine all in an attempt to establish Hindavi Swaraj Shivaji, even at that age, knew that he had to work cautiously and to employ artifice, if necessary, as the Mahabharata showed how S'ri-

Krishna himself employed artifice against artful and iniquitous foes. And the maxim that every thing was fair in war was especially applicable to a weak but just party, fighting against powerful enemies, and was accepted among all peoples. But he never forgot the immortal truth preached by the Mahabharata[1], "Victory comes only to the righteous," as will amply appear from the manifold incidents in Shivaji's eventful life.

The first thing that Shivaji did after this resolve was to secure friends and co-workers among the Deshmukhs and landholders of the twelve Mavals which formed part of his jagir and though we have as yet no contemporary record to prove it, Tanaji Malusare, Yesaji Kank and Baji Pasalkar were among the first to join him and swear allegiance to his scheme of establishing an independent Hindu kingdom. The next thing was to form an army of Mawalas who inhabited the several khores or valleys. They were an indigent lot of weaklings, but independent in spirit like all peoples of mountainous lands, such as the Pathans, the Bhils, the Swiss or the Highlanders. They were also accustomed to climb steep hills and descend them with ease. Shivaji himself acquired all the qualities of a mountaineer in his constant movements among the hills. The Mawali infantry was most useful in mountain warfare where

1. यतो धर्मस्ततो जयः ।

cavalry and artillery could not be employed. Thirdly, Shivaji took possession of all the neglected forts in his jagir and even built new ones on impregnable hill-tops. Among such forts was the fort of Rajgad built at a little distance from the old fort of Torana in the Muse khore. We have no direct contemporary evidence to show that Shivaji began his career by seizing Torana as the Bakhars relate and by representing to the Bijapur Durbar that he was working for their benefit, as Kafikhan represents. For even Duff states that the jagirdars were entitled to keep in repairs old forts in their jagir. forts in such distant and out of the way places being usually neglected by the central government; and thus there was apparently no necessity of making any representations to the Bijapur Durbar.

Shivaji soon gained the confidence and respect of the people and his friends by his just and generous administration and stern and speedy justice. PS 510, dated January 1646, gives interesting details of a case in which he dealt out stern punishment tempered with generosity even at the age of 16. It is an order issued from the court of Shivaji Raje to the Deshmukhs and Desh-Kulkarnies of Taraf Khede Bare, declaring that the Mukadami of village Ranze was vacant, as the Mukadam Babaji Gujar had committed criminal breach of trust in respect of revenue and on being called before the court had been found guilty and punished by the cutting of his hands and feet, but that Babaji Gujar of Kille Purandar having applied for the post was given it as he was Babaji's relative and undertook to take care of him. We must remember that punishments awarded in India from the most ancient days down to Mahomedan times were severe and included the cutting off of hands and feet, especially of thieves caught red-handed.

This order must have been confirmed by or given with the consent of Dadaji Konddev. But the veteran administrator died in 1647 A. D.[1] and at the age of 16 Shivaji was full master of his jagir. He began to put into execution his plan of founding Hindavi Swaraj. The first thing he had to do was to take possession of the government forts which in a manner overawed the country. He took possession of Kondhana easily as successor and master of Dadaji Konddev. The Havaldar of the fort was a Siddi Mahomedan and it is said that he was bribed to acknowledge Shivaji's authority. Then again Nilkanthrao, the Brahmin keeper of fort Purandar for government, also died at this time and his sons fighting among themselves invited Shivaji as a friend to arbitrate. Shivaji with his Mawalas went to the fort and inducing the bro-

1. Phalgun S'. 11 S'. 1568 (7 March)—D. V. Kale in B. I. H. M. Quarterly, X, p. 53.

thers to accept inams from him elsewhere took possession of the fort. These two acts were in open rebellion against the Bijapur Durbar which now thought it necessary to take strong measures against Shivaji's rebellion, so to speak.

Note :—It is often argued that Shivaji could not have had, at this early age, the high ideal of freeing Maharashtra from Mahomedan yoke and establishing Hindavi Swaraj. Two documents, however, show that Shivaji had already formed this plan. PS 645 is a sanad issued by Shivaji to a Brahme of Chakan dated July 1653 and states "I have become entitled to a Rajya through the power of your Anushthana (continuous prayer to God) and have obtained whatever desire I had." Shivaji had formed the plan of acquiring Rajya thus before this and had asked Brahme to perform Anushthana for him for the same. PS 631 is another interesting sanad issued earlier in February of the same year to a Brahmin of Mahabaleshvar granting inam for performing a similar Anushthana of the sun for 'Abhyudaya' (prosperity) and this was sanctioned by his mother, who thus seems to have sympathised with Shivaji in his high design. These two documents prove to our mind that Shivaji, at least from 1647, had begun to work for the liberation of Maharashtra. The word Rajya here cannot mean his own jagir which he had got already before any Anushthana was begun; nor can the word Abhyudaya mean ordinary prosperity, which had already come under the able administration of Dadaji. And in 1653 he had already become, as we shall find later on, a *de facto* independent king.

IX. IMPRISONMENT AND RELEASE OF SHAHAJI

It is not necessary for us to describe in detail the arrest of Shahaji about this time, narrated with such poetical fulness in *Shiva-Bharata* and historical exposition in *Muhammadnama*. As stated already, when Shahaji finally entered the service of Adilshah in 1636, he was employed by him in extending his dominion into South India from west to east, called by the general name of Karnatak; and Ranadullakhan, Shahaji's friend, was his commander or nominal superior in these operations. Ranadullakhan died soon after; but Rustam Jama as also others who succeeded in command were well disposed towards Shahaji. Shahaji conquered so many chiefs and places in Karnatak that Muhammadshah rewarded him with the territory and fort of Bangalore worth five lakhs of Hons. There Shahaji usually hereafter resided and carried on his expeditions against many Karnatak 'polygars' who had become independent after the fall of Vijayanagar. When Mustafakhan was sent as commander in January 1648 to conquer Jinji, Shahaji with his army of 12000 horse assisted him. Differences arose between them and Mustafakhan secretly obtained an order from Adilshah to imprison Shahaji for insubordination, as *Muhammadnama* relates. *Shiva-Bharata* suggests that Shahaji had become so popular among the Hindu chieftains of Karnatak that " they gave up all fear of Mahomedans."[1] Virabhadra who had been dispossessed by Ranadullakhan was thus reinstated in his jagir by Shahaji. It is probable that Muhammad Adilshah also thought that Shivaji was rebellious through the connivance of Shahaji who himself was also getting too strong. Whatever the motive of the king in ordering his arrest, Mustafakhan with the help of Maratha chiefs who were inimical to Shahaji, especially of Baji Ghorpade, succeeded in suddenly surprising Shahaji in his camp one morning and, overpowering him, arrested him. He was sent a prisoner to Bijapur together with the plunder of his camp, and there he was placed in respectable confinement, as *Muhammadnama* relates.

But after a time, Muhammad Adilshah had to release Shahaji on certain conditions, as his endeavour to conquer Sambhaji and Shivaji was unsuccessful. Sambhaji sallying from the fort of Bangalore and Shivaji from that of Purandar defeated Faradkhan and Fattehkhan respectively sent against them. In this his first regular encounter with Bijapur forces, Shivaji was fully victorious. *Shiva-*

1. SB 11, 7.

Bharata describes this battle near Purandar with Fattehkhan with imaginary details, in the fashion of the Mahabharata, though with many real names of captains fighting on both sides. The Bijapur force encamped at Shirval beyond the Nira was attacked by Kavaji, Shivaji's commander, and was first dispersed. Fattehkhan who next advanced himself against Shivaji invested the fort of Purandar and attempted to scale the walls from the 'machis,' or lower hill plain stretches, but in a sally from the fort, Fattehkhan was defeated and his lieutenant Faraskhan was killed. Gunfire is mentioned in *Shiva-Bharata* as employed by Shivaji in this battle, besides volleys of stones thrown from slings by Mawalas. This success proved that Shivaji was now fully equipped with arms and men to fight the forces of Bijapur with all their preparation and practice of long standing. Though not mentioned in *Muhammadnama*, this campaign is confirmed by a parwana to the Deshmukh of pergana Shirval[1], dated 10th August 1649.

Shiva-Bharata relates that Muhammad Adilshah after weighing the pros and cons decided to patch up the quarrel by pardoning Shahaji and releasing him on condition that Shahaji remained loyal to him and Shivaji gave up the fort of Sinhgad and Sambhaji that of Bangalore. He was afraid

1. PS 562.

that if he did any harm to Shahaji, his two valiant sons would carry on the fight with greater vigour and not only his new possessions in Maharashtra and Karnatak would be lost, but he would lose even his own kingdom.[1] To these two enemies coming from the west and the south would be added, he thought, a third more powerful one from the north, namely the Mogul. Shahajahan was watching for an opportunity to devour Adilshahi in the same way as he had already done Nijamshahi. We have evidence that Shivaji at this juncture requested Shahajahan to move for the release of Shahaji, in two letters[2] from Murad, son of Shahajahan, subedar of the Deccan at this time, dated November 30, 1649, and addressed to Shahaji and Shivaji respectively; the one to Shahaji speaks of Shivaji's request to intercede for the liberation of the former forgiving his former faults. Muhammad Adilshah must have thought it prudent to pardon Shahaji rather than incur the enmity of three powerful adversaries and accordingly released him. Shahaji must have been kept waiting in Bijapur for some time hereafter, before he was employed again, pending the delivery of the forts demanded from Shivaji and Sambhaji, as also for watching their conduct.

It seems probable that when Shahaji was sent again into South India, he assured Muhammad Adil-

1. SB 15, 23. 2. PS 574 and 575.

shah of his loyalty, but that as for Shivaji, he must have told the king that he was no longer responsible for him and that the king might punish him, if rebellious, in whatever manner be thought proper.

Among the supporters of Shahaji, imprisoned and released along with him, were Kanhoji Jedhe of Kari, his most trusted captain, and Dadaji Krishna Lohakare. In the army of Shahaji, there were naturally many Maratha captains from among the Deshmukhs of the Mawal country and the Jedhe family was most intimate with him. Jedhe Karina[1] states that Shahaji at this time asked Kanoji to join Shivaji and support him through thick and thin. Shahaji foresaw that Shivaji would incur danger in the pursuit of his high plan, of which he must have been already cognisant and with which he probably sympathized; and now that Dadaji Konddev was no more, Shahaji in his fatherly anxiety, transferred the services of Kanhoji Jedhe to his son. Indeed Shahaji must have been pleased with his son's heroic defence of Purandar against Faraskhan and must have also thought of rewarding him by the transfer of his most trusted lieutenant Kanhoji Jedhe as also of Dadaji Krishna.

Note—Shahaji was released on 16th May 1649, according to the Jedhe S'akavali and this date is borne out by PS 566 & 568. The first is a sanad issued by Bijapur

1. *Shiva-Ch. Pradip*, p. 46.

officers to Moroba Gosavi on 5th September 1649, and in it Shahaji is styled Maharaja and Farjand and the second is a sanad issued by Maharaja Shahaji to Deshmukhs of pergana Rane Bennur in favour of Mulla Hussein. These show that the title Maharaja was also bestowed upon Shahaji on his release and also Farjand. How long Shahaji remained in Bijapur after his release cannot be determined.

J gives the account of the release of Shahaji and the reasons therefor as follows :—Kanhoji Jedhe and Dadaji Krishna Lohakare who were also in prison were released at this time. When Shahaji met them, he said, "We have settled a 'Tah' (treaty) with the Padashah that we will pay respects from 12 villages (probably given in Inam) and will serve in the oprations in Karnatak where Bangalore prant with 5 lakhs of Hons has been conferred on us in jagir. So we are going to Karnatak. Your vatan is in Mawal prant. Our son Shiuba is in Khede Bare and Poona. You should remain in his service with your force. You are powerful in that prant. You should, therefore, forcibly compel all Deshmukhs of the whole of Mawal to obey him. If a Mogul force or even Adilshahi force attacks him, you should remain loyal to him and fight with these forces." *Oath* was administered to Kanhoji and he with Lohakare was sent with a letter to Shivaji. This also means that while Shahaji absolved himself from all responsibility for Shivaji, he at the same time gave strong forces for his protection.

X. THE SUPPOSED MORE-MURDERS

Shivaji felt very strongly for being compelled to hand over the fort of Sinhgad to Bijapur, which could thence watch his movements; but he was consoled by Sonajipant Dabir (adviser) who advised him to look, for the present, to the consolidation of his power by strengthening the forts he had, including Purandar and Chakan, for the return of which Bijapur did not ask. Shivaji remained inactive for seven years, but he took advantage of every opportunity of bringing together the Maratha captains in the Mawal prant adjoining his own jagir. He had already secured the friendship of Chandrarao More of Javali. (More is a surname and Chandrarao is a title like Vishvasrao, Sarjerao etc. astutely conferred by Bedar and Bijapur kings on Maratha captains for bravery in battle). *Shiva-Bharata* states[1] that Chandrarao had been dispossessed by some one but had been reinstated by Shivaji probably a few years before this. This Chandrarao died without a son about 1649, as we find from a letter of Afzulkhan to Jedhe dated July 1649.[2] The Bakharkars had forgotten all about this Chandrarao and the real nature of the Javali incident, as

1. SB 13, 43.
2. PS 557.

they had forgotten all about Babaji and the real cause of the greatness of Maloji; and they invented a story about the capture of Javali, multiplying Shivaji's artifices, as they had done about Maloji. The above document is a key to the proper understanding of this episode in Shivaji's life. When Shahaji was sent after his release to Karnatak, Afzalkhan who had taken Shahaji captive to Bijapur, it seems, was sent by Muhammad Adilshah as subedar of Wai, in order probably that the two might not come together. Afzalkhan as subedar of Wai writes in this letter to Kanhoji Jedhe, "Old Chandrarao being dead, other people have taken possession of Javali. I have been ordered (namjad) in this connection. As you are a loyal servant, collect Hasham (foot-soldiers) and come." It appears that the name of this old Chandrarao was Daulatrao (Moryanchi Bakhar) and that he died childless. There were many More relatives, who posed as claimants and Hanmantrao, one of them, had already taken possession of Johar Khore. It was the duty and the right of Bijapur, the sovereign power, to settle the succession to the jagir of Javali. Afzalkhan, as subedar of Wai, was, therefore, ordered to go to Javali and settle the matter. Kanhoji Jedhe, who had been imprisoned and released along with Shahaji and who was in his Deshmukhi at this time under Shivaji but who had also Deshmukhi in Wai prant, was properly called upon by Afzalkhan to come to his assistance. Kanhoji having just passed through a calamity brought about by Afzalkhan was naturally distrustful. He asked Shivaji what to do and Shivaji in his reply directed Kanhoji to secure a kaul (promise of safety) and then to go himself or send his son.[1] Kanhoji promised to go to Afzalkhan's help but asked for the Deshmukhi of Johar Khore which he would conquer, and also for permission to maintain a force of 200 men for Javali from his own Deshmukhi. Afzalkhan granted him this request[2]. There are no papers found which can show what subsequently happened; but it seems clear from the Bakhar of Mores and later documents that eventually a son was adopted by the widow of Daulatrao, presumably with the consent of Afzalkhan. His name was Krishnarao and he, with his father and brother, became master of Javali and Hanmantrao remained in possession of Johar Khore, probably as a concession to his claim.

Shivaji was on friendly terms with the deceased Daulatrao and tried to maintain the same relations with the new master. We have already stated that Shivaji in his plan of establishing Swaraj wished to take all Maratha jagirdars within the confederacy; but many of them refused, either

1. PS 558.
2. PS 564 and 567, dated September 1649.

through loyalty to the Bijapur Durbar or through fear of losing their long enjoyed jagirs. We witness a similar phenomenon in Italy, when in 1871 the Duke of Piedmont threw his lot with the revolutionaries and revolted against Austria. The Duke of Piedmont, like Shivaji, called upon other Italian states to join him, but many of the Dukes refused to do so and remained neutral or fought on the side of Austria. The present master of Javali, Krishnarao, and his own father (janaka) who was his guardian, being installed by Afzalkhan, were naturally all the more loyal to Bijapur and gave contemptuous replies to Shivaji's proposals. The Bakharkars relate that Shivaji then resolved to acquire Javali by fraud and force and sent Raghunath Ballal Sabnis, as his agent, with the ostensible purpose of demanding in marriage Chandrarao's daughter but with secret instructions to murder him. Sabnis while in a conclave with Chandrarao stabbed him and his brother Suryajirao with a dagger. In the consequent consternation, he succeeded in getting out safely and reached the camp of Shivaji, who already was prepared with an army to attack Javali. With his own army, assisted by contingents of the forces of Kanhoji Jedhe, Bandal, Selimkar and other Deshmukhs, Javali was conquered and annexed. But all this story of the Bakhars is a myth and a blasphemy. There was no daughter to be married at Javali. Even Sabhasad who gives the same story does not say that Raghunath Ballal went to arrange a marriage, but says that he went there as a Hejib (a political ambassador) from Shivaji and told Chandrarao that he had to speak on several matters and to settle a treaty (Tah rah karane ahe).

The real incident appears to be as follows from the above letter, *Shiva-Bharata* and *Jedhe S'akavali*. When the new Chandrarao refused to join Shivaji in his plan, Shivaji decided upon attacking Javali, as it was an important place on the way from the ghat-matha of Wai to Konkan and could impede Shivaji's movements. He, therefore, as challenged by Chandrarao, attacked Javali[1]; and in the sally made from the town, Chandrarao's (janaka) own father was killed; but Krishnarao, the real Chandrarao, and his brother escaped to the fort of Rairi in Konkan which was in their possession. Shivaji pursued them and invested the fort. Eventually, by the intercession of Selimkar who was a devoted follower and friend of Shivaji, Shivaji allowed the two princes to come down and on promise of their entering his service took them to Poona in May 1656 (J). Krishnarao and his brother, however, breaking their promise, entered into treasonable correspondence with Bijapur secretly. But their letters were

1. Pausha V. 14 S'.1577 or 15 Jan. 1656 (J).

intercepted and shown to them. Shivaji ordered their execution for treason and they were accordingly beheaded near Poona.

That Chandrarao (janaka or real father) was killed in battle is apparent from *Shiva-Bharata* wherein the word battle is used and that Bajraj and Krishnaraj were defeated is also stated therein.[1] Their beheading was an execution and not a murder. Sabhasad relates that Hanmantrao, who had taken refuge in Chaturbet, was murdered by Sambhaji Kavaji who gained admittance to the fort on the excuse of his marriage relationship. But this is doubtful as *Shiva-Bharata* relates that other adherents and relatives of More who opposed Shivaji were killed presumably in open fight.[2] In any case Hanmantrao could not have been murdered by Sambhaji Kavaji by an artifice, if Chandrarao and Suryajirao had previously been murdered by Sabnis by a similar artifice.

The acquisition of Javali was extremely valuable as it held a strategic position. *Shiva-Bharata* properly describes its importance when it says,[3] " Whoever has Javali, has Wai prant, the whole range of Sahyadri, and the corresponding sea-coast. " Shivaji could not have founded Svarajya without first acquiring Javali. The Javali jagirdars, like other Deshmukhs of Mawal prant, were usual-

1. SB 18, 4. 2. SB 18, 7. 3. SB 18, 18.

ly fighting with others, sometimes even imprisoning tenants and we have evidence that Javali committed aggressions at this time on other Deshmukhs who were in Shivaji's favour. There was certainly a cause for attacking Javali; but we believe that Shivaji made this acquisition with the sole motive of founding Hindavi Svarajya. As Sabhasad puts it, "Svarajya cannot be founded", thought Shivaji, "without destroying Javali."[1] Indeed we think the episode of Jarasandha in the Mahabharata, in which Jarasandha was attacked by the Pandavas, may have been before Shivaji. Yudhisthira wished to perform Rajasuya or the sacrifice of declaration of empire and Shrikrishna said, "You cannot do so unless Jarasandha is conquered." Even on modern principles the attack on Javali was justifiable. The acquisition of independence by Maharastra could not be achieved without subjecting the recalcitrant Mores of Javali; and Shivaji had either to win over Javali or extinguish it. Why Bijapur Durbar and Afzalkhan were oblivious of these proceedings may be explained by the fact that Muhammad Adilshah was ill at this time and there were factions at the Durbar in view of his impending death. Shivaji immediately made arrangements for the prosperity of the jagir by assigning lands to Mawalas and also for its safety by building a fort

1. जावळी मारल्याविना राज्य साधत नाही. (S)

on a high hill near the source of the Krishna, the fort which is known as Pratapgad. Shivaji also built here a shrine dedicated to his tutelary deity Tulja-bhavani. Moropant Pingle to whom this work was entrusted, it is said, executed it expeditiously. This must have taken, however, some time and we do not know the exact date of the opening of this shrine. J does not mention it and the papers of this shrine have not yet been available for inspection.

Muhammad Adilshah died soon after this event in November 1656 (J).

XI. TIME AND PLACE FAVOURABLE FOR SHIVAJI'S PLAN

Javali territory was not directly under Bijapur. The jagirdars also often fought among themselves. Bijapur, therefore, was not much moved. But emboldened by this acquisition, Shivaji committed aggressions on territory directly under Bijapur and even under Delhi. Circumstances, both by time and place, were favourable for such aggressions. It would be proper to stop here a while and examine in detail what these circumstances were.

The Mahomedan kingdoms also fought constantly among themselves. Maharashtra was conquered by Allauddin Khilji and Malik Kafur about 1300 A. D. and in the dismemberment of the Delhi empire after Muhammad Taghluk, Deccan declared independence under Ahmedshah Bahamani in 1347. Gulbarga, and subsequently Bedar, was chosen as capital on the frontiers of Telangan or Warangal and Karnatak or Vijayanagar. The Hindus who never had any national sentiment were happy under Bedar kings as they did not interfere with their religion and also left leading Maratha captains in the enjoyment of their fiefs. The revenue administration was entirely in of hands of the Hindus and we find devout Hindus like Damajipant and Janardanpant appointed governors of provinces like Mangalvedhe and Daulatabad. Weak kings succeeding, the kingdom of Bedar fell to pieces and five kingdoms came into existence after the death of the last able minister of Bedar, Muhammad Gawan, about 1489. The Nizamshahi of Daulatabad and subsequently Ahmednagar, comprised the most part of Maharashtra and was generally tolerant. The people were contented, especially under Malik Amber, the able minister of Chand Bibi. But the five kingdoms were also usually at war with one another, except at one time when they combined against Vijayanagar and obtained a signal victory over it at Talikot in 1563. The Mogul kingdom in the north founded by Babar in 1526 soon became powerful and four successive able emperors extended its dominion over the whole of Northern India. The Moguls now aspired to conquer the southern Mahomedan kingdoms. They first easily swallowed Imadshahi of Berar and then Nizamshahi of Daulatabad in 1636. The question why the North failed to conquer the South in ancient times, when Vikrama or Harsha made an attempt to conquer it and why it succeeded under Allauddin or Jehangir may be explained by the fact that the Deccan was now divided, while the Mogul empire in Northern India was united, the Mogul emperors being always able to keep subordinate generals and subedars under control. The centrifugal forces were at work even in the north and they succeeded after Muhammad Taghluk and again after Aurangjeb when the Mogul empire fell to pieces. But for about 200 years, the personal ability of the emperors was too strong for these forces and kept the empire united. Shivaji saw clearly that Bijapur and Govalkonda, like Ahmednagar, were bound to fall sooner or later before Delhi and he rightly argued that he could carve out a kingdom from Bijapur territory during its struggle with Delhi. Even at this time Aurangjeb, the Mogul viceroy of the Deccan, in conjunction with Mir Jumla, the erstwhile Peshwa of Govalkonda had almost destroyed that state. At Bijapur Muhammad Adilshah died at this juncture and Ali Adilshah succeeded. Aurangjeb alleging that he was not a son of Muhammad Adilshah invaded Bijapur with the consent of Shahjahan and invested that city. He had almost accomplished his object when news of the severe illness of Shahjahan reached him and patching up a treaty with Bijapur and securing a large treasure from it as tribute, he started for the north to try conclusions with his three brothers in the struggle for the throne.

Besides this constant fight between the Mahomedan kingdoms, there was another weakness in them in that succession to the throne was usually contested. Probably the Mahomedan law did not lay down hard and fast rules for kingly succession and princes almost always fought among themselves, the successful prince usually murdering all other claimants. Even the powerful Mogul empire became weak at this time owing to the struggle between Dara and his brothers. And Shivaji found an opportunity for making aggressions even on the Mogul empire at this juncture.

A third cause of weakness in the Mahomedan kingdoms was the corruptibility of high officers; and even Mogul officers were not above corruption. How terribly disloyal were Mahomedan officers generally may be seen from the results of the treachery of Fattehkhan in Nizamshahi, Mir Jumla in Kutubshahi and Khan Muhammad at this very time in Adilshahi. He was the prime minister at Bijapur (May 1657) "and shamefully neglected every opportunity of impeding the march of the Moguls," (Duff), who reached Bijapur and invested it. The feeling of nationality was as absent among the Mahomedans as among the Hindus.

The fourth circumstance which favoured Shivaji's cause was the religious intolerance of the Mahomedan kings at this time and their oppression of the Hindu religion. Fortunately for the success of Shivaji's Hindavi Swaraj, Aurangjeb, it may even be said, succeeded in his ambition and became the Mogul emperor by imprisoning his father and murdering his brothers. Had Dara succeeded, the intolerance of Aurangjeb could not have had an opportunity to inflame and unite the Hindus to whom the cry of religion in danger alone appealed. The British government in India is accepted by all people because, taking a lesson from the evil results of Mahomedan and Portuguese intolerance, it abstains from all religious oppression. Indeed, it does not encourage any one religion. Akbar set this example of religious tolerance and by placating the Hindus, the Jains, the Parsis and others, he even became popular with all. This principle of religious tolerance was at this time given up to some extent by Shahjahan as pointed out by my friend Mr. D. V. Apte, "In 1633 Shahjahan issued a proclamation forbidding the building of new temples or the repairing of old ones. In the Panchakroshi of Benares alone 76 temples, old and new, were thrown down." Prisoners again who accepted Islam were liberated while those who refused were slaughtered.[1] In the Deccan Muhammad Adilshah in a private circular addressed to his provincial governors directed among others (1) the confinement of Hindus to karkuns' places and prohibition of their appointment to mamlats, (2) the prohibition of the public

1. *Padshah-nama*, J. I. H., VIII, 1, p. 45.

celebration of Hindu festivals like Dassera and Divali, and (3) the imposition of a tax like Jijaya on Hindu workers and traders and rich men in proportion to their income, Mahomedans and converted Hindus being exempt.[1] These circumstances were favourable to Shivaji's plan for founding Swaraj.

A few further facts which favoured Shivaji's plan may be given from our paper on the Mahomedan kingdoms in the Deccan before Shivaji. (1) Another weakness of these Mahomedan kingdoms was the frequent struggle between minister and master to obtain power. When the prince was weak and did not lead armies, he was usually supplanted by the minister who often ascended the throne himself. We find the Peshwas following this course in later Maratha history though they did not ascend the throne themselves. The reason why ministers or governors succeeded in their ambition is found in the fact that the people had no idea of nationality and ambitious aspirants found supporters not only among the people but also among nobles and captains who joined them for their own advancement. This explains why in countries like England where the national feeling is strong, no governor [illegible] ister aspires to the throne or becomes trouble[illegible] and [illegible] ous. (2) The foreign rulers had not su[illegible] foreign force to compel obedience of the native tr[illegible]us. Even important forts were entrusted to Maratha con[illegible] from Persia and Arabia had near[illegible] ceased and [illegible]

1. Apte's paper in S. M. Quar[illegible] Vol. II. quoting from Parasnis' Historical Writing. I [illegible] based on an unpublished Bakhar of Adilshah.

turers from these were absorbed by the Mogul armies. The Siddis alone often came and reinforced Deccan armies; but the Maratha contingents chiefly kept up their strength. (3) These Mahomedans were accustomed to live in open plains though hot. The plains of the Deccan were more fertile and more paying than the hilly Mawals; (they were also easy of attack though difficult of defence). The capitals of these states were, therefore, in the open plains. The Mawals of Poona, being difficult of attack and easy of defence, were thus the proper place for unfurling the banner of independence. (4) Lastly the system of ryotwari tenure which obtained in Maharashtra from the days of Bedar rule, treats the individual cultivator as the owner of the soil and as in direct connection with government without an intermediary Zamindar. This difference of tenure in Northern India and Maharashtra has an influence on the character of the people and to some extent explains why the movement for independence arose and prospered in Maharashtra. The Zamindar being rich feels himself bound up with the existing rule and usually supports it like feudatories. The cultivators under him being tenants at will and rack-rented are apathetic in any change of government as it does not affect their lot. Peasant proprietors, on the other hand, are interested in self-government as it means fixity of and leniency in taxation. The peasants of Maharashtra, therefore, forwarded Shivaji's attempt for founding Swaraj which thus was not like a jungle fire appearing and spreading haphazard but has launched in the place best fitted for it.

XII. CONQUEST OF KONKAN

Shivaji was now strong and experienced enough to take advantage of these favourable circumstances and resolved to extend his dominion. He saw that the dissensions among the Mahomedan kingdoms were his opportunity; but he also realised that he must maintain a large army if he wished to extend his power and a large army required an overflowing treasury. He decided upon acquiring money by raids on the neighbouring prosperous Mogul empire. The right of a conquering power to plunder enemy-country has been recognised throughout human history, from the most ancient times down to the modern, along with the right of the strong power to attack the weak one without cause. Even at this time, Aurangjeb had attacked Govalkonda on a paltry excuse and without a just cause. (The son of Mir Jumla was imprisoned by Kutubshah, but Auranjeb had no right to interfere in his behalf). Seeing Aurangjeb engaged in this affair, Shivaji suddenly attacked and plundered Junnar. This town was near his frontier in Mogul territory at this time. He acquired much wealth and captured several horses which were specially useful as they were needed to increase his cavalry, a force best fitted for sudden and speedy expeditions. This happened in May 1657[1], the year next after the conquest of Javali.

Shivaji did not stop with plundering Junnar, but proceeded to Ahmednagar and succeeded, though partially, in plundering that town also. All this plunder was safely taken to Rajgad which Shivaji had properly made his capital, having lost Sinhgad. He had also fortified Pratapgad and Javali was also a safe place. Shivaji now had a compact territory from Poona to Javali and even had the ghat portion to the east, as he had removed Sambhaji Mohite from Supa in the previous October[2], because he being a brother of Shahaji's second wife was disobedient to him. The story of the Bakharkhars is that Shivaji arrested Sambhaji in Phalgun after gaining admittance to the fort of Supa on the pretext of asking for Holi Bakshis; but this is as usual an exaggeration of Shivaji's tricks and J gives the date of this event as As'vin and not Phalgun.

When Auranjeb after patching up a treaty with Bijapur went hastily towards the north in January 1658[3], he left strong instructions to Nasirkhan, subedar of Ahmednagar, and also to Mir Jumla to take care lest Shivaji might make a sudden plunder-

1. Vaishakh S'.1579 (J).
2. As'vina Vadya S'.1578 (J). 3. Paush S'.1579 (J).

ing raid[1]. By his letter to Ali Adilshah[2] he returned to him the fort of Parenda, Konkan territory and Vengi Mahal which had been ceded to the Moguls by Bijapur and also remitted one fourth of the tribute of one crore of rupees exacted from it, in return for helping him against his brothers. He also ordered him not to take Shivaji into his service and if taken at least to employ him in Karnatak. It was probably feared that Shivaji, like his father, would offer to serve one king against another and thus safely offend the weak ; for Shivaji had even now offered to enter Mogul service and attack Bijapur. Shivaji, profiting now by the absence of Aurangjeb in the north, attacked and took North Konkan which as stated in the above letter had been ceded to the Moguls but had been just returned by Aurangjeb to Bijapur. North Konkan with Kalyan as its capital was thus open for attack. This part of the country had, before 1636, belonged to the Nizamshahi and had only been under Adilshahi for twenty years and was, therefore, not yet well assimilated. It was, therefore, ceded to the Moguls without much difficulty. Shivaji attacked and took Kalyan, with its fort on the Durgadi hill looking over its port, without trouble. There while repairing the fortifications, Shivaji got it is said, buried treasure. This happened just on the eve of Diwali

1. PS 743. 2. PS 744, dated 1657-1658.

or November 1657[1]. Bhivandi was also taken as also the fort of Mahuli which was the most important fort in North Konkan where Shahaji had made his last stand for the puppet Nizamshah against Delhi and Bijapur. Shivaji immediately made arrangements for the administration of the territory by appointing Dadaji Bapuji as Subedar of Kalyan and Sakho Krishna Lohakare as Havaldar of Bhivandi, and gave them sufficient Hasham or infantry force (J).

A letter from Aurangjeb to Shivaji written on 14th February 1658[2] has been found which is important as it refers to these events. It was written after Aurangjeb had defeated Jaswantsingh near Ujjain in his progress to the north. It was in reply to a letter from Shivaji in which the latter probably had explained to him his conquest of Kalyan and had offered to hold it for Aurangjeb along with other territory that he might be permitted to conquer from Bijapur. Aurangjeb says in reply that Shivaji's offences, though unpardonable, would be forgotten and that he should send Sonajipant with such proposals as he wished to make. Aurangjeb was a match for Shivaji in dissimulation. Shivaji in the meanwhile pushed on his conquest as far as Chaul and even further in South Konkan. On the sea-coast were Portuguese

1. As'vin Vadya 12, S.' 1579 (J). 2. PS 739.

settlements at Bassein, Revadanda, Chaul, Dabhol and Goa. The governor of Goa in a letter dated 5th May 1658[1] refers to Shivaji's activities in South Konkan at this time and mentions the sending of a force of eighty sepoys to Chaul for its protection. But Shivaji was astute enough not to molest the Portuguese and create strong and fresh enemies in Konkan. He appears to have pushed on and conquered the refractory chief of Shringarpur named Surve with the help of Shirke (Sabhasad). Lakham Sawant was favourable to Shivaji's plan of founding Swaraj and entered into correspondence with Shivaji, as we learn from the next Goa letter dated 5th May 1658, stating that Bijapur had sent Rustum Jama specially to punish Lakham Sawant, but that the latter had defeated him with a loss of 1500 men. Rustum Jama, the letter stated, had, however, siezed the fort of Rangana. Lakham now openly joined Shivaji's cause and the latter naturally confirmed him in all his possessions and rights and titles. The terms of the treaty settled between them on March 5th 1659 are very important[2] and were as follows:

1. Lakham Sawant agrees to maintain an infantry force of 1500 men for half the revenue of the jagir and to send it to help Shivaji whenever needed.

1. PS 547. 2. PS 765 dated Phālgun Vadya 7 S'. 1580.

2. Shivaji keeps to himself the fort of Phonda with its territory and Lakham should help to defend the fort whenever needed.

3. Lakham would fight against the Turuks (Mahomedans) along with Shivaji, keeping touch with him through his Vakil for the establishment of Swaraj (this word used here is specially worth noticing).

4. The officers of Shivaji who would visit the jagir from time to time for settlement of revenue should be assisted in their work.

5. The Desagat or Lordship of the territory and vatans and the title Bahadur of the Sawant are confirmed and the forts and the thanas would remain in the possession of Sawant.

These articles clearly show that Shivaji was now a king *de facto* and was looked upon as such by Maratha jagirdars in Konkan and Ghat-Matha who threw in their lot with his cause. The exemplary punishment inflicted by Shivaji on Javali and its Mores who refused to come under Shivaji's Swaraj scheme probably confirmed the wavering Maratha captains and from this time, they helped him with their whole heart and might, as will appear further on. Even the English soon realised that this was a movement by the Hindus to establish their Swaraj, as Revington addresses his letter dated 13th Feb. 1660 to Shivaji as "The Captain of the Hindu forces."[1]

These exploits and aggressions on Mahomedan kingdoms are brought together with the usual poetical artifice, in a speech of Adilshah in *Shiva-Bharata.* Says he to Afzalkhan, "Shivaji does not respect my orders. By his treacherous movements, the Sahyadri territory has become asahya (intolerable) to me. Shivaji might have drowned the lord of Rajapur (Siddi) in the sea, if my father had not helped him in time. He has conquered Chandraraj with his sons and ministers and has taken possession of Javali. (These events happened in Muhammad Adilshah's time.) He has now conquered and annexed that province of Nizamshahi which I had given to Aurangjeb in treaty together with all mines, forests and forts, thus insulting me and also Aurangjeb. He plunders my towns and villages, following a bandit's life, by sudden and unexpected raids. He has levied contributions from towns in Mogul territory including even Ahmednagar. Even the lord of Delhi does not, therefore, feel secure in the possession of the Nizamshahi territory taken by him. My father was compelled to release Shahaji in fear of his prowess. Chieftains are flocking to his standard hoping for preferment, as his power and wealth are daily increas-

1. PS 801 ER 4.

ing. He threatens to take the whole of my kingdom[1]." We give this long extract from *Shiva-Bharata* to show that that contemporary poem also refers to these exploits of Shivaji and thus confirms their authenticity.

Note A—It would be proper to bear in mind here the following dates given in the Thana Gazetteer regarding Kalyan: (1) The Senale tank, with its basalt masonry bank, was built in 1506 A. D. (Nizamshahi rule). (2) The Portuguese once conquered the town in 1536. They burnt the suburbs again and carried away booty in 1570. (3) In 1648 Shivaji took the town.[2] In 1674 he granted lease to the English to establish a factory there. (4) The wall about the city was begun by Mahatbarkhan, Minister of Shahajahan, and was completed in 1694 A. D. His tomb or makarba is on the other side of the above tank. (5) The Jumma mosque in the city was changed into Ramji's temple between 1760 and 1772 in Peshwa times. (It was changed with the consent of the Mahomedans, as we have heard from old men, the mosque being now in the midst of the Brahmin quarters). (6) In the citadel on the creek (Durgadi fort) the Marathas built a Durgadevi temple behind the mosque. The image in the temple was stolen away in 1876.

It seems from the above dates that when Shivaji took the town there was no wall around it and that though he plundered the rich Mahomedan traders, he did not pull down any masjid, as is wrongly stated in Marathi translation of a verse in SB. महासिद्धिनिलया: means not Masjids, but houses, full of great wealth. (SB 18, 52.) It is admitted by all that Shivaji never pulled down any masjid.

1. SB 17, 12–29. 2. This date is not correct (J).

Note B—Jedhe S'akavali states that Kalyan was taken by the king on A'svin Vadya 12 (25th November 1656). Bakharkars mention that the town was taken by Abaji Sondev; this, however, may not be inconsistent as the words 'by the king' include his lieutenants. The story of the beautiful daughter of the ruler of Kalyan taken prisoner and sent to Shivaji by Abaji Sondev and her being sent back with honour and presents by Shivaji to her relatives is also related by Bakharkars and may be accepted as adding lustre to Shivaji's character, though *Shiva-Bharata* does not mention it and thus in a way creates doubt about its truth. This poem cannot be expected to be silent about it. Silence, however, is not positive proof unless mention is absolutely necessary.

XIII. THE MOMENTOUS MEETING

The aggressions of Shivaji had now reached a point where they could not be safely overlooked and Bijapur, being now at peace with Aurangjeb and the Portuguese, resolved to punish and destroy him. The young Ali Adilshah[1] and the Badi Sahebin or Dowager Queen (S), spoken of also as the Rani of the Deccan in an English letter from Rajapur dated 10th December 1659[2], sent Afzalkhan against Shivaji on that mission. *Shiva-Bharata* gives the account of this conflict in great detail in several chapters and many contemporary letters, Indian and foreign, also refer to it, but with details differing in several points. We will in this chapter give the history of this momentous meeting from these several documents.

Afzalkhan started from Bijapur with a very large force, estimated as 10,000 horse and foot in the above Rajapur letter,[3] with many captains under him such as Ambar, Yakut, Musekhan, Ankushkhan, Hasan Pathan. Many Maratha captains such as Ghorpade, Pandhare, Kharade, Mambaji Bhosale and others joined him with their contingents[4]. The

1. SB 17, 40. 2. PS 721. 3. ER I Revington.
4. SB 17, 55-58.

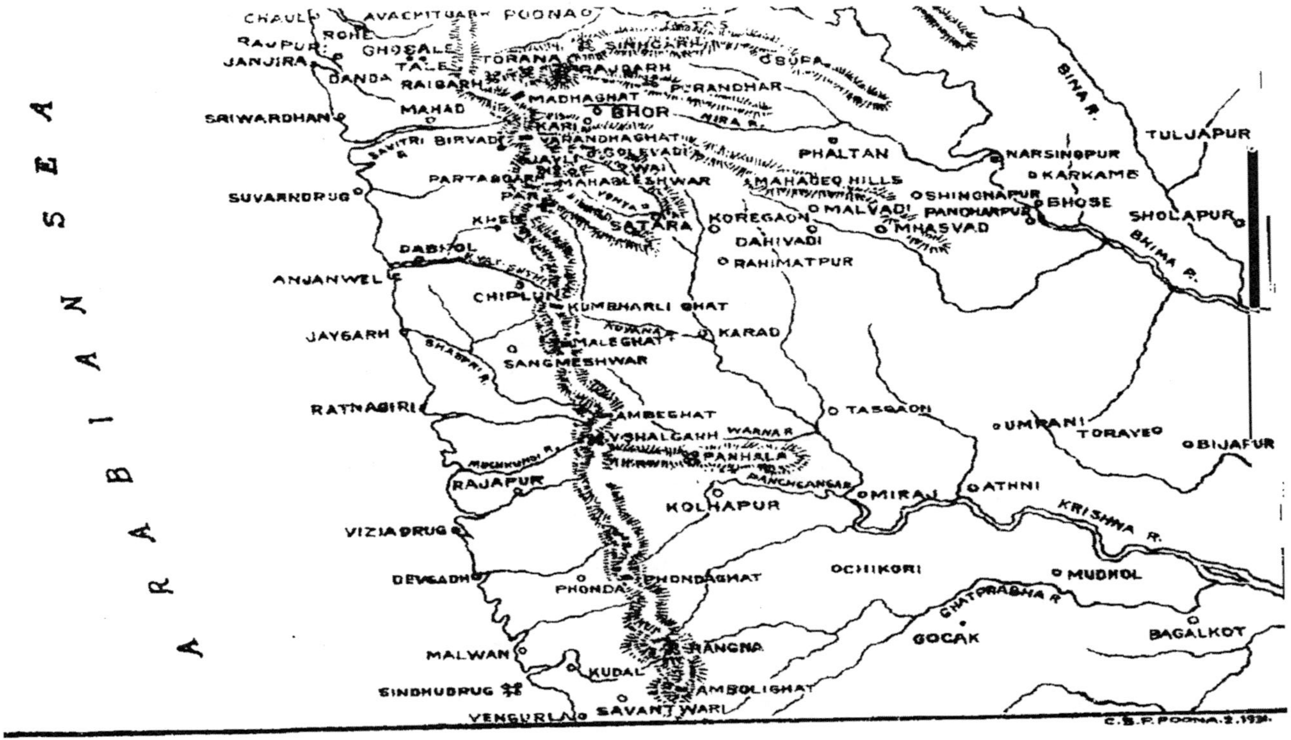
ARABIAN SEA
CHAUL
AVACHITGARH
POONA
ROHE
RAJPUR
JANJIRA
GHOSALE
TALE
TORANA
SINHGARH
RAJGARH
SUPA
DANDA
RAIGARH
PURANDHAR
MADHAGHAT
SRIWARDHAN
MAHAD
BHOR
NIRA R.
BINA R.
TULJAPUR
KARI
SAVITRI
BIRVADI
PHALTAN
NARSINGPUR
KARKAME
PARTABGARH
MAHABLESHWAR
WAI
MAHADEO HILLS
SHINGNAPUR
SUVARNDRUG
PAR
SATARA
KOREGAON
MALVADI
PANDHARPUR
BHOSE
SHOLAPUR
KHED
MHASVAD
DAHIVADI
BHIMA R.
DABHOL
RAHIMATPUR
ANJANWEL
CHIPLUN
KUMBHARLI GHAT
JAYGARH
KARAD
MALEGHAT
SANGMESHWAR
RATNAGIRI
AMBEGHAT
TASGAON
UMRANI
TORAVE
BIJAPUR
VISHALGARH
WARNA R.
PANHALA
RAJAPUR
PANCHGANGA
MIRAJ
ATHNI
KOLHAPUR
KRISHNA R.
VIZIADRUG
DEVGADH
PHONDA
PHONDAGHAT
CHIKORI
MUDHOL
GHATPRABHA R.
GOCAK
BAGALKOT
MALWAN
RANGNA
KUDAL
SINDHUDRUG
AMBOLIGHAT
SAVANTWARI
VENGURLA
C.S.P. POONA. 2. 1931.

expedition was determined upon already in May, as farmans issued in the name of Adilshah himself to the several Deshmukhs of Wai prant to join Afzalkhan with their forces, prove. Among these that issued to Kanhoji Jedhe dated 16th June 1659[1] is before us and it clearly says that the object of the expedition was to destroy Shivaji (निर्मूल फडशा करावा). It was thus a struggle for existence for Shivaji and also for his idea of Hindvi Swaraj. Some Deshmukhs, like Khopade of Antroli, thought it safe to join Afzalkhan, but others like Kanhoji Jedhe loyally stuck to Shivaji's cause. He was warned by Shivaji that he might lose his vatan (hereditary holding); but he swore allegiance to Shivaji even at the risk of his vatan and joined him with his force (J). Afzalkhan started probably in Kartik (October) when the rains usually cease and taking Tuljapur and Pandharpur on the way came to Wai.[2] He insulted the idol of Tulja Bhavani at Tuljapur, the tutelary deity of Shivaji, as *Shiva-Bharata* says,[3] and broke it into pieces accord-

1. PS 774.

2. Some relate that when Afzalkhan started, he slaughtered his 63 wives in johar; but this statement is absurd as he was not a Rajput nor was he going to immolate himself. On the contrary, he was so puffed up and confident of success that such an idea could not have entered his head.

3. दुर्नयेन भृशं येन निशुंभसमतेजसा। अवाज्ञायत वै देवी तुळजापुरवासिनी॥

ing to Sabhasad. People at Tuljapur do not, however, think that the present idol at Tuljapur is a new one. Afzalkhan similarly desecrated the holy city of Pandharpur and the temple of Vithoba, as a document dated 8th October 1663 distinctly states.[1] It is certain that the present idol of Vithoba at Pandharpur is older than Afzalkhan and, therefore, also certain that the idol must have been removed and concealed by the Pujaris when Afzalkhan came to desecrate the temple.

Shivaji hearing of his moving towards Wai left Rajgad and went to Javali. He left his capital in charge of his mother and also of his son, Sambhaji, enjoining all his officers and sardars to fight on in the name of his son, if the worst happened to him. *Shiva-Bharata* explains this movement of Afzalkhan towards Wai by noting the importance of first taking the possession of Javali which was the key to both Konkan and Ghat-Matha and also by the fact that Prataprao More, who alone of all Mores had escaped and taken shelter with Adilshah, suggested this move, as the capture of Javali would be of greatest importance strategically. Perhaps Afzalkhan went to Wai first because he had personal knowledge of the district, being its Subedar even then (PS 756, 758) and did not per-

1. PS 984. This simply mentions अफझलखानाची तसवीस क्षेत्रास लागली.

sonally know the district about Poona, which he could easily attack from Wai and Javali.

Afzalkhan may also have intended to take possession of Javali and the neighbouring pass of Parghat while undefended, by making a feint of advancing against Poona and then suddenly turning towards Wai; but Shivaji with his army forestalled him and was already at Javali. Afzalkhan, therefore, probably thought it prudent, instead of fighting with Shivaji in the high mountains, to secure his object by apparently peaceful negotiations and asking Shivaji to submit. He had, no doubt, artillery with him, called Gulikayantra in *Shiva-Bharata*, to attack forts. The poem also speaks of camels in Afzalkhan's army and thus supports the possession by him of "a number of swivels mounted on camels" (Duff); but in the difficult passes, they might prove more a hindrance than help and Afzalkhan wished to try to secure his object by negotiations. It seems probable that the first envoy for peace went from Afzalkhan[1]. The message given in *Shiva-Bharata* again enumerates, by poetical artifice, Shivaji's aggressions and is worth reproducing here[2]. Says Afzalkhan, " You have seized the Nizamshahi territory given by Adilshah to the red (the Moguls are always differentiated in SB from other Mahome-

1. SB 18, 46, and (J). 2. SB 18, 48, 58.

dans by the epithet Tāmra) with its hill-fort (this refers probably to Shivaji's taking of Mahuli). You have confined and surrounded the Lord of Rajapuri. (This refers to Shivaji's attack on the Siddi of Janjira and his taking possession of the plain part ot his territory). You have seized the prosperous kingdom of Chandrarao. You have taken Kalyan and Bhivandi and dismantled the palaces of Mahomedans full of riches in them. Those Mahomedans whom you have despoiled of all their possession there, are still enraged against you like serpents. You have barred the road of Muslim religious men by stopping them (from pilgrimage). You have assumed the emblems of a Chakravarti (independent king ruling over others) fearlessly and even sit on a golden throne." These facts we have already recorded and they are proved from other documents also and thus confirmed by them.[1]

"Conclude peace by humbly giving up the hills with the forts, Sinhgad, Lohgad, the lofty basalt rock (probably Rajgad) and Purandar and the territory between the Bhima and the Nira to the Lord of Delhi. The Adilshah begs of you also that you should give him Javali which you have seized

1. E. g. PS 777, dated 6 August 1659, mentioning also Shivaji's having built fighting ships in the creeks of Kalyan and Panwel.

from Chandrarao More." This message mentions Sinhgad which, it appears, after being returned to Adilshah for the release of Shahaji, had subsequently been taken back by Shivaji. It also shows that the territory about Sinhgad had been ceded by treaty to the Moguls and hence was to be delivered to Aurangjeb and Javali was to be returned to Adilshah, as it was in his territory. Here Afzalkhan is made to use the word 'begs.' showing his anxiety to conciliate Shivaji.

It may be noted that Shivaji's attack on Danda Rajapuri or Janjira must have taken place after the taking of Kalyan which is referred to in a Portuguese letter of the time. Adilshah's speech already referred to speaks of a previous attack by Shivaji when "he had almost drowned the Siddi in the sea." The Siddi first held the Janjira jagir under Nizamshah, then under Adilshah, when Muhammad Adilshah helped him against Shivaji's attack. This second campaign of Shivaji against Janjira does not appear elsewhere.[1] He subsequently sent Shamrajpant Peshwa against it but he was defeated. The Siddi, thereafter, offered allegiance to the Moguls. This little Mahomedan fief continued to be a thorn in the side of the Maratha empire throughout its history and it often committed acts of cruelty on the Hindu inhabitants of the neighbouring villages.

1. PS 791, Dec. 1659, mentions Shivaji's taking the town.

Shivaji was counselled submission by his advisers as fighting with such a force armed with cannon was unthinkable. But Shivaji felt that submission meant death at least to his high ideal of Hindvi Swaraj and he must have remembered the maxim of the Mahabharata, "Unless you brave danger, you cannot see prosperity."[1] He, however, consented to accept Afzalkhan's proposal for a meeting, personally to settle the terms of submission. He suspected treachery, but he was ready to meet stratagem by stratagem. It appeared that he might even lose his life in a physical tussle with his tall and powerful adversary. But Shivaji had more confidence in himself than his advisers and he resolved to brave even death. He artfully asked Afzalkhan to come up to Javali as he was afraid to meet him down in the plain, surrounded by his army. He sent his own Vakil, Pantaji Gopinath, to assure Afzalkhan of hospitable and honourable reception at Javali (about 12 miles from Wai).[2] The Pant was also commissioned to secretly ascertain the real motive of Afzalkhan in asking for a personal interview, instead of settling the terms of submission through Vakils as usual.

On being assured of proper reception, Afzalkhan, against the advise of his captains, like Shivaji, in self-confidence resolved to march into the moun-

1. न संशयमनारुह्य नरो भद्राणि पश्यति. 2. SB 19, 18.

tainous region with all his army and to meet Shivaji near Javali. His army, infantry, cavarly, canon, elephants, camels, etc., (the *Shiva-Bharata* poetically describes) marching with great difficulty and loss through the Radtondi Ghat from Wai, reached Par, near Javali and encamped there. At a safe distance of about 3 miles from this camp the place of meeting was fixed at the foot of the Pratapgad fort where Shivaji was. Each party, being distrustful of the other, the details of everything connected with the meeting were settled. Afzalkhan, armed as usual, was to arrive with his attendants at the mandap set up for the meeting, accompanied by ten body-guards, who were to stay at a distance of an arrow throw[2]. Afzalkhan was to arrive first in a palanquin taken by four bearers. Shivaji was to come next, also armed as usual, and also with ten body-guards to be kept at a distance and to meet Afzalkhan in the mandap, each one taking 2 or 3 attendants with him inside. Afzalkhan accordingly came to the mandap a little before midday and Shivaji soon after came to the momentous meeting. On that noon of Margashirsha S'uddha 7th S'. 1581, Thursday, a date specially recorded in *Shiva-Bharata* and also exactly the same in Jedhe S'akavali, corresponding to 10th November 1659, and at that juncture, trembled in the balance the

2. SB 27, 7.

fate of Maratha independence as also of Bijapur rule. As poetically expressed by *Shiva-Bhārata*, "Shivaji knew what was in his opponent's heart and he knew what was in Shivaji's. God alone knew what was in the mind of fate and the people knew that a peace was being arranged."[1]

१. शिवस्याफजलो वेद हृदयं स च तस्य तत् । तं विधिं तु विधिर्वेद वेद सन्धिंविधिं जनाः ॥ (SB 20, 57).

Bhawani Temple, Pratapgad.

XIV. THE TERRIBLE TUSSLE

Destiny declared its decree within half an hour. A terrible tussle took place at the meeting which is described by *Shiva-Bharata* as follows :—Both came to the meeting armed. They had probably the same arms usually taken by sardars, namely, a sword in the left hand, and a dagger in the waist band. Bakhars mention a Vaghnakh or tiger's claw in the left hand of Shivaji and a Bichva, scorpian tail, concealed by Shivaji in his sleeve. But this is not possible as a tiger's claw put on the right or left hand could not have escaped notice, even though the sword might not have been held by that hand. Moreover, *Shiva-Bharata* does not mention it and it is as usual an exaggeration of later writers. Both had at least two men with them inside the Mandap, one body-guard and the other the Vakil, Krishnaji Bhaskar on Afzalkhan's side and Pantaji Gopinath on the other. The body-guard of Afzalkhan was Sayyad Banda and of Shivaji, Jiva Mahala. They were no doubt chosen for their tried physical strength and bravery and their names deserve to be recorded in history. Having a white Maratha turban on his head surmounted with a Tura (crest) and a saffron-colour-ed long coat over a steel corslet, and bearing in one hand a sword and in the other a patta, Shivaji advanced to the meeting. Afzalkhan seeing him rose and giving the sword in his hand to his attendant, in order to induce confidence in Shivaji, advanced; and with a loud but kind voice said, " You impertinent boy, you neither serve Adilshah nor the Lord of Delhi but follow a crooked path. I will catch hold of you and taking you to Bijapur bend your neck before Adilshah." Suiting his action to his speech and adding " You, Shahaji's son, give me your hand and embrace me," Afzalkhan caught hold of Shivaji's neck with his left hand and drawing him near thrust his dagger into his side. The blow was evaded by Shivaji wriggling his body. But other documents say that it was of no effect owing to the corslet Shivaji wore. Expert in the art of wrestling, Shivaji succeeded in disengaging himself and freeing his head from Afzalkhan's grip and saying, "Take this sword," thrust it into the Khan's belly. It went through his belly upto the back and coming out brought out his entrails. Afzalkhan caught them in his hand and cried aloud, " I am struck, kill him ". His Brahmin attendant advanced, aiming a blow with the sword Afzalkhan had given him. But Shivaji parried the blow away with his sword. Shivaji then with a sudden movement struck Afzalkhan on the neck and the head rolled down. Sayyad Banda with his patta ran to the attack and would almost have killed Shivaji with his trenchant blow; but Jiva Mahala with one stroke of his sword severed Banda's arm with the uplifted sword from the shoulder. The outsiders, now hearing the melee, came, but they were met by Shivaji's body-guards and a regular fight ensued. Shivaji, in the meanwhile, whizzing about him his patta in the wield of which he was an expert, reached the foot of the fort and safely went to the top. The names of the ten body-guards of Shivaji are given by *Shiva-Bharata* as Sambhaji Kavaji, Patoji Ingle, Yesaji Kank, Krishnaji Gayakwad, etc. It appears clear that none of them nor Afzalkhan's men had guns with them. Probably they were not allowed to have them or else they did not know their use.

The question who began the tussle is rather difficult to decide, as the two sides give different accounts of what happened at the beginning though they agree in other details. It is a common experience that even eye-witnesses to an event give different accounts owing to wrong impressions, as also their own biases and even motives. The well-known historain, Sir Walter Raleigh, even thought that it was impossible to write true history, when witnesses to a murder he himself had seen gave different accounts of it. The Mahomedan accounts state that Shivaji treacherously with his dagger wounded

Afzalkhan who was innocent of any desire to harm him. However, it is almost certain from the following considerations that Afzalkhan must have begun the affray. In the first place he had received orders to kill Shivaji as is proved by a farman of Bijapur actually sent to Kanhoji Jedhe already referred to. Secondly, it is impossible that Afzalkhan could have believed that Shivaji would give up all his acquisitions, go to Bijapur and accept a small jagir, without struggle, by a mere show of force or a personal appeal. Thirdly, the conditions laid down for the meeting show that each side expected treachery. Lastly, if Shivaji had intended to murder Afzalkhan from the beginning, he would have effected his purpose, without endangering his own life, by concealing men near the place of meeting and setting them to fall upon Afzalkhan when he came to the Mandap. Even if it be believed that Afzalkhan intended merely to seize Shivaji and take him to Bijapur as prisoner in the same way as had been done to his father, it must be admitted that Shivaji could not have been seized without a struggle in which many persons would be killed. Shivaji's act, therefore, cannot in any case be looked upon as murder.

Afzalkhan's death in the conflict naturally gave rise to the rumour that Shivaji had inveigled him into a trap and murdered him. Both Shivaji and Afzalkhan had met together knowing each other's mind and it was possible that Shivaji might have lost his life in the struggle. In that case the rumour would have started that Afzalkhan had entrapped Shivaji and then murdered him. Indeed, in one of his expeditions in Karnatak, Afzalkhan had similarly invited the Nayak of Shira to a conference and murdered him.[1] As the report travelled, time and distance added new embellishments. Thus Henry Revington, writing from Rajapur a month after on 10th December[2], wrote that the Rani of Deccan sent Afzalkhan with 10,000 men to crush Shivaji, but knowing the force to be insufficient counselled him to pretend friendship, that Shivaji also did the same and to induce full confidence in him, "sent his mother as hostage," and that the two embraced each other in the presence of others, but when they retired to talk alone, Shivaji suddenly thrust his dagger concealed in his coat into Afzalkhan's heart. Revington also adds a third concocted rumour that Shahaji with a large force was advancing on Bijapur.[3] In a Dutch letter[4] written five months later (April 1660) the same exaggerated account of Shivaji's conflict with Afzalkhan is given with many details such as Shivaji's sending his mother as hostage and his first thrusting a dag-

1. Modern Review, July 1929, p. 9.

2. PS 791 and ER 11. p. 3. 3. (*Ibid.*). 4. PS 812.

ger into Afzalkhan's stomach. But even this letter states in the beginning that the Badi Sahebin had sent a message to Afzalkhan to call Shivaji by sweet words to a conference and then kill him. She had, we knew, similarly murdered three ministers in Bijapur itself. A still later story is that given by Grant Duff, namely, that Shivaji heavily bribed the Brahmin Vakil of Afzalkhan sent to him and through him induced the latter to leave Wai and come to Javali for personal discussion. This idea seems to have arisen from a confounding of names in a copy of the Sabhasad Bakhar. Grant Duff gives the name of Shivaji's agent as Krishnaji Bhaskar while really his Vakil was Pantaji Gopinath who was not Afzalkhan's agent. Krishnaji Bhaskar was a Deshpande of Wai and was properly enough Afzalkhan's agent. Shivaji certainly handsomely rewarded his own agent, Pantaji Gopinath, for his valuable service in this affair and this was perhaps wrongly looked upon as a bribing of the Vakil of Afzalkhan wrongly said to be Pantaji Gopinath. His Vakil Krishnaji Bhaskar was so deserving of Afzalkhan's confidence and loyal that he gave him his sword when he advanced to meet Shivaji and *Shiva-Bharata* relates that this Vakil fearlessly advanced to attack Shivaji with that very sword to kill Shivaji when Afzalkhan was wounded by him. Pantaji Gopinath was a Kulkarni of Hivre near

Saswad and Purandar and was naturally with Shivaji. The Bokil family to which he belonged got Hivre in inam, not at this time but long hereafter.

The successful emergence of Shivaji out of this duel enhanced his reputation for intrepidity among his captains and soldiers. It made his cause of Swaraj prosper among the Hindus generally who looked upon him as under the special protection of heaven. Shivaji's success was hailed with great delight by Hindus; Brahmins especially "were pleased at the deliverance of the basin of the sacred Krishna river from the Mahomedan forces of Afzalkhan" (SB). Destiny is no doubt working in the concerns of this human world; but the historian may explain Shivaji's success by two reasons. Following the sound advice given by the Mahabharata, "Do not trust even a trustworthy man, much less an enemy,"* Shivaji had put on a steel corslet while Afzalkhan relying upon his strength had failed to take this precaution in over-confidence. Secondly, Shivaji was young, only 29 years old, agile, skilled in wreslting, undaunted and wary, while Afzalkhan was old, probably more than 50 and though powerful, unwieldy. Shivaji had also wisely taken every precaution and had reliable men about him. He thus escaped not only from Afzalkhan, but also

* न विश्वसेदविश्वस्ते विश्वस्तेऽपि न विश्वसेत्।
विश्वासाद्भयमुत्पन्नं मर्माण्यपि निकृन्तति॥

from his army which he had requested him to keep at a safe distance.

It was an extraordinary incident in the annals of history and caught the imagination of the people throughout India. Sabhasad compares the fight between Shivaji and Afzalkhan to the duel between Bhima and Duryodhan of Mahabharata fame, but this is a wrong simile, Bhima being so much the stronger and bigger. If a similar Puranic incident is to be quoted, the fight between Shri Krishna and Chanura would be the proper one, as Shri Krishna, like Shivaji, was much younger and smaller than his adversary. When Sabhasad and the Jedhe S'akhavali state that Shivaji killed Afzalkhan by making *ekangi* they probably refer to a trick in wrestling by which a combatant disengages himself from the clasp of his opponent.

XV. TAKING OF THE FORT OF PANHALA

The peel of a war-drum (Dundubhi) from the fort of Pratapgad announced the safe return of Shivaji there, to the several detachments of his army which were kept concealed on all sides of the army of Afzalkhan encamped on the Par plain. It was a signal, as already notified to them, to attack the enemy. Detachments led by Tanaji Malusare on the east, by Moropant Peshwa subsequently coming from the Konkan on the opposite side by Parghat on the west, and by Yesaji Kank and by others[1] on other sides, suddenly fell upon Afzalkhan's army. The encounter was fierce but Afzalkhan's army being surprised was naturally defeated. Many escaped with the help of Prataprao More who knew the hilly passes, but many were taken prisoners while many others were slain. Fazalkhan, who escaped, reached Wai, but his two younger brothers with other captains were taken prisoners. Shivaji, both manfully and discreetly, did no harm to them, but sent them all with presents back to Bijapur. Those of the soldiers taken prisoners, both Hindu and Mahomedan, who wished to enter Shivaji's service were so engaged, while others who like Ghatge

1. J mentions Kanhoji Jedhe and Bandal.

refused and remained loyal to Bijapur, were let go with their wounds attended to. It is creditable to Shivaji that throughout his life, he never committed acts of cruelty and believed in the noble maxim of the Ramayana that enmity ceases with the defeat or death of the enemy[1].

Shivaji obtained enormous plunder in cash, jewels, horses, elephants, camels and other things like tents etc. He also got cannon and guns. The plunder is detailed as follows in Sabhasad: 65 elephants, 4000 horses, 1200 camels, many carts, bullocks etc., besides jewelry worth three lakhs and seven lakhs in cash and gold mohurs. This does not seem to be an extravagant estimate. Shivaji from this plunder did not fail to reward his men. The widows, especially, of soldiers fallen in battle were given pensions and the wounded soldiers were attended to and given sums of money. To the captains he gave horses, elephants, golden ornaments and mokasas of villages (Sabhasad).

Shivaji naturally took advantage of this signal victory to at once extend his dominion. He at once came to Wai where he was joined by his commander Netaji Palkar who had been called back from the pursuit of parties sent by Afzalkhan against Shirval, Saswad, Poona and Konkan. He came rather too late to intercept Fazalkhan who

1. मरणान्तानि वैराणि (रामा. युद्धकाण्ड).

took away the remnant of his force at Wai.[1] *Shiva-Bharata* details the towns in the Krishna valley he next took and annexed to his kingdom, such as Khatav, Mayani, Ashte, Masur, Karhad, as also Karavir or Kolhapur. But the greatest acquisition was that of the fort of Panhala which was the dominant fort in that part of the country. The fort was stormed and Shivaji, when he surveyed it, was pleased to find within its extensive wall circuit, palaces, wells, gardens and well-built tanks.[2]

The taking of the fort of Panhala, following soon after the destruction of Afzalkhan and his army, caused the Bijapur Durbar great anxiety. They at once sent Fazalkhan who had escaped, to join Rustum Jama who was the general in charge of Rajapur, Kolhapur and Raybag districts and ordered them to forthwith attack Shivaji. Rustum Jama, though of wavering loyalty and favourably inclined towards Shivaji, as letters from European traders in Konkan show[3], led his army augmented with forces from Bijapur against Shivaji. But he was defeated signally near Kolhapur in a pitched battle, described in detail in *Shiva-Bharata*, chapter 24, mentioning the names of generals on both sides in the centre and flanks, as in the Gita and Mahabharata. Rustum Jama and Fazalkhan escaped

1. SB 23, 58-61. 2. SB 23, 72.
3. PS 790, 791, 800, 812.

and were not pursued. Shivaji remained master of the territory he had acquired, consisting of the present Satara district and the greater part of the present Kolhapur state as also of the controlling strong and extensive fort of Panhala. This battle near Kolhapur was fought on December 28, 1659, as mentioned in the Rajyabhisheka Shakavali, (the date of the taking of Panhala being a month before and time, early in the night, according to the same authority). J gives the date of the taking of Panhala as Margashirsha Vadya 9, Monday[1], and it also mentions (without specifying the date) the battle near Kolhapur with Rustum Jama and the seizure of 12 elephants and 2000 horses.

A Rajapur letter, dated 19th November 1659[2], speaks of Shivaji's advancing against Panhala, while another letter dated 9th December[3] speaks of his having taken the fort. The battle between Rustum Jama and Shivaji is also spoken of in another Rajapur letter.[4] It describes the battle as follows:— "Fazalkhan, joining his force with that of Rustum Jama who was in Rajapur, advanced against Shivaji. His force which was in advance was totally defeated, many soldiers being slain; but Fazalkhan himself escaped. Rustum Jama was also defeated but not with much loss and he retreated towards

1. S′ 1581 (Nov. 28,1659). 2. PS 781.
3. PS 790. 4. PS 800, ER 3, p. 5.

Hukeri." This suggests his being favourably inclined towards Shivaji, a fact actually mentioned further on in this letter.

While Shivaji returned to Panhala, Netaji was sent in pursuit of the fugitives and also to conquer territory towards the east. He took many towns, such as Kundal, Kagal, Miraj, Sangli, etc. (names of about 36 towns are given in SB). Jedhe S'akavali mentions that Shivaji himself went on this plundering expedition in Bijapur territory as far as Gada Lakshmeshvar in Magh Shudha 14 (February 1660). Ali Adilshah now determined to send a third army against Shivaji, under a reliable commander. He called Siddi Johar, commander of Karnul in South India, and also many contingents of forces of the Nayaks in Karnatak and sent him, thus enforced, against Shivaji together with Rustum Jama and Fazal who had returned defeated.

While Bijapur was collecting an army, Shivaji availed himself of his victory to extend and reimpose his dominion in the Konkan also. He had taken Kalyan and Bhivandi long before (three years back) and had also annexed their territory. Southwards he had by this time taken the territory from Chaul to Dabhol ; for even *Shiva-Bharata* relates that when Afzalkhan started against Shivaji, he sent detachments to take, besides Supa, Sasvad and Poona, Tal Konkan also."Saifkhan Habsi (Siddi) forcibly recovered Tal Konkan".[1] Dabhol must have been lost thus for a time, but Shivaji now sent a force to Konkan to retake the towns lost, as also seize Bijapur property lying there in its ports. 3 ships of Afzalkhan laden with property in the port of Dabhol were taken to Rajapur by the subedar, (port officer), as related in a Rajapur letter[2] dated 4th February, 1660. We must remember that there were settlements for trading of three European powers in the ports of Dabhol, Vengurla and Rajapur, namely, English, Dutch and Portuguese. These often intrigued against one another by bribing the authorities at Bijapur and their transactions with the various fighting powers are also referred to in their letters. It is not necessary to mention these transactions here; it will be sufficient to note their testimony in connection with Shivaji's doings. Thus the long Rajapur letter[3] already referred to and dated 10th December 1659, speaks of Shivaji's taking the ports on the west coast and also the inland towns in Konkan. This evidences Shivaji's retaking Dabhol at this time.[4] The ships of Bijapur in the several ports were taken by the subedars of those ports to Rajapur which was a strong and safe place in the possession of Bijapur. But Shivaji's

1. SB 23, 12.
2. PS 800; ER 3.
3. P 791.
4. Ditto (ER 3.)

army even went to Rajapur and tried to seize Bijapur property. A Rajapur letter[1], dated 14th January 1660, mentions Shivaji's army being in Rajapur. This must have been after the defeat of Rustum Jama in December 1659. The English who naturally usually sided with the suzerain power, on the plea of their own claim for money lent, did not deliver the ships of Afzalkhan to Shivaji's captain. He thereupon imprisoned Gyfford and kept him confined at Kharepatan[2]. On receiving a complaint, Shivaji ordered his release[3] and also directed his soldiers to return every thing taken by them. Revington in his letter[4] says, " Shivaji is so great and noble a person that he would do no injustice," a remark worth noticing here.

A Goa letter, dated 12th March, mentions Shivaji's plundering the country as far as Bijapur itself and defeating some Bijapur captains. It also mentions that Shivaji's men attacked Banda and that he was now master of all the Konkan territory from Chaul to Banda[5]. A Rajapur letter dated 19th March speaks of about three to four thousand men of Shivaji moving about in the Konkan and taking towns and tributes.[6] A Dutch letter, dated April 1660 from Vengurla, gives interesting details

1. PS 790, ER 2.
2. Ditto and ER 3.
3. PS 804.
4. ER 3.
5. PS 810.
6. PS 811.

of operations which may be accepted as correct as the operations were conducted near Vengurla. " Shivaji's men attacked Kudal fort in February. Lakham Sawant who was still a jagirdar under Bijapur and who was now against Shivaji collected men and attempted to raise the siege. They were unsuccessful, many allies leaving Lakham. Kudal fort was taken, but Lakham Sawant made a second attempt and took it on March 18th. Rustum Jama, taking advantage of this victory, reported that he had taken Kudal. He also took possession of the fort of Phonda ".[1] It thus seems that when Shivaji was invested in Panhala in April or June, as we shall presently see, he had lost the fort of Phonda which had been long in his possession.

1. PS 812.

XVI. THE THERMOPYLÆ OF INDIAN HISTORY

Bijapur, at this time, also applied for help to Aurangjeb. Aurangjeb was, until now, with consumate diplomacy, playing a policy of alternately patronizing the two parties. In a letter dated 3rd April 1657, written before he became emperor, he had allowed Shivaji to keep with himself the forts he had taken from Bijapur and had also given him the fort of Dabhol with the territory about it[1]. When he started for the north, he asked Bijapur to look to Shivaji and not to take him into its service, as already stated. After he became emperor, he informed Shivaji, in a letter dated 14th July 1659, of his ascending the throne and asked him to carry out his former proposal. A Goa letter, dated 18th December 1659, mentions that Shivaji was supported in his aggressions against Bijapur by Aurangjeb[2]. He thus wished to weaken Bijapur through Shivaji and then to destroy both in their weakness. But after the success of Shivaji over both Afzalkhan and Rustum Jama, he thought that Shivaji was getting too strong and hence decided to send an overwhelming force into the Deccan to

1. PS 724. 2. PS 792.

crush him and thus in a way to assist Bijapur. His maternal uncle Shaistekhan, in command of a force of 70 thouand horse, with artillery, and assisted by many Rajput and Maratha captains with their contingents soon arrived on the banks of the Bhima, the boundary between Mogul and Maratha territory. The names of these captains are given by *Shiva-Bharata* in a long list[1], which it is not necessary to copy here in detail. But we may state that five Bhosale captains, one of them being Trimbakji, son of Sharifji, who were probably jagirdars in Mogul territory, were present as also the Maratha heroine Raibagin, widow of Uderam of Raibag. The force crossed the Bhima and invested the fort of Chakan; but Shivaji's men who held the fort, gallantly defended it, declaring that " while Shivaji fights with Johar at Panhala, we will fight with Shaistekhan at Chakan."[2]

Shivaji's kingdom was thus invaded at the same time by two powerful armies and seemed threatened with extinction. Shivaji was confined in the fort of Panhala by the large army under Siddi Johar, assisted by many Maratha captains who were opposed to Shivaji, like the chief of Pali and that of Shringarpur. It seems from Parnālākhyāna that Venkoji, Shivaji's half-brother, who was a jagirdar in South India was

1. SB 25, 40-45. 2. SB 25, 66.

also among the Maratha captains who joined Siddi Johar in the investment of Panhala. This force, in spite of sallies of detachments of Mawalas from the fort, invested it closely. Shivaji's heroic mother who was at Rajgad saw her son's kingdom attacked on both sides and Shivaji unable to move from Panhala. She, therefore, asked Netaji Palkar, Shivaji's commander-in-chief, to relieve Shivaji by attacking the investing army, instead of ravaging the country about and trying to cut off the supplies of Siddi Johar. He, thereupon, made a sudden attack on Siddi Johar's army in company of Hilal, a Siddi captain, who had joined Shivaji after Afzalkhan's destruction. In spite of the bravery of both, they were defeated, with the loss of Hilal's heroic son who was killed in battle.[1] This happened about June 1660 and the army of Siddi Johar, under orders from Bijapur, continued the investment with greater rigour even in the rainy season. In the meanwhile, the Mogul army "destroying temples and mathas, pillaging and pulling down the houses of Patels and Deshmukhs and laying waste towns and villages"[2], took Shivaji's country about Chakan and Saswad. Shivaji became very anxious and resolved to leave the fort of Panhala in charge of a trusted captain[3] and go to

1. SB 26, 36. 2. SB 25, 60, 61.
3. Trimbak Bhaskar, SB 26, 54.

Vishalgad breaking through the investing line of guards. *Shiva-Bharata*, as usual, states that the goddess Bhavani, the protecting deity of Shivaji, advised him to do so in a dream. It was Ashadha Vadya 1, July 13, 1660 (J), the middle of the rainy season. (SB mentions S'ravan, perhaps not taking into account the intercalary Jyeshtha of that year which makes the period of Shivaji's confinement one of 5 months). The foreign letters of that time do not give, and we cannot fix, the exact date. On this night, rendered dark by clouds, Shivaji started on this dare-devil march, seated in a palanquin and escorted by 600 trusted Mawalas. The unwavering devotion of these foot-soldiers which was beyond all praise and their intimate knowledge of hill-paths were the two staves on which Shivaji depended. The party, starting about 9 p. m., avoided the investing guards (who were further put up in thatched huts owing to the rains) by hilly crooked paths; and notwithstanding the rains and the swollen streams illumined now and then by lightening flashes, as *Shiva-Bharata* poetically describes, reached, the next evening, the foot of the Vishalgad fort which was in Shivaji's possession. When Johar learnt, from spies, of Shivaji's escape, some hours after his departure, he was aghast and intensely vexed. He, however, sent in pursuit a party of horsemen and soldiers under Masaudkhan Berber. They saw Shivaji's men ascending the hill in the evening light and the horsemen pressed on and also the footmen. They might have caught Shivaji before he ascended the hill and entered the fort. At this supreme crisis, Baji Prabhu Deshpande of Hirdas Maval was placed by Shivaji in a narrow khind or defile which has to be passed before reaching the fort and asked him to hold the pursuers till he was apprised of Shivaj's safe arrival on the fort by the boom of a cannon. The heroic and devoted Baji with the help of the equally heroic and devoted Mawalas under Bandal, opposed the rushing onset of horsemen and footmen in the defile and held them till the boom of a cannon was heard. Baji Prabhu, as he heard the boom, gladly died, being cut down at that moment in this Thermopylæ of Indian history, like Leonidas; and his name deserves to be immortalized in the history of Maratha independence.

The news of Shivaji's safe escape was heard by the Hindus in Maharashtra with the greatest glee and by Bijapur with the greatest grief. The Sultan of Bijapur was wroth with the Siddi and as usual suspected him of being bribed. Some accounts state that Shivaji had lulled the Siddi into supineness by proposing, on the evening before his escape, to hand over the fort to him with permission to retire. But this is not believable as

Johar would not have slackened his vigilence for a mere proposal. The real reason why Shivaji successfully went out, in spite of the vigilance of the investing guards, was that it was a raining night and the Mawalas by their intimate knowledge of hilly paths succeeded in avoiding the guards altogether. Shivaji arrived at the fort of Vishalgad about five in the evening, as *Shiva-Bharata* states that he had gone five yojanas (40 miles) in seven yāmas[1]. Shivaji next day was invested in Vishalgad itself by a contingent sent by Siddi Johar who could not or would not give up the siege of Panhala. This force, being insufficient, was attacked by Shivaji in a sally and utterly routed and Masaudkhan fled back to Panhala[2]. Shivaji thereupon, taking with him trusted and faithful contingents, left Vishalgad and went to Rajgad to meet his anxious mother. The safe arrival of Shivaji at Rajgad must have intensely gladdened the heart of that anxious and heroic mother. One can imagine the immense joy which Jijabai felt as a mother and a sympathiser in Shivaji's sacred plan for the deliverance of Maharashtra and for the relief of oppressed Hinduism. She clasped her darling heroic son to her bosom and bathed him with tears of joy, "the milk of love flowing out of her breasts."[3]

1. SB 27, 13. 2. SB 27, 30-35. 3. SB 27, 40.

Siddi Johar, accused of being bribed by Shivaji, was dishonoured and dismissed and after a time he returned to his original charge, namely the district of Karnool. *Shiva-Bharata* relates that he was subsequently despatched by poisoning, which may be believed, the Bijapur Durbar being already blackened by such acts of treachery against three ministers. The king of Bijapur, after the rainy season, himself went to Panhala for prosecuting the siege of the fort. Trimbak Bhaskar, the commandant, by Shivaji's order, however, handed over the fort to Salabatkhan himself on 22 September, 1660.[1]

It seems strange, it may be stated again, that the combatants in the Pavan Khind defended by Baji Deshpande had no guns with them. At least the Mahomedans were expected to have these weapons which could have been procured from Europeans settled on the west coast. Perhaps these weapons could be had for high prices only. The Mahomedans had manufactured cannon, but why they could not manufacture guns is inexplicable. They did not also use cannon much for want of expert gunners. The Marathas certainly wholly depended for these fire-arms, cannon and guns, on foreigners and apparently did not manufacture even gunpowder. The Mawala foot-soldiers usually seem, therefore, to have only used swords up to this time

1. Bhadrapada Vadya 13 S'. 1582 (J).

It is again strange that *Shiva-Bharata* does not mention the memorable self-sacrifice, on the altur of patriotism, of Baji Prabhu. No mention is no proof, however, of the non-existence of a thing unless mention is absolutely necessary; and the *Shiva-Bharata*, written mainly to glorify Shivaji's exploits, may have unconsciously failed to notice this incident. But it mentions fights of even Sardars repeatedly and with great detail, following the example of the Mahabharata. This exploit of Baji Prabhu is, however, unquestionably historical, being mentioned in Jedhe S'akavali and other documents such as a Dutch letter of Vengurla, dated 5th September 1660, which speaks of Shivaji's keeping men in a defile and their defending the pass against odds till cut down by a party coming in their rear by a difficult route as at Thermopylæ.[1] Indeed a Sanad granted to the family by Shahu refers to this incident and we have no hesitation in glorifying this hero of the important Prabhu community of Western India.

Some Minor Controversia l Points

1. PS 831, a Dutch letter written on September 5th 1660, two months after Shivaji's escape, mentions that Shivaji, through his vakil Gangadhar, proposed to Siddi Johar alias Salabatkhan that he would deliver all his kingdom to Ali Adilshah if the former who was like his father would plead for him and that Shivaji next day on a

1. PS 31.

stormy moonless night left Panhala with 1000 men. Such rumours which exaggerate matters were, however, natural after Shivaji's successful escape.

2. It is suggested by some that Vishalgad was already invested by the chiefs of Pali and Shringarpur in behalf of Bijapur. But this does not seem correct. Shivaji who had plenty of sources of correct information would not have gone to such a place. These two chiefs were probably with Siddi Johar at Panhala and they were sent to assist Masaudkhan after Shivaji had gone to Vishalgad. SB 27-28 seems to suggest this idea, but as the previous verse 25 speaks of Shivaji being already on the Vishalgad fort, the coming of these two Maratha chiefs must be for helping Masaudkhan and there can be no possibility of or reason for Johar's sending them to invest Vishalgad on the Ghat-Matha, of all forts, before Shivaji reached it.

3. We have already noticed the controversy as to whether Baji Deshpande fought and died in the Pavan Khind, as SB does not mention it. Some have suggested that he had come of his own accord to assist Shivaji, as his being in the latter's service is not mentioned. But as often stated elsewhere, no mention leads to no inference. His dying there is mentioned by J and also a contemporary foreign letter. This also disposes of the idea of the chiefs of Pali and Shringarpur having already invested the fort, as Baji could not have then defended the defile.

4. The story given in PS 831, namely that Shivaji formed two parties, one of them taking his barber who was named Shivaji and his own and that the first was caught while the other reached the fort safely, is absurd, to say the least. It is an imaginary multiplication of Shivaji's devices.

5. The more difficult question whether Shivaji went to Vishalgad or Rangana confronts us here. Chitnis Bakhar mentions Rangana, and Grant Duff naturally follows it; but *Shiva-Bharata* which was found later clearly mentions Vishalgad. The Dutch letter PS 831 also mentions Khelna which was the original name of the fort before Shivaji named it Vishalgad. But Captain Modak of the Gwalior army who has studied this question on the spot gives his opinion in favour of Rangana. He says that Ghod Khind, Gajapur, Badshah Mal, Pandhare Pani are names to be found on the way to Rangana also. But Vishalgad is nearer than Rangana and the argument that Shivaji would not have brought the enemy against the fort which was his kothi, is not of much avail. The nearest fort was the safest and the enemy might have followed him even to Rangana. Shivaji knew that the investing force at Panhala would not be weakened and Johar could only send small detachments against him. Moreover, his ultimate object was not to stay at Vishalgad but to go to Rajgad. The most cogent reason is that SB and the Dutch letter, being contemporaneous and much earlier than Chitnis Bakhar, deserve to be followed.

XVII. MOGULS MOUSE-TRAPPED IN UMBERKHIND

Having thus discomfited the Bijapur force, let us now see how Shivaji also discomfited the greater force of the Moguls. Jedhe S'akavali has the short note, "Shaistekhan took Chakan and then encamped in Poona, September 1660." *Shiva-Bharata* also notes the event of the taking of the fort of Chakan, after describing the excesses committed by the overwhelming force of the Moguls in its march, as already described[1]. The movements of this Mogul force are noted in Mahomedan accounts in detail as follows:— Alamgir-Nama states that Shaistekhan started from Ahmednagar on February 25 and crossed the Bhima after five days. He captured small forts near Sonavadi, Supe, Baramati etc., and came to Shirval on April 18th. He went thence to Khede Bare (a village where Shivaji often passed the days of his childhood in a big house specially built there) which was near the village of Kondhana which gave its name to the fort near by, also called Sinhgad. He could not, however, take that fort and he came back to Saswad, May 1st. He could not also take the

1. SB 28, 27-29.

important fort of Purandar near Saswad. He, therefore, went to Poona and thence to Chakan and invested its fort. After two months of investment, he took this ground-fort of Chakan on August 14th. There is a difference here of about a month (which is not of much importance) between J and Mahomedan accounts.

Shivaji had in the meantime come to Rajgad, and his ministers advised him to try for peace with the Moguls, as it was difficult to fight with such a strong force. J has a note that Sonajipant returned from Shaistekhan with his message in Kartik (October), which means that Shivaji had sent him with proposals of peace. The reply not being satisfactory, the war continued. Shaistekhan, hereafter, sent a strong detachment under Kartalabkhan, assisted by some Maratha chiefs, Raibagin included, through the Ghats to attack Shivaji's possessions in Konkan, such as Kalyan, Bhivandi, Panvel, Chaul (Champavati) and Nagothna.[1] The army passed through the Umber Khind Ghat by a road which was so narrow that the men could descend one by one only. Shivaji knew of this invasion but did not attack the invading force at this place and allowed it to collect in a plain at the foot, surrounded by such high mountains that "there was not even a breath of wind in the plain encir-

1. SB 28, 59.

cled by a thick jungle" (SB). Shivaji had kept detachments of his force concealed on all sides of this plain, as at Par near Pratapgad before. The sound of war-drums, suddenly beat, gave the Mogul army notice of an attack and the army was soon enveloped and plied with shot and arrows. It was mid-day and "the extreme heat increased by absence of wind added its arrows." The army not even seeing the enemy was thrown into confusion. At this juncture, the Raibagin advised Kartalabkhan to save the army by beseeching Shivaji for safe retreat. Shivaji probably did not wish to carry matters too far and enrage Shaistekhan or Aurangjeb and granted truce. The soldiers of Shivaji who had begun falling upon the confused army were countermanded by Shivaji's mace-bearers and the army eventually returned by the path it had come by, leaving much property on the battle-field[1]. This event happened on Magh S'uddha 14, S'1582, corresponding to February 2, 1661 (J). Shivaji asked Netaji Palkar, his commander-in-chief, to follow the army and see that it did not break the conditions of the truce.

1. SB 29, 53-60.

XVIII. CONQUEST OF SOUTH KONKAN

Having taken this precaution, Shivaji resolved to make a sudden raid into southern Konkan and plunder Rajapur and other towns and thus punish the English for having supplied cannon and shot to Salabatkhan at the siege of Panhala and also the chiefs of Pali and Shringarpur for investing Vishalgad. These sudden resolves and movements of Shivaji prove Shivaji's great genius for war. He was already in Konkan with a large force and instead of returning to Rajgad to watch Shaistekhan, he suddenly started on this momentous expedition. He found towns and villages abandoned by the enemy and plundered them. He came to Dabhol and took that place.[1] Next he came to Pali, the chief of which fled to Shringarpur. He next came to Chiplun and thence to Sangameshwar which were immediately abandoned by the Mahomedans. He was joined here by Tanaji Malusare and Pilaji Nilkanth.[2] Finally he reached Rajapur and, defeating the Mahomedan force posted there, took that place, well-known for its riches obtained by maritime trade.[3] Shivaji compelled all the traders, Hindus and Mahomedans, English and Dutch,

1. SB 29, 67. 2. SB 29, 81. 3. SB 29, 89.

to pay to him heavy tributes. Even treasure buried underground was dug out.[1] *Shiva-Bharata* gives a highly poetical account of the rich plunder obtained by Shivaji and a long list of the articles of merchandise seized which is important for commercial history. But what is more important to us here is that it properly praises the valour of the Europeans though considered " lower in rank than Mahomedans." "The valour of these foreigners is heightened by their unerring aim with fire-arms. They are expert in attacking fortifications. They surpass the god of riches by their wealth. They have all the arts of delusion of Mayāsura. They are daring navigators of the mid-ocean."[2]

Ali Adilshah was pained to hear of the plundering of Rajapur; but he could do nothing to punish Shivaji, being engaged in war with Johar in Karnatak. He, however, directed the chief of Shringarpur or Prabhanavalli to attack Shivaji as that chief was already inimical to Shivaji and was near by, as also accustomed to hill fighting. He suddenly fell upon the army of Tanaji Malusare at Sangameshwar at night; but he was signally defeated. Shivaji on his return from Rajapur attacked him with all his force and took his prosperous town. The country was full of various artisans whose avocations given in SB are worth noting[3]. The chief called

1. SB 30, 6. 2. SB 30, 1-2. 3. SB 31, 17-24.

Suryarao fled and his whole prosperous state was conquered and annexed. Shivaji built a fort at Pali and named it Mandanagad[1]. He built a fort at Shringarpur also and called it Pratitagad[2]. Trimbak Bhaskar was appointed governor and was kept there with a strong force for the protection of the newly acquired territory. Shivaji then returned to Rajgad; he did not proceed against the Sawant of Wadi as he proffered submission and again joined Shivaji (Duff).

J mentions the plundering of Nizampur (Rajapur) and the taking of Dabhol and Prabhavali after the Mogul defeat in Umber Khind in the same month, Magha (February), and the taking of Shringnarpur and the flight of Suryarao in May 1661. This latter date is confirmed by an English long letter[3] which states that Shivaji "has lately enlarged and strengthened his country by overcoming the two Rajas, the Dalvi and the Chief of Shringarpur, by which means he now commands all the coast from Danda Rajapur to Kharepatan". A Dutch letter, dated April 20 1661,[4] mentions that Ali Adilshah has concluded peace with Shivaji and that Siddi Johar has rebelled against him, proclaiming himself servant of the Moguls. This conclusion of peace must have been merely a

1. SB 31, 26. 2. SB 32, 4.
3. PS 848 dated 10th June, 1661. 4. PS 845.

proposal made after the plundering of Rajapur, as we shall presently show. It is rather strange that the plundering of Rajapur does not find mention in English letters until the 10th of June 1661, when the above long letter from Revington and others[1] first refers to it as follows :—" Shivaji has sent us as prisoners to Vasota. He robs and demands money from all men, Banias, Moors, Persians and Arabians "[2]. Probably they could not write earlier, being imprisoned. They wished that negotiations should be opened from Surat for their release and for compensation for plunder, at least for their release only. This latter clause shows that the plunder was justifiable. Indeed, a Surat letter from President Andrews, dated 10th March 1662, clearly admits the justice of Shivaji's action in plundering the English and imprisoning Revington[3]. He writes from Surat to the 'disconsolate prisoners' on Rairi castle:— " How you came to prison you know very well. This punishment is not for your defending company's goods. It is for your going to the siege of Panhala and firing cannon under English banner. Anybody who is strong enough would have punished you in these circumstances. Merchents have no business to sell ball and powder nor fire on enemies."

1. PS 848, ER 26, p. 23. 2. SB 26, 23, also.
3. PS 874, ER 36, p. 37.

'Shivaji had even asked Revington not to sell ammunition to Bijapur.' In this just manner the authorities at Surat condemned Revington's action. It also seems from this letter that Revington was not released up to March 1662. Another letter of Escaliot, dated 20th January 1664[1], mentions Shivaji's digging the English factory and carrying away buried treasure. It mentions the release of English prisoners after about eight months.

1. Siddi Johar

1. Siddi Johar was in no way guilty of allowing Shivaji to escape. And he rebelled against Ali Adilshah, because he was unjustly charged and Ali Adilshah went personally against him. As stated in J, Siddi Johar, being defeated, fled to Kelosi and there died after two months. *Shiva-Bharata*, however, states that he was besieged in Kurnool and when he could not be taken, he was secretly poisoned by the mother of the Adilshah (SB 28,21). J does not give the date of his death or defeat.

2. Pali and Shringarpur

Pali according to SB is to the south of Dabhol (SB 29, 68). Pali, a town in the present Bhor State. is north of Dabhol and it cannot, therefore, be identified with the above Pali in SB. But Palvan seems to be the Pali of SB. The name of its chief is given as Jaswant (SB 29, 76) and he is called Dalvi in PS 848, (the English letter of Revington to Surat dated 10th June 1661 already referred to). Shringarpur is to the north of Sangameshwar

1. ER 79, 74.

in the present taluka of Ratnagiri. The name of its chief is given as Suryaraj (SB 29, 71). It is not clear if this is a surname and is equivalent to Surve. The name Surve is well-known in the Konkan, but it is not to be found in Desh. PS 843 speaks of Harji and Suryaji as chiefs of Prabhavali and of their fleeing from Shringarpur to Lakham Sawant for protection. The name Prabhanvali is of the district and is given in SB as Prabhavali, as also in PS 857 and 871. Pilaji Nilkant was the Subedar of Prabhavali in 1661 and 1662. The date given in J of the defeat of Surve of Shringarpur, *viz*., May 1661 (Vaishakh S'uddha 11 S'.1583 Monday) is proved by PS 848, which mentions Dabhol and Prabhavali as taken possession of in March.

3. Peace with Bijapur

Dutch register, dated April 20, 1661 (PS 845), states " The Sultan of Bijapur went against Panhala with a large army but eventually concluded peace with rebellious Shivaji. Salabatkhan has rebelled against him and declared himself to be a servant of the Moguls. " J states "Panhala was given to Salabatkhan on 13 Bhadrapada Vadya (Sept. 22) and peace was concluded." Putting the two together it seems that Ali Adilshah, finding the fort of Panhala still not taken, though Shivaji had escaped, and suspecting Johar of treachery, himself marched against Panhala ; but before he reached it, Shivaji concluded terms of surrender with Johar and handed over the fort to him. The peace spoken of in the Dutch letter of April 20 does not seem to be a recent event but seems to be the peace concluded with Johar in September. There was thus no peace with Bijapur itself when Shivaji took South Konkan and sacked Rajapur in the possession of Bijapur in February. But a peace appears to have been concluded between Shivaji and

Ali Adilshah himself after this event, because the latter had to proceed against Johar and punish him for his treachery and subsequent rebellion. Shivaji, therefore, appears to have taken rest hereafter and remained quiet for a time at Vardhangad as J notes "Shivaji went to Vardhangad in Kartik (November 1661) and remained there the whole summer (June 1662). J records that in Bhadrapada (September 1661) Narhar Anandrao was appointed Peshwa and Annajipant was appointed Wakenavis while Sarkarkoons (Divisional officers) were given Palkhis. This shows that Shivaji concerned himself at this time with the civil administration of his state. In April 1662, J next records, Moropant was appointed Peshwa. This position he enjoyed very long, while there was frequent change before him. Thus while in September 1661, Narhar Anandrao was Peshwa, PS 871 of January 1662, an order by Shivaji to Pilaji Nilkantrao Subedar, Prabhavali, bears the seal of Shamraj Nilkant who was thus Peshwa from 1661 December to April 1662. Shivaji found in Moropant a trusty man both as soldier and administrator.

Shivaji must have concluded peace with Bijapur because he had to fight with Shaistekhan who was encamped in his Poona territory. Rajapur English letter from Rudolf Taylor to Surat, dated February 6, 1663,[1] clearly states that Ravji Pandit, Shivaji's agent, explained that Shivaji plundered Rajapur because it was then Bijapur territory and 'his master was at war with the

1. PS 917, ER 53, 47.

king of the Deccan.' 'But now Shivaji had a farman from Bijapur for Rajapur and the places he had conquered in Konkan and thus Shivaji was master of Rajapur and the English need have no fear of being molested.' This means that Shivaji had consented to hold his conquests in South Konkan as a jagirdar under Adilshah. This also justifies the expression in PS 857, dated August 3, 1661, that 'at present Tal Konkan had been granted to Saheb.' This peace and the farman must be placed between March and August 1661.

XIX. MIDNIGHT RUSH OF MOGUL CAMP

Shaistekhan, the lord of 70,000 horse and artillery and several contingent forces, "the encampent of which covered the area of two villages"[1] was established at Poona on the Mutha river. He had conquered Chakan and thus had clear communication with the Mogul territory beyond the Bhima wherein lay Ahmednagar, his base. He not only checked Shivaji's operations in the Deccan, but also watched what was happening at Bijapur and Govalkonda so that he might pounce upon them at the opportune moment. He had sent Kartalabkhan to take possession of the fort of Parenda which probably was given at this time again by Bijapur to Aurangjeb for assisting it against Shivaji. It was taken by him probably in November 1660 (J). We also find that he tried to extract tribute from Govalkonda also as per Dutch letter dated November 20, 1661.[2] Since the disaster in Umberkhind in February 1661 till April 1663 for about two years, he appears to have done nothing worth noting against Shivaji. But he must be supposed to have retaken, by sending detachments under his lieutenants in May 1661,

1. S & SB. 2. PS 863.

Kalyan and the adjoining district as we find from contemporary English letters, probably while Shivaji was absent in South Konkan. An attempt was made by Bulakhi in 1661 (probably June) to take Dehrigad near Pen by besieging it, but the siege was broken through by Kavaji Kondhalkar (J). Pen itself had probably been taken by the Moguls and, as J mentions, Shivaji himself went against Jamdarkan (Mogul captain) suddenly and plundered Pen. In this hard-fought battle, Waghoji Tupe and other captains of Shivaji were wounded (J). In the Poona district itself, detachments were often sent to harass the Deshmukhs who were, therefore, advised by Shivaji to send their families and even the people under them to safe places in the Konkan after the rainy season.[1] Shivaji himself remained outside the Poona territory apparently not even residing long in its forts, Rajgad or Sinhgad. Shaistekhan tried to take Sinhgad by treachery ; but the attempt was discovered in time and Shivaji sent Moropant Peshwa to the fort with a sufficient force[2]. Mogul cavalry detachments were posted by the Moguls at Chaul in Konkan and at Rahimatpur in Desh as mentioned in the English letter from Gyfford to Surat dated 30th March.[3] Mogul cavalry also pursued Netaji Palkar, who had gone on a

1. PS 905 of 23 October 1662.
2. PS 925 April 3, 1663. 3. PS 923, ER 56, p. 52.

plundering expedition into Berar, as far as Bijapur. But these were unimportant affairs and it seems that Shaistekhan himself remained in Poona inactive, enjoying the cool and equable climate of Poona so different from that of Delhi and even Ahmednagar.

One night, however, in April 1663, he was suddenly roused from his inactivity in his own camp and in his own bed by Shivaji. The details of this midnight rush of the Mogul camp, given differently by different writers, appear like those of a thrilling chapter in a romance. We lose from here the guidance of the well-informed contemporary *Shiva-Bharata*, in relating the story of Shivaji's life and have to rely on foreign reports which though exaggerated are at least contemporary.

It is possible that this midnight attack might have suggested itself to the intrepid Shivaji from the Mahabharata account of the midnight rush of the camp of the Pandavas by Ashvatthama and the merciless massacre perpetrated by him of the victorious allies. The points of similarity are these. Shaistekhan was established in Shivaji's house, Lal Mahal, every inch of which was known to Shivaji. The Pandavas similarly, in the arrogance of victory, were established in Duryodhana's *S'ibir* or camp palace, every inch of which was known to Ashvatthama. The Mogul army was encamped in and around the town of Poona, every outlet or inlet of which was known to Shivaji. So was Ashvatthama thoroughly familiar with the whole of the encampment of the Kauravas spread over many square miles. Thirdly, owing to their secure stay for about two years, the Mogul army and guard-posts were not alert, never expecting any hostile attack at night. So also the victorious Pandavas and their partisans felt themselves completely secure, having destroyed the whole of the Kaurava army and they too did not expect any midnight attack. Lastly, that was the only way left to Ashvatthama to wreak his vengeance on the Pandavas, especially on the Pānchala Dhrishtadyumna who had murdered his father. Similarly Shivaji could not hope to fight with such a vast force openly and a midnight surprise was the only way by which he could frighten it or make an impression on it.

How exactly the rush was carried out cannot, we think, be now determined as the accounts vary and each of them seems faulty or exaggerated. The substance of all, however, is the same. Shivaji with some men entered the Mogul encampment probably in the evening as ordinary men who could not have been challenged. It was Chaitra S'uddha 8 Sunday, ([illegible] and other Shakavalis). About midnight, when it was dark, the moon having gone down, Shivaji and his men approached Lal Mahal and cutting down the guards entered the sleeping apartments. The women in Shaistekhan's seraglio raised an alarm and Shaistekhan tried to escape through a window when a sword stroke on his hand cut off three fingers. Shaistekhan's son attacked Shivaji and his men but he was killed. Shivaji got out safely and mounting a horse which was kept ready, rode away in the tumult caused by the surprise attack and joining his men kept outside of Poona at a distance of about 2 miles, reached Sinhgad safely.

This successful raid into the Mogul camp was unquestionably the most daring feat in Shivaji's life and is unsurpassed in the history of the world for intrepidity, careful planning and successful execution. It created so much consternation in the enemy* that Shaistekhan with his army soon retired from Poona to the Mogul territory (Ahmednagar), as we shall presently see, while at the same time it spread the fame of Shivaji among his countrymen. Indeed as he had himself planned the raid and executed it successfully putting his own life in danger, it increased his hold upon his captains and his people. Jasvantsingh who was encamped near the Mogul army was accused, as usual, of complicity in that he did not pursue Shivaji. He could,

* Strange notions arose about Shivaji's prowess, such as the idea that he could jump forty feet.

of course, do nothing when all of a sudden Shaistekhan's camp was attacked at night. But even pursuing Shivaji in a dark night and in a country which Shivaji well knew and the pursuers did not, was an impossibility, especially as Jasvantsingh did not know in which direction Shivaji had retired, and there was the danger of being ambushed as Afzalkhan's army had been at Par.

Different versions of the surprise attack

1. PS 930, a Rajapur English letter dated 12th April 1663, gives the earliest and clearest contemporary account of this event. "Raoji Pandit says he has got a letter written by the Raja himself which states that Shivaji with four hundred picked men entered Shaistekhan's camp, that he went into his tent to salam him and presently slew the watch, his eldest son, his son-in-law, 12 of his chief women, 40 great persons, and their general and wounded Shaistekhan with his own hand and left him for dead. Shivaji on his side had six men killed and 40 wounded. Jasvantsingh, captain of 10,000 horse, did not pursue Shivaji ; so it is generally believed it was done with his consent. But Shivaji tells his people that his Permeshwar bid him do it. "[1] Subsequent letters like PS 938 dated 25th May from Surat[2], tell this story with further exaggerations. This account, however, cannot be entirely true, from the fact that Shivaji would not have got admission for salaam with so many armed men and at such an awkward time. And if this incident had happened in daytime or even up to 10 p.m., Shivaji could not have escaped. The letter itself says that the pretext by which Shivaji got entrance [illegible] given in Shivaji's letter.

1. ER 60 p. 54.

The statement of Raoji Pandit that he had a letter from the Raja himself may be true, but the contents of it may have been misunderstood by the factors. This letter, however, confirms the date of this event (given in J) namely about a week before 13th April 1663, as will be just noted.

2. The next account we have is that of the Jedhe S'akavali. It gives the date as Chaitra S'uddha 8 Sunday S'. 1585 or 5th April 1663, and notes that " the hand of Shaistekhan was cut off and his son Abdul Fatteh was killed." Shivaji as soon as he got out of the Lal Mahal Dindi (door), mounted a horse and rode towards Karyat Mahal with some horsemen, joined by batches of others kept from place to place. There is nothing unbelievable in this story ; but it says nothing as to how Shivaji got into the camp of Shaistekhan as also into his palace. It, however, mentions Lal Mahal, it must be noted, and not a tent.

3. A still later account is that of Sabhasad-"The king came down from Rajgad alone and took choice men with him ; Babaji and Chimnaji, Kulkarnis of Khed (Bare), two brave and discreet men, walked in front. Two armies, the cavalry under Netaji and the Infantry under Moropant, were placed on the two sides of the Mogul camp at a distance of one mile. The king armed with a sword and buckler and followed by one thousand men entered the camp. They were challenged at several guardposts ; but Babaji and Chimnaji who preceded, replied, ' We are men of the camp returning from our posts, being relieved.' They reached Nawab's tent at mid-night. Keeping parties of his men on the four sides, Shivaji tore the tent cloth with his dagger. There were tents within tents and men on guard. They were struck down as they were lying asleep. The women being awakened caused alarm and the Nawab

as he was taking up his sword was attacked by Shivaji and his fingers were cut off. The row was now great and the men in the camp got ready and called aloud, 'Where is the enemy?' Shivaji's men getting mixed in the crowd also cried, 'Where is the enemy?' and thus safely got out. Shivaji joining his forces returned. The Nawab suspected his sardars of treachery and defection and left for Delhi after three days." It is, however, strange that one thousand men could pass challenge on the plea that they were guards returning from their posts and such guards could not have gone so near the Nawab's tent. Babaji and Chimnaji might have spoken in Urdu but the others must have been detected by their language as also by their dress. General Wolfe, when he conquered Quebec, used a similar artifice with success; but his English soldiers could easily have passed as French and could have spoken French well. Marathas could not be expected either by their appearance or language to pass as Mahomedan guards. Round about the Nawab's tent further, surely there must have been Mogul and Pathan guards and no Maratha guards. It goes without saying that Shivaji through his spies had information about everything in Shaistekhan's camp including the posting of guards and the sleeping place of the Khan.

4. The last and the strangest account is that given by Grant Duff from later Bakhars. "Shivaji left Sinhgad one evening in April and keeping small parties of Infantry along the road as he passed, reached Poona. Yesaji Kank and Tanaji Malusare with only 25 Mawalas entered the town with Shivaji. A Maratha foot-soldier of the camp who had been gained over, celebrated a marriage and obtained permission for a procession with tom tom

and armed men dancing as usual. Shivaji and his party joined the crowd, Poona being an open town. When all was quiet, Shivaji who was acquainted with every avenue went with a few pickaxes and broke into the cook-room. The women there raised an alarm. Shaistekhan was in the act of lowering himself from a window when he received a blow on his hand. Shivaji safely got out and having gone four miles lighted many torches to show the enemy that they were many in number." The foremost objection to this is that there could be no marriage celebration in Chaitra in which month this surprise raid undoubtedly took place. This cuts off the whole ground from the story and Sinhgad is about 15 miles from Poona and even a thousand torches ascending the fort cannot be seen from Poona, as the account absurdly relates at the end. The artifice of sending some torch-men one way while the men sought for, escaped by another and opposite way has been used and is found in history. But this account of the torches is not such an artifice.

It is suggested by some that the difficulty about a tent or a palace may be solved by holding that Shaistekhan lived in a tent pitched in the open ground inside Lal Mahal. But his tent was so big that "it required 66 elephants to carry it." In the old town of Poona and in Lal Mahal, there could hardly be room in any open space for even a moderately sized tent.

XX. CONQUEST OF KUDAL

Kudal territory is to the south of Rajapur and forms the present state of the Sawants of Wadi. The language of the people is Marathi and it forms part of Maharashtra like North and South Konkan, which form the present Thana[1] and Ratnagiri districts. Further south is the territory of Goa which is also in Maharashtra by language and further south is Karwar the people of which speak Marathi mixed with Kanarese. Kudal was unquestionably a part of the territory wherein Shivaji wished to establish Swaraj. He had already conquered the present Thana and Ratnagiri districts; and he now turned his attention to Kudal, the Desai of which, Lakham Sawant, had proved false to him more than once. He was a jagirdar under Bijapur, but he early acknowledged Shivaji's leadership and joined his plan for founding Swaraj, as stated already. He, however, assisted Bijapur whenever Shivaji was weak and he had recently helped the chief of Shringarpur against Shivaji. He had also obtained from the Dutch, powder and ammunition for fighting with Shivaji and the Dutch also thus deserved to be punished.

1. Thana includes Kolaba District.

The main Mogul army in the Deccan had retired to Ahmednagar beyond the Bhima, as Shaistekhan was suspicious of his captains. Shivaji thus found himself free to make a sudden dash against Kudal and Vengurla, in the same way as he had suddenly raided Rajapur after his escape from Panhala.

It may be noted here that the three European powers which were settled in the several ports on the western coast were already taking active part in the politics of the country, assisting one party against another and even planning to acquire dominion. The opportunity was favourable. The powerful Hindu state of Vijayanagar being destroyed, the western coast from Dabhol southwards came easily under Bijapur. In South India, wrongly called Karnatak, however, Bijapur had not yet established its authority and the petty chiefs who ruled patches of territory there, were too weak to oppose the disciplined forces and the fire-arms of the west. The Portuguese had already established their dominion in the territory of Goa in the teeth of the opposition of Bijapur, as also at Bassein and Chaul and were building forts there. The Dutch were established at Vengurla and had just conquered Quilon and Cannanore and fortified the latter place (English letter dated 17th April 1663[1]). The English were established at Rajapur as traders

1. PS 933; ER 61, p. 54, strangely omits this.

and they had just acquired Bombay from the Portuguese, hoping to lay the foundation of their future *empire*, as indeed their king, in his order (dated March 1662) to Sir Abraham Shipman to take possession of the island, prophetically said, "This would extend both the commerce of our subjects and our dominions in these parts[1]." The French, however, had no settlements on the west coast though they had some on the east. It is true that these western powers were constantly fighting with one another; but they were all shrewd enough to take advantage of the weakness of the country and as one means of acquiring dominion, they assisted one side against another in the country's internecine disputes, especially by the supply of cannon and ammunition. Shivaji also took advantage of the jealousies among these western powers, and before attacking the Dutch at Vengurla for assisting the Sawant, he concluded an alliance with the Portuguese[2]. The governor of Bassein had previously also been instructed from Goa to keep on friendly terms with Shivaji and not to assist the Moguls with supplies of provision and provender (Pisurlekar). The English, however, were at this time against Shivaji for keeping some of their men still confined and had even ordered reprisals against him on the sea.

1. PS 88, ER 39, p. 38. 2. PS 932 of April 1663.

Ali Adilshah with his foster mother, the Badi Sahebin, having also left for the south in March to punish Bahilolkhan and his mother, Shivaji properly decided to make a sudden raid on Kudal. A Dutch letter from Vengurla, of November 4th 1663,[1] six months after the event, describes this raid as follows: " Shivaji with four thousand horse and ten thousand foot came to Kudal Prant on 23rd May, 1663 (this date may be a little earlier, as Gyfford writes on 24th May from Kolhapur that Raoji had gone to Kudal and Vengurla with Shivaji)[2]. The people of Vengurla fled." "Sawant has burnt some villages of the Portuguese." (Dutch letter dated 11th June 1663.)[3] Some plunder was obtained by Shivaji and some Dutch houses were destroyed as the Dutch had removed their property on board steamers. "Shivaji sent a letter that the Kudal Prant had been given him by the Padshah." "Some najarana was sent to Shivaji by the Dutch which he accepted. Having made arrangements for the good order of the district, Shivaji has returned." "The Portuguese were joyful at the news of Shivaji's attacking Vengurla." "Lakham Sawant with six hundred men has left Wadi and is staying at the foot of Balaghat."[4]

Shivaji appointed Raoji Pandit as Subedar of Kudal as is noted in a Goa letter[5] dated 23rd July,

1. PS 959. 2. PS 937, ER 63, p. 55.
3. PS 940. 4. PS 959. 5. PS 948.

1663. Apparently he did not pursue and punish the Sawant, because he was a Bhosale himself and was likely to return to allegiance. Shivaji must really have obtained a farman from Bijapur for taking possession of and keeping this territory, as he had obtained one for Rajapur. The Bijapur king, being engaged in war with the refractory Bahilolkhan of Bankapur, must have thought it convenient to keep Shivaji satisfied as he was at peace with him at this time. Shivaji probably returned to Rajgad soon, not because the Moguls had come after him, as was supposed by some, but because the rainy season was approaching and the rains are always early and heavy in South Konkan.

Jasvantsingh was no doubt preparing to attack Sinhgad and did attack it after the rains; but he was defeated and he returned. Both Jasvantsingh and Shaistekhan were recalled by Aurangjeb in his rage at their incompetency and Jasvantsingh must have raised the seige for this reason also. He left Kondhana on Jyeshtha S'uddha 14 S'. 1584 or 28th May, 1664 (J).[1]

1. Monday is wrong here, but if it is correct we must take Ashad S'uddha 14 which fell on Monday and which corresponds to June 27.

XXI. SHIVAJI NOW A DE FACTO INDEPENDENT KING

It would be convenient to take here a survey of what Shivaji had achieved by this time. He began as a petty jagirdar under Bijapur, enjoying the fief of Poona, Supa and Indapur, acquired by his father Shahaji, originally under Nizamshahi, and then under Adilshahi in 1636, when he finally entered its service. Shivaji was installed as jagirdar in this fief in 1642 when he was in his 12th year and for some years he remained in tutelage under Dadaji Konddev, Shahaji's agent. He began his career in his 15th year (Amatya's Nītiśastra) in 1644 by forming a resolve to establish Hindwi Swaraj and collecting sympathisers in the cause of the founding of this Hindu kingdom in Maharashtra. He began actual work by taking in 1648 the forts of Sinhgad and Purandar which were usually kept by the suzerain power under its own officers. We have not yet found any contemporary document in support of the story that Shivaji began his career by taking Torana fort. Perhaps the word Torana suggested this idea. He next conquered Javali and added that jagir to his own in 1656. He next took North Konkan in 1658 and then South Konkan as far as Rajapur in Nov. 1661. He lastly took the Kudal territory (Nov. 1663). He had to give up Sinhgad for a time for securing the release of his father Shahaji in 1649; but he retook the fort some time after. His small kingdom thus at this time (1664) comprised all the Konkan from Bassein to Vengurla[1] and the corresponding Ghat-Matha, with all the important forts in both of them. Wai and Satara were, however, not in his possession[2] as also Kolhapur, though probably Bhor was.

It may be noted here that while Shivaji held the Rajapur and Kudal territories as mokasa under

1. A Dutch letter, dated 17th November 1663 (PS 963), says that Shivaji has sent some soldiers to Vengurla for its protection. Karwar English letter, dated 5th November (PS 961), shows that Rajapur was in Shivaji's possession. The Dutch long letter already noted (PS 959) speaks of Shivaji's control over Vengurla since it was reported that the Portuguese offered 15,000 hons to Shivaji for driving out the Dutch from Vengurla, but Shivaji did not accede to this request. On 20th July 1663 (PS 946, ER 67, p. 57), Gyfford writes to Surat that he had heard that "Adil-shah had ordered the Subedar of Phonda and the Sawant of Wadi to drive away Shivaji from Rajapur and Kharepatan which he had given to Mahomedkhan." A Dutch letter from Goa, dated 19th March 1660, says that all the territory from Chaul to Banda is in Shivaji's possession (PS 810). Thus these letters show that Shivaji acquired the whole Konkan from Kalyan to Kudal from 1660 to the beginning of 1664 and had it in his possession at this time.

2. PS 953, September 1664.

Bijapur, with respect to the other territories he was practically independent. He did not hold them under Bijapur as mokasa, as seems clear from hiso rder dated 18th December 1660[1], which directs cash payments to the Inamdars, Hindu and Mahomedan, who held *inams* in Poona, Indapur, Chakan, Supa and Baramati " when *formerly* these were held in mokasa by us before Afzalkhan. " The word peshji (formerly) is here important and shows that these places were now held by Shivaji independently, though before Afzalkhan they were held in mokasa under Bijapur. What the status was of North Konkan is not quite clear; but that part also was not in mokasa; for it had been ceded to the Moguls and had been conquered by Shivaji. The territory was more than once taken by the Moguls and was retaken by Shivaji. We must, therefore, look upon this territory also as independently held. Thus Shivaji's small kingdom consisted, at this time, of Poona, Indapur, Supa etc., to the north of the Nira ; and of Bhor, Javali etc., to its south, with the corresponding Konkan territory with the exception of Janjira or Danda Rajapuri.

That Shivaji was looked upon at this time as an independent king is also clear from the letters of foreigners. Thus the Viceroy of Goa in a letter to Shivaji dated 26th April 1663 styles him as Maratha

1. PS 837.

monarch (Pisurlekar). That his movement was a Hindu movement started for the deliverance of the Hindus from the yoke of a Mahomedan power is also apparent from the fact that English letters of this time style Shivaji as *Hindu* captain. Thus Revington's letter[1] written from Rajapur dated 13th February 1660 and addressed to Shivaji calls him General of Hindu forces. The English no doubt in their letters to one another describe Shivaji as a rebel against Bijapur. But successful rebellion is *de facto* independence, though not as yet recognised by the suzerain power. Shivaji acquired this position clearly enough when he destroyed Afzalkhan and his army, sent to suppress his rebellion.

This status is also supported and proved by the possession of strong forts and also a strong and numerous army. As described poetically by *Shiva-Bharata* and as stated in the Nīti of Amatya, the strength of a king lies in forts and in an army, for without an army, even forts are of no avail (SB). The importance of forts was realised even in the West till the last European war, though owing to the development of aeroplanes, it is now gone. For this reason, Shivaji maintained in good condition and even strengthened old forts such as Sinhgad, Purandar etc., and built new ones in Ghat-Matha such as Rajgad and Pratapgad and on the

1. PS 801, ER 4, p. 2.

sea-coast such as Vijayadurga and Suvarnadurga. (Hill forts were called 'gads,' ground forts 'kots' and forts in islands in the sea, 'durgs' or janjiras which is an Arabic word for island). The chief fort which Shivaji upto this time treated as his capital was Rajgad newly built by him on the Konkan side of the Sahyadhri range (now in Bhor state). The extensive fort of Rayari, subsequently called Raigad, was taken by Shivaji from the Mores in 1659, as already stated, and rebuilt. It was treated as capital by Shivaji after some years.

It would be interesting to give here the details of the administration and the military arrangements for the guarding of forts noted by Sabhasad. There were three heads on each fort : Havaldar, Sabnis and Sarnobat. A store officer called Karkhannis kept note of all stores. The rampart was divided for watching purposes into portions which were under sub-Sarnobats. The soldiers were put into parties of ten, nine men with one Naik. They were classed into four sorts according as they carried guns, swords, bows or other weapons. Each soldier was enlisted after personal inspection by Shivaji himself, The Havaldar was keeper of the fort and the Sarnobat was commander of soldiers; and these officers were to be Marathas of good family. The Sabnis was keeper of records and was to be a Brahmin and the Karkhannis was to be a Prabhu. This recognition of caste capacities and this enrolment and adjustment of the higher castes in Maharashtra is remarkable and was a new system, as Sabhasad remarks. It shows the genius of Shivaji for civil and military administration.

The army consisted of cavalry and infantry. The cavalry was divided into two sections, the Paga and the S'iledars. The Paga was cavalry maintained by the state itself and Shiledars were horsemen who joined in times of war and who maintained their own horses. Paga or state cavalry was made up of squadrons of 25 horsemen under a Havaldar and 5 such squadrons formed a company under a Jumledar whose pay was 500 hons yearly and a Palkhi was given him. 10 Jumlas formed a cavalry force of 1,000 under a Hazaria who got 1,000 hons. This force was provided with a Mujumdar or accountant who was a Brahmin, a Jamnis who was a Prabhu and a Karbhari or minister who was a Maratha. The Sarnobat or Commander-in-chief had 5 such units under him and his pay was 5,000 hons and he also had under him a number of spies and messengers. The S'iledari force was similarly constituted but it was under the control of the state Sarnobat. In dry season, that is from October to June, the cavalry was usually employed on foreign expeditions. It came back, for quarters in the rainy season, to certain fixed places where there were huts already erected for shelter of both man and horse and where grass and provisions had duly been collected. When on service, the cavalry was to subsist on forced contributions and whatever plunder was obtained was to be accounted for on return, portions of the same being allotted as of right to the men; but the rest was to be credited to the state. All valuable things such as jewels, costly cloth etc., were to be placed before Shivaji himself by the commander and then credited to the state.

The infantry of Mawalas and others consisted of units of ten men under a Nayak, 5 units being under a Havaldar and 10 under a Jumledar. 10 Jumlas formed a company of 1,000 under a Hazaria. A Jumledar got 40 hons yearly and a Hajaria got 500. The infantry Sarnobat or Commander-in-chief had under him 7,000 men, (the first Sarnobat of infantry being Yesaji Kank). The pay was paid in cash either from the Huzur treasury or from the treasury of Subas or districts and by varats or orders. Pay was paid punctually. Shivaji never gave any revenue power or mokasas to military officers, in order to protect the subjects from oppression and to prevent the military officers becoming too powerful. The revenue administration was left entirely in the hands of Karkuns or civil officers.

The state was divided into mahals for revenue administration and there was a Mujumdar (accountant) for each mahal and the head officer was called Havaldar, a word not now used. Several mahals formed a district or Suba which was placed under a Subedar. These words were taken from the existing system, but the Suba stood for the province in the Mogul empire. Shivaji's provinces were naturally districts. This word is still in use in some Maratha states like Gwalior. The revenue of a district was about 1 lakh of hons (or 3 lakhs of rupees) and the pay of a Subedar was 400 hons. The Subedar could keep a Palki in his own pay. Mahomedan higher officers used chhatri (umbrella); but this was now reserved for the king (Shivaji) himself and officers could only use abdagirs.

Land of all villages was measured by bighas and the revenue demand was fixed and taken in kind from the actual produce. Sabhasad's different copies give different proportions for the share of the state, such as one-fifth, two-sevenths or two-fifths. One important innovation introduced by Shivaji was that the village hereditary officers, Kulkarnis and Patels, were not under Deshmukhs. The latter were paid cash for their rights and the revenue was paid by the village officers direct into the Diwan (Government Civil Office). The Deshmukhs were thus kept under control and could not become powerful by collecting the whole revenue and paying a fixed sum like a farmer to the state.

Sabhasad notices at the end how all religious places and persons, temples and masjids, monks and fakirs, were provided for. New yearly grants in cash were made to learned Vaidika Brahmins and even saintly men living in jungles or villages, in order that they might bless the new Hindu kingdom.

The whole state had a Peshwa (foremost) or prime minister, subsequently called Mukhya Pradhan, and a Mujumdar (Accounant) subsequently called Amatya. These were officers with every jagirdar and were the most important officers now of the state. They were placed higher than the Sarnobats (subsequently called Senapatis). But even these civil officers had often to do military duty and to lead armies. They had seals of their own. The Jedhe S'akavali hence mentions the persons appointed from time to time as Peshwa and Mujumdar.* They did not get any territories or mokasas as pay, but were paid in cash like all other officers.

* Chitnis and Surnis were officers probably not yet appointed, as they are not noticed in papers yet.

XXII. THE SACK OF SURAT

Shivaji now entered upon a new phase of, and a more daring enterprise in, his life than hitherto, namely, an open and offensive conflict with the most powerful empire in the world of that time. The Mogul had harassed and harried his home, the town and district of Poona for two years; and Shivaji now exacted a fitting retribution for it. He performed the fourth extraordinary exploit of his life and plundered the richest city under the Moguls to the north of his kingdom. While Jasvantsingh was still prosecuting the siege of Sinhgad, Shivaji with his usual suddenness of resolution and celerity of execution, led an expedition against Surat and sacked that city without hindrance for four days. And he safely returned with all his plunder as suddenly as he had gone and by a route as unthought of as the one he had taken. He thus not only recompensed himself for what he had suffered by the Mogul incursion into his country, but acquired sufficient means to equip a strong army beyond the means of his small state.

The accounts of this sack of Surat recorded by the Dutch and English factors there, who were eye-witnesses to it, are full and may be summarised from their letters as follows. We have no contemporary Marathi records about the event except the short note in J that Shivaji plundered Surat on Paush Vadya 4 S'. 1585 (6th January 1664), Jasvantsingh's investment of Kondhana commencing in the preceding month *viz.*, Margashirsha (J). Shivaji who was then in North Konkan, passing by Bassein without molestation by the Portuguese, suddenly arrived at Gandevi, a few miles from Surat, on January 5th, 1664. Consternation seized the people and the Mogul Subedar, perhaps not having sufficient forces, retired within the fort where many rich merchants also took refuge. The Dutch and the English remained in their walled factories defended with cannon, but did not assist the people or the Subedar (though the English did a little), as that would have involved them in the affair. Indeed, Shivaji expressly said to Antony Smith, taken prisoner, that he wished to revenge himself on Aurangjeb "for invading his state and killing his people," but that he had no cause to molest the Dutch or the English. (Escaliot's long letter dated 20th January 1664).[1] The principles of international law are the same all over the world, being based on natural justice. Shivaji well stated his position and the Dutch also understood properly enough that they would incur Shivaji's enmity if they assisted the Moguls. The

1. PS 977, ER 79, p. 76.

city was, therefore, at the mercy of the invader and Shivaji's soldiers plundered its rich palaces and peoples without hindrance. Fires were also started every day by bands of soldiers of Shivaji who entered the city. Shivaji himself remained outside the city and had laid before him piles of silver, gold, jewels, etc. He did not care for other articles, which being heavy in weight and insignificant in value were given away. Torture by the chopping off of hands and even the cutting off of heads are described as resorted to by the order of Shivaji for securing treasure or extracting ransom.

A Dutch letter[1], dated January 10, gives daily account of this event and shows that Shivaji plundered the city from 6th, Wednesday, to 9th, Saturday, and left on the 10th, Sunday. It also states that the Dutch did not send any men to assist the Subedar though called upon to do so, pleading that they had to defend themselves and had not spare men. They also declined to protect the property in a house near their factory though requested to do so. This letter speaks of the English sending some men to assist the Subedar. Another Dutch letter of the same date[2] states that the Dutch refused to take a box sent by the chitnis of the local court. None of Shivaji's soldiers had any shelter in their camp and even Shivaji was under a cloth fastened to a tree. Sudden expeditions cannot be made with heavy tents and other paraphernalia. A Portuguese letter[3] gives Shivaji's army as 8 to 10 thousand men and suggests that Shivaji removed the plunder in

1. PS 968. 2. PS 969. 3. PS 972.

ships previously kept ready at a distance (this does not seem probable). An English letter, dated 25th January[1], states that Shivaji sacked the city for four days from Wednesday to Saturday. He demanded a tribute from the English but they refused it and defended their factory. Antony Smith fell into Shivaji's hands but he was released. He saw 26 men's hands cut off and even some heads. (The English were not quite friendly to Shivaji and having assisted the Subedar, tribute was demanded from them). Antony Smith was let off on the small ransom, however, of 300 rupees, without any personal injury, as stated in Surat letter dated 16th February[2]. A Surat English letter, dated 28th January[3], states that Shivaji first proposed that a ransom for the whole city should be settled by three rich men named but received no reply from the Subedar. The loot obtained was estimated at about ten millions of rupees (English letter ER 76, p. 64). It consisted of gold mohurs, pearls, jewels etc., and it was taken away in bags by 3,000 coolies.

It also appears[4] from Escaliot's letter that a man sent by the Subedar for parley suddenly attacked Shivaji but he was cut down. Shivaji fell covered with that man's blood but escaped unhurt. Shivaji probably returned with the plunder to Rajgad, though some documents state that he sent his plunder to Raigad which had been recently strengthened. Shivaji's immediate return to Rajgad, however, seems doubtful as will appear from the succeeding chapter.

1. PS 974, ER 76, p. 64. 2. PS 979, ER 83, p. 84.
3. PS 975, ER 78, p. 66. 4. PS 977, ER 79, p. 79.

The acts of cruelty which Shivaji committed at Surat in securing ransom or discovering treasure, as described above, ought not to prejudice us. Such cruelties are the inevitable accompaniments of war. The question is whether the cruelty was needless and excessive. Shivaji did not at any time resort, it will be seen, to unnecessary cruelty if we compare his action with that of others in history. The plunders and massacres recorded in history, both Indian and Western, not only of those centuries but of even the 19th, are almost revolting. We have thus the cruel massacre and plunder at Jhansi, after it was taken, by General Havelock in 1858 before us and it must be set down as wholly unnecessary and inflicted solely for striking terror. We have again the massacre of one lakh of inoffensive Hindus perpetrated by the Ahmednagar Sultan after the battle of Talikot. In European history we have many accounts of cruelty resorted to by various peoples unnecessarily after sieges. The Spaniards and the Germans thus under Charles V in 1527 plundered Milan and Rome and inflicted nameless miseries on the Italians. The Spaniards in Milan inflicted such cruelties that "prisoners died or committed suicide, under blows or tortures." The account of the sack of Rome by the Germans is still more terrible. "It is impossible to estimate the extent of this spoil, because of the accumulation of riches in the city and the number of persons for whom heavy ransoms were paid. Thus the palaces of Cardinals were all sacked except those for which heavy sums of money were paid. Many who had compounded with the Spaniards were pillaged by the Germans or had to compound with them also. The Cardinal of Sienna was taken prisoner by the Germans who sacked his palace, though he had compounded with the Spaniards and they led him bare-headed with many blows through Borgia. The prelates of Minerva and Pongette were similarly treated, being led through Rome in a vile procession, though they had paid their ransoms." (Historian's History of the World, Vol. IX, Italy, Page 453.)

But the full horridness of the event is laid bare when we further read, " On every side arose the cries and lamentations of Roman ladies and nuns dragged off by bands of soldiers to satisfy their lust. Everywhere arose the wails of those who were being horribly tortured to force them to pay ransom and reveal where their property was concealed. " (*Ibid*). The moral grandeur of Shivaji's character rises before us when we remember that such scenes never disgraced his plundering or even ravaging of town and country. Not only did he not inflict unnecessary harm, much less death, but neither he nor his men touched women or sacred persons either from lust or greed. Shivaji's orders were so stern and his influence so great that even in the detailed Dutch and English letters, describing the sack of Surat from eye-witnesses, there is no mention of any women being ill-treated or even seized. The English no doubt in plundering and massacring the innocent inhabitants of Jhansi had given strict orders to soldiers not to touch women and for this credit is due to them. But this was an event in modern civilized times. When the Mahomedans in the 17th century and the Europeans in the 16th as described above, seized women for lust and ill-treated and dishonoured holy men, Shivaji's conduct must be eulogized and his greatness acknowledged, as he and his soldiers systematically desisted from touching women and holy men under the influence of the high teaching of the Mahabharata contained in S'antiparva.

> अयुध्यमानस्य वधोः दारामर्षः कृतघ्नता
> ब्रह्मवित्तस्य चादानं निःशेषकरणं तथा ।
> स्त्रियामोषः पतिःस्थानं दस्युष्वेत्तद्विबर्हितम् ॥ १३४–१७.

Even Greeks and Romans in ancient times inflicted nameless miseries on women of conquered towns. The ancient Indo-Aryans never killed people not fighting or seized or violated women or plundered religious men and this noble practice and teaching of the ancients was strictly followed by Shivaji.

XXIII. OTHER SURPRISE ATTACKS IN 1664-65

The discomfiture of Shaistekhan and Jasvantsingh so much incensed Aurangjeb that he not only decided on sending another general with an overwhelming force to crush Shivaji, but he also wrote to the Bijapur Durbar to attack him on their side. Bijapur accordingly sent a force against Shivaji directing it to take all the Konkan from him upto Chaul, as noted in a Karwar English letter of 4th May 1664[1]. North Konkan being treated as Mogul territory was left to the Moguls to conquer. The commandant at Phonda and Lakham Sawant were asked to join the force. At this time, Shivaji led a sudden attack against Mudhol as described in his own letter[2], which purports to be written by him to his father and which gives the account of this raid from his own mouth. This letter may be taken to be genuine, being first published by the Alienation Department. It is doubted whether this incident happened at this time or later and some think that this letter was written by Shivaji not to his father but to his mother. The contents of the letter, however, appear to us to show that the letter was addressed

1. PS 992, ER 67, p. 87. 2. PS 1041.

to his father. His father had written to him, as the letter says in the beginning, that "Khavaskhan had started from Bijapur against him, that Baji Ghorpade and Lakham Sawant had sworn to assist him with their armies and that as a good son Shivaji should carry out his (father's) desire." This information, we think, could only have been given by Shahaji and not by Jijabai who was at Rajgad and who could not have known these movements earlier than Shivaji. Shivaji says further on in this letter that "he, on hearing that Baji Ghorpade was at Mudhol with some followers suddenly attacked him there and took and plundered that town," and that "Baji Ghorpade was killed in the fierce battle which ensued." Thus was terrible revenge taken on Baji Ghorpade who had treacherously arrested Shahaji as already related.

It is true that the history of Mudhol does not mention this event (see history recently published by the state). But this incident is mentioned in J though it assigns a different date to it.

Note :—The date of this event is given by J as Kartik S'. 1586 (November 1664). But J begins with the statement that 'the peace between Adilshah and Shivaji being broken, Khavaskhan came to Kudal but he was defeated.' Now this same incident is detailed in Shivaji's letter also; for it says further on that Khavaskhan was also subsequently defeated and pursued back towards Bijapur and that Shivaji then entered Sawant's territory to punish him and harried it with fire and sword. J also mentions that Khavaskhan fled to the Ghats. Thus it seems that J has mistaken the proper date of this event and has confounded the first invasion of Khavaskhan with a subsequent one by the same commandant, as we shall presently see. Then again J mentions that Shivaji came to the fort of Rajgad *again* on Magh Vadya 4, S' 1585 or February 5, 1664. Thus it seems probable that Shivaji, after having sacked Surat from 6th to 9th January 1664, returned the first time to Rajgad after four or five days, but that he left it again on receipt of Shahaji's letter to attack Mudhol and having taken revenge upon it, he returned a *second time* to Rajgad on February 5th. The punishment of Baji Ghorpade of Mudhol should, therefore, be placed towards the end of January 1664. Even if it be granted that the letter PS 1041 was in answer to Jijabai's letter, there is no necessity of changing the date of this event.

Shahaji died in consequence of a fall from his horse while hunting, on Magh S'uddha 4, S' 1586, or January 22nd, 1664, and the news must have reached Shivaji at Rajgad, after some days. The necessary obsequies being performed, Shivaji started again for Kudal as Lakham Sawant had, as above stated, changed sides and assisted a Bijapur general. In the above noted letter of Shivaji to his father, we are told that the fort of Phonda opposed him but that it was mined and taken. The Firangis who helped Sawant were also attacked but they concluded peace and presented some guns.

The Sawant also sent Pitambar Shenvi as Vakil and requested Shivaji to pardon him, promising to pay half his income as before and these terms were accepted as he was a Bhosale.

These incidents are supported by contemporary documents, though they speak of a fresh invasion by Bijapur forces assisted by Lakham Sawant. A farman[1] from Bijapur to the Sawant dated 29th July 1664 states that "Pitambar Shenvi, envoy of Lakham Sawant (mentioned in Shivaji's letter also) had assisted Azizkhan with a good army." The next general sent by Bijapur against Shivaji was thus Azizkhan, a name mentioned in two subsequent letters. Karwar English letter[2], dated 16th February 1664, speaks of Goa preparing against Shivaji and of the rumour that Shivaji would come against Karwar. A Dutch letter, dated 3rd August[3], gives a budget of news extending over months. "The Sar-Subedar of Shivaji, Raoji Pandit, invited the Dutch Vakil on the 22nd (July ?) and asked him to induce the English to come to Rajapur for trade, but the latter did not trust Raoji and refused to come." "Kudal being *constantly* overrun has suffered. Shivaji has returned some villages to the Sawant. Adilshah returned from Kannada in January after exacting tribute. The people of that part honour and love Shivaji." Thus it seems that Shivaji again

1. PS 1001. 2. PS 980, ER 81, p. 81. 3. PS 1002.

visited Kudal and drove away Azizkhan. Azizkhan died on June 10th and he was replaced by Rustum Jama.

While thus Shivaji was engaged in resisting frequent invasions of Kudal, he did not forget to strike at the Moguls. Shivaji, seeing that the Mogul forces had left the Deccan, suddenly went against Ahmednagar and plundered that town advancing even as far as Aurangabad. In fact, Shivaji in this year, like a consummate swordsman, attacked and defended himself against two foes with wonderful activity, striking now one and now the other, so that Oxenden said in a letter[1] from Surat dated 26th June 1664, "a report has made Shivaji an airy body and added wings also, so that he was in one place to-day and in another several miles away to-morrow."

This raid must have happened several months before August, though it finds mention in an English letter[2] from Karwar dated 8th August, as such raids were usually made in the dry season though, in Ahmednagar district, the rains are never heavy and continuous as in Konkan. This raid must have incensed Auranjeb still further and Dag Register of 1664 on September 14th contains the report that Aurangjeb "intends himself to march against Shivaji and is sending out forces daily,"

1. PS 996, ER 89, p. 88. 2. PS 1003, ER 91, p. 90.

(probably as reinforcements to Jaisingh who had already started). But he sent more urgent calls upon Bijapur and promised to remit the yearly tribute of 30 thousand hons from it, if it made a strong effort to put down Shivaji. Bijapur was hitherto carrying on only a half-hearted campaign against him. We have seen how Azizkhan Sarnobat had moved as far as Kadoli and how he had defeated Raoji Pandit who fell back upon Rajapur.[1] But Azizkhan was driven back by Shivaji probably in May and he died in June. The Dutch Viceroy even thought that the Adilshah was simply making a show of fighting with Shivaji but had inwardly agreed with him for a share of plunder. This does not seem to be true, though it may be granted that neither Azizkhan nor Rustum Jama who succeeded him in the business worked sincerely[2] and hence the Mogul emperor was justified in bringing strong pressure on the Bijapur Durbar.

Taylor's letter from Karwar, dated 29th October[3] 1664, states that Vengurla was burnt to the ground and Bijapur forces were repulsed. This shows that a strong force was sent by Bijapur but that it was defeated before this date by Shivaji's army. Alinama which gives no dates and which describes all events introduced by imaginary dramatic speeches, details how Khavaskhan took up the

1. PS 1011. 2. PS 1030. 3. PS 1015, ER 93, p. 91.

gauntlet thrown by Shivaji, when asked by Ali Adilshah who would go against Shivaji, how he went to the Konkan where a battle was fought, introduced by vaunting speeches and finally how Shivaji who had surrounded the Bijapur force failed to achieve anything. This was looked upon as a defeat of Shivaji and the Adilshahi vakil informed the Portuguese Viceroy at Goa that Khavaskhan was victorious in the conflict between him and Shivaji. This letter, dated 3rd December 1664[1], shows that this conflict must have taken place about the end of November. It may be the same event as is noted in J or a different one previous to it, as the date given in J is Kartik S'.1586 and this month of Kartik extended from 10th October to 7th November 1664 and as J mentions that Khavaskhan was defeated.

Whether there was a defeat or a mere discomfiture or even a partial success of the Bijapur army, it is certain that Shivaji took advantage of Khavaskhan's army being in Konkan and sending up the Ghats a strong force or himself going there sacked Hubli and other towns in Bijapur territory in the month of December as stated in a Karwar English letter dated 14th December 1664.[2] J states that the king plundered Khudavantpur in Margashirsh S'. 1586 (Dec. 1664).

1. PS 1020. 2. PS 1024, ER 99, p. 94.

Shivaji next took another and a more daring plundering expedition against Barcelore. Going there in his own navy he plundered that town in the month of Magha (February 1665, J). While returning he did not fail, as a devout Hindu, to visit Gokarna where there was the famous Shiva shrine of Mahabaleshwar. When returning from Mahabaleshwar he was delayed by an adverse wind for some days. The account of this raid given in Karwar English letter, dated 14th March 1665[1], is worth repeating here: "In the beginning of February, Shivaji started from Malvan in person with a fleet of 85 frigates and 3 great ships and sailing by Goa, without impediment, arrived at Barcelore and plundered that town. While returning, he stopped at Gokarna where he washed his body according to the ceremony of that place and then came to Ankola with 4,000 men. On 22nd February he came to Karwar; but, thank God, all the property and cash of the Company was already removed to a ship." Finally, it is related that after a stay of one day, a truce was arranged with the governor, Sherkhan, by which the merchants of the place paid a tribute to Shivaji, the English bearing their part of it, and on the 23rd Shivaji departed, saying that "he had spoilt his Holi hunt." (23rd February 1665 fell on Phalgun 15 of S'. 1586).

1. ER 107, p. 97.

Thus from January 1664 to March 1665, Shivaji carried out raids on several places both in Mogul and in Adilshahi territory, plundering many towns and acquiring the means of maintaining a large army. Kudal was more than once taken by Bijapur and Shivaji retook it every time and in addition raided Hubli and Barcelore. The Konkan territory thus remained in Shivaji's possession including Vengurla, Rajapur and several other ports on the Konkan coast[1]. Shivaji remained at intervals at Pratapgad, Raigad, Rajgad, Purandar or Sinhgad; but it was always difficult to know where he was and what were his designs, these being known only after their execution (फलानुमेयाः प्रारंभाः 'Kalidasa'). Thus while it was known that he would again plunder Surat, he instead went southwards to Barcelore. He had a very efficient service for spying and he got accurate information about the movements of his enemies. He, therefore, in Chaitra S'. 1587 (March) went to Purandar where Jaisingh arrived in Vaishakh (April 8th) with his overwhelming force (J). The exact date of Jaisingh's arrival according to Persian papers was 31st March, 1665.

Note:—**BARCELORE**

There is no port of this name on the West Coast of India now. The Imperial Gazetteer indentifies Barcelore

1. 1010 Dag R. Oct. 6th.

with Basrur which is a village in Coondapoor Taluq of South Canara. " It had a wall and a fort. It carried on trade with Malabar and Persia. When the Portuguese settled at Coondapoor in the 18th century, the town declined. "

Mr. Shejavalkar doubts this indentification and suggests that the town plundered was Bārkur. Imperial Gazetteer describes Barkur as a village in Udipa Taluq of South Canara. " It was the capital of the Tulu-speaking people. When Vijayanagar was founded (in 1336) it placed a viceroy here. On the fall of Vijayanagar Bednur asserted its authority over the village. The Jains were almost extirpated and it fell into ruin. It has a fort and some Jain shrines only remain. " Under Coondapoor, Imperial Gazetteer says that it was fortified by the Portuguese in the 16th century and that it stands on an estuary of three rivers. It is thus a good port. Bednur kings held sway here.

The difficulty thus remains of deciding which was Barcelore. Shejavalkar says that *c* ought to be pronounced *k* and the name was really Barkilore. But it is not still Barkur as it cannot be explained. Basrur and Barkur are both inland towns, probably connected with the sea by creeks like Kalyan or Rajapur. The settlement of the Portuguese at Coondapur is given as 18th and 16th century. The former would show that Basrur was still prosperous. Finally J names the town plundered as Besnur.

XXIV. THE MOGUL AND THE MARATHA

Now came a turn in the fortunes of Shivaji which threatened to destroy his work of 20 years (1645–65), by which he had built up a Maratha kingdom, practically independent of either Delhi or Bijapur. He was now faced with the prospect of a fight with a force which was likely to crush him in spite of his bravery and resourcefulness. Indeed, the game of chess which the two craftiest and most powerful men of India of the time were playing on the board of Maharashtra, had come to its critical point. Of the two, the Mogul Aurangjeb and the Maratha Shivaji, the latter was, however, bound to succeed, according to the immortal maxim of Mahabharata, 'Where there is righteousness there is victory'—'यतो धर्मस्ततो जयः ।.' The former was trying to impose slavery on another nation, while the latter was trying to free a nation from foreign slavery. By what several stages, Shivaji eventually succeeded in this critical year (1665), we will recount in this and the next chapter with the help chiefly of original letters.

Garry's letter from Surat, dated 22nd March[1] 1665, states that "Aurangjeb has sent to the Deccan

1. PS 1028, ER 108, p. 100.

an army of one lakh of horse and it was likely that the Mogul would take from Shivaji the whole country from Bombay to Chaul which would benefit the trade of the English." The Portuguese were, however, rather afraid of the Moguls, for they had helped Shivaji and the Viceroy of Goa wrote to Jaisingh that the Portuguese never assisted Shivaji though there were several Portuguese in his service as of other states[1]. He at the same time privately instructed Bassein officers to secretly sell to Shivaji powder and provision, as it was not good that Shivaji's country should be occupied by the Moguls[2].

Before Jaisingh arrived in the Deccan, he had been instructed to destroy both Bijapur and Poona though he might sometimes use one against the other. The fear that Jaisingh would first invade Konkan was removed when he encamped between Purandar and Poona for the reason given in his letter to Aurangjeb,[3] namely, that he believed that Shivaji and Adilshah were friendly and might combine against him, whereas from Saswa. he could keep an eye on both. These arg[illegible] supported by rumours mentioned i[illegible] letter dated 14th April.[4]

1. PS 1047, dated 21st March (P[illegible]kar)
2. PS 1055, 8th April (Hiras.).
3. PS 1051, Jaisingh's letters in Modern Review, vol. [illegible]
4. PS 1056, ER III, p. 101.

Unable to fight with or outwit Jaisingh, Shivaji thought it prudent to submit to the Mogul on honourable terms and he began correspondence with both Jaisingh and Dilerkhan, his second in command, on the subject.* But he did not remain in Purandar and moved about and even plundered some enemies like the Dutch and the ships of Kashiba in the port of Kharepatan where he was about the end of May[1].

Jaisingh was chief in command unlike Jasvantsingh who, in the preceding Mogul invasion, was the second of Shaistekhan who was his chief and he thought it convenient to secure honourable peace without sacrificing men and money. It was almost impossible to subdue Shivaji with his army of 10 thousand horse and 50 thousand foot[2], with his

* It is supposed by some that Shivaji first appealed to the Hindu feeling of Jaisingh and then proposed terms of peace. A long letter of Shivaji to Jaisingh (PS 1042) has been published by the Nagari Pracharini Sabha; but this letter is not quite reliable as it contains at the end a statement by Shivaji (in fact an admission) that Shivaji first struck Afzalkhan, which is not correct, as we know from SB and all Marathi accounts. Moreover, Shivaji must have known that Jaisingh was not the man to whom such patriotic and religious sentiments could appeal.

1. PS 1060, Dag Register dated 12th June and PS 1063, dated 29th June.

2. PS 1023. This Dag Register, dated 7th Dec. 1664, further mentions that Shivaji had 40 fast-going ships at

(Continued on the next page)

strong forts from Trimbak to Vishalgad, with his intricate, sudden and constant movements in the mountainous country, every pass and defile of which was known to him. Above all, Jaisingh did not think it advisable to fight with Shivaji in the mountains where Afzalkhan had found his grave and Shaistekhan's lieutenant had lost his honour. Dilerkhan, Jaisingh's second in command, however, was anxious to visit these defiles and passes and to try conclusions against Shivaji's forts.[1] As Sabhasad relates, differing from Jaisingh, he at once proceeded against the fort of Purandar with 5,000 Pathans and some chosen Rajputs. Morar Baji Prabhu, commandant of the fort, made a sally with 300 Mawalas and courageously attacked him; and after killing many men he fell in the fight. The men on the fort, however, still defended it with vigour against Dilerkhan who came thus to know the difficulties of taking Shivaji's forts and eventually gave his consent to the peace proposals which were being carried on between Jaisingh and Shivaji.*

hand and had laid 60 more in Kharepatan and Rajapur creeks and that he had not yet been divested of Kudal by Bijapur.

1. PS 1065, Jaisingh's letter.

* Jaisingh accepted proposals of peace, because he saw the difficulty of an armed conflict and not because he was

(Continued on the next page)

Terms were finally settled and accepted by Aurangjeb. Shivaji was to hand over 23 forts with the territory commanded by them of the yearly income of 4 lakhs of hons and Shivaji was to keep 12 forts including Rajgad, Raigad, and Torana and the rest of his territory of the income of 1 lakh of hons, for loyally serving Aurangjeb as a subordinate chieftain.[1] It was subsequently proposed that Shivaji should keep the Tal Konkan with an income of 4 lakhs of hons and also have the corresponding Ghat-Matha to be conquered from Bijapur worth 5 lakhs of hons, paying as *peshkash*, 40 lakhs of hons in 13 years. Jaisingh recommended this proposal, as 40 lakhs of hons meant 2 crores of rupees and as the troublesome hilly country could best be managed by Shivaji alone. It was, of course, intended in this suggestion that the Mogul and the Maratha were to combine against Adilshah.[2] Shivaji accord-

(Continued from the last page)

appealed to as a Hindu and as a Rajput, as stated already. We have even evidence that he tried to create defection in the ranks of Shivaji's followers. That he resorted to 'bheda' is certain from his letter to Aurangjeb (PS 1053) in which he tells him that he had invited Chandrarao More's relative and the son of Afzalkhan and the Mahomedan servants of Shivaji who were manufacturing guns for him as also Shivaji's comrades, on promises of mansab.

1. P 1064, Haft Anjuman, Benares.
2. PS 1060.

ingly submitted a petition to Aurangjeb, expressing contrition and promising obedience in all matters.[1] A letter from Dilerkhan[2] also states that Aurangjeb has accepted Shivaji's petition and has sanctioned a mansab of six thousand horse to Shivaji's son Sambhaji and the grant of a reward of 2 lakhs of rupees.[1] Sambhaji was at this time 8 years old, being born on Jyeshtha S'uddha 12, S'.1579, corresponding to 14th May, 1657 (J), and he was made a mansabdar even at this age according to the custom of the time.

A florid account is given by many, of the personal visit of Shivaji to both Jaisingh and Dilerkhan, the latter especially being on his guard at the time of the visit, remembering Afzalkhan's fate; but as there was nothing wrong in the minds of either, the negotiations were successful. This momentous visit took place on Ashadh S'. 10, S'. 1587, or 12th June 1665, as is specially noted in J. It was also settled that the three should proceed against Bijapur on the plea that it had not paid the annual tribute for several years. The imperial farman which has been printed[3] repeats the above conditions and adds the provision that Shivaji should faithfully assist Jaisingh against Bijapur and Bijapur should be conquered. The farman details the 12 forts

1. PS 1067.
2. PS 1068, Dilerkhan's letter, Riasat.
3. PS 1083.

which were to be retained by Shivaji. Shivaji, as was customary, went three miles to receive the gracious farman in company of Jaisingh's officer on the 30th of September 1665[1]. It seems from the list of the 12 forts given to Shivaji, including as they did Rajgad, Raigad and Lingamgad, that he retained now only the territory about them to the south of the Nira and that he handed over to the Moguls his original jagir of Poona, Supa and Indapur as also the Nizamshahi Konkan from Kalyan to Chaul, as is clear from a Bombay letter[2] and also from a Surat letter dated 1st January 1666[3]. Though apparently he remained master of about 10 lakhs of hons territory, 5 lakhs worth had to be acquired and the loss of Sinhgad and Purandar with the surrounding Poona district, his home, must have been a great sacrifice.* Shivaji promised to keep 5,000 horse for the mansab of Sambhaji and the pay to be received for it was to be counted as paid in the yearly instalment of 3 lakhs of hons for *peshkash*.

1. PS 1088.

2. PS 1098. The English expressed their satisfaction that the Moguls were now in possession of the territory adjoining Bombay, as their trade would prosper.

3. PS 1103.

* The district of Poona was already under the Moguls from 1660 when Shaistekhan invaded it and took up his quarters in the town of Poona. Mr. D. V. Kale has shown

(Continued on the next page)

As soon as the rains ceased, Shivaji with his usual vigour and celerity drove away the Bijapur army which was in Tal Konkan and even advanced into the Ghat-Matha territory of Bijapur.[1] But Muhammad Ikhlaskhan returned to Kudal and attacked Shivaji's men and retook this territory. The task of taking Bijapur territory in Tal Konkan and Ghat-Matha was thus not an easy thing.

Jaisingh was anxious to settle matters with Bijapur also peacefully according to its proposal; but Dilerkhan was, as before, anxious to fight and vowed to conquer Bijapur and drink water inside that city.[2] But he failed as before, as will just be seen. The Mogul army marched no doubt against Bijapur and Shivaji joined the force and conquered Phaltan, his Mawalas escalading its fort for which

this from a letter to Deva of Chinchwad, dated Jyeshtha 6, S'. 1586 (published in B. H. S. M. Quarterly, XI, 4), which proves that the rule of Shaistekhan was acknowledged by the people. It is further proved by No. 13, Khand XVIII, dated S'. 1588, describing Poona as in Sarkar Junnar, Suba Aurangabad. Thus though Shaistekhan had returned, Moguls remained in possession of the Poona District. Shivaji had, however, the possession of the dominating forts of Sinhgad and Purandar. Even these Shivaji had to deliver when he concluded peace with Jaisingh in 1666.

1. PS 1096, Pisurlekar, Goa letter dated 27 Nov.

2. PS 1097; Karwar English letter dated 27th Nov. 1665; ER 116, p. 106.

Aurangjeb expressed his satisfaction[1]. Ali Adilshah made a strong effort to defend Bijapur. He, however, called his best generals and all his army and laid waste the territory about it for about 4 miles in order to prevent the Mogul army from obtaining provisions and even water[2]. Bijapur had an army of 35 thousand horse and 5 thousand foot encamped outside the city. Alinama describes with flourishes how this Bijapur army inflicted a defeat on the Moguls and how Dilerkhan was made conscious of the fact that Bijapur at bay was difficult to be conquered. Eventually a truce was settled between the belligerents. Bijapur secretly paying a large sum as tribute (J). probably 9 lakhs of hons offered in the beginning[3] and the Mogul army returned without achieving much.

The game which the Mogul and the Maratha were playing on the board of Maharashtra with the help of armies was thus over to the discredit of neither ; but a more difficult game with the help of deception and diplomacy now began on the plain of Northern India with a far different result, as will be shown in the next chapter.

1. His letter dated 25th December, PS 1099.

2. PS 1101, Gyfford's letter from Karwar, 29th December ; ER 118, p. 107.

3. PS 1102, Oxenden from Surat, 29th Dec. 1665 ; ER 117, p. 108.

XXV. THE MOST ROMANTIC EPISODE IN INDIAN HISTORY

The visit of Shivaji to Aurangjeb at Agra, his imprisonment there by Aurangjeb and his escape form the most romantic episode in his life and in the history of India, if not of the world. Diplomacy and deception were met successfully by deplomacy and deception and the work of the uplift of the people of Maharashtra, which Shivaji had taken up as the business of his life, was not only not destroyed but was strongly furthered and soon accomplished. We have not many records to tell us the true story of this extraordinary incident and have consequently to rely much on conjecture. We will tell the story, however, as far as possible, from original records arranged and published in Patrasārasangraha.

The letters of Jaisingh to Aurangjeb and *vice versa* have been published; and the first letters, which embody the negotiations for peace, do not tell us that paying respects to the emperor by Shivaji personally was one of the conditions of peace. The proposal was, however, talked about in September 1665, as a Karwar English letter[1]

1. PS 1085; ER 115, p. 105.

tells us. It does not clearly appear who made the suggestion; but Jaisingh seems to have made it, probably to ensure Shivaji's reconciliation and to secure his employment in the Imperial service. Shivaji, however, refused to take any mansabdari for himself, though he consented to take one for his son. Jaisingh's letter dated 16th February 1666 mentions a further reason, namely, that Shivaji should go to the north and not remain in the Deccan where Govalkonda and Bijapur had combined against the Moguls at this time and Shivaji had to be prevented from joining the two.[1] Aurangjeb, with a purpose of his own, accepted this suggestion and, according to the recommendation of Jaisingh, issued orders for Shivaji's being treated with the honour due to royal princes, on his way to the north. Aurangjeb's letter to Shivaji himself, dated 6th April 1666, expressly contains the assurance that he would be received with honour and then granted permission to return[2]. This means that Shivaji had a suspicion that he might either be detained in custody or on pretext of some service. Public talk told him that he might be employed on service in Kabul. It is quite possible that Aurangjeb intended from the first to inveigle Shivaji into his clutches and then keep him imprisoned. Nothing was beyond him who had

1. PS 1112, Bhandarkar Volume.
2. PS 1128.

imprisoned his own father and Shivaji had specially affronted him and opposed him from the beginning. In his first letter to Jaisingh, Aurangjeb took him to task for allowing Shivaji to go away when he had himself come to see Jaisingh. This letter, dated 6th August 1665,[1] is important as giving us an insight into his mind. "Why did you allow Shivaji to go?" said he. "What oaths has he taken so that you did not take into consideration his faithlessness?"

Shivaji must have foreseen all this and must have resolved to go after full consideration. The question why Shivaji consented to go is difficult to answer. It is sometimes supposed that Shivaji wished to obtain the viceroyalty of the Deccan after conquering Bijapur and Govalkonda and then to offer a bold front to Aurangjeb. He also, it is thought, intended to personally impress on the Rajput princes the necessity and feasibility of combining and subverting the Mahomedan power. But Shivaji, we think, knew Aurangjeb and the Rajput princes too well to have entertained any such idea. It is possible that Shivaji wanted to see the state of things in the Mogul empire for himself and to find out its weaknesses as well as to get into touch with Rajput princes. But more than this, we think that Shivaji well knew that he had

1. PS 1077.

no other alternative but to go and decided upon going. He relied upon his own strength, his own resourcefulness, his own capacity to meet deception by deception. Further he had implicit faith in his high destiny and in the righteousness of the cause he had taken up. He had also full faith in the loyalty and devotion of his followers who were ready to lay down their lives for him and his great cause. In fine, we think, there was no go for him but to go and he saw that he must take the risk involved, according to the maxim of the Mahabharata already noted.

> " A man sees not good things with't dangers braved ;
> He sees them only, if through danger saved. "

He, therefore, finally resolved to risk the undertaking and prepared for his long journey. A Surat letter[1] already speaks on 29th December 1665, that Shivaji was preparing to go with his son to see the emperor taking many rich presents with him.

He had joined the Mogul camp though he was usually out of its reach for fear that he might be arrested and sent as a prisoner and he moved about taking Bijapur territory round Panhala[2]. He took leave of Jaisingh and came to Rajgad. He called a council of his followers, made known to them his resolve and took the necessary measures for the

1. PS 1102; ER 117, p. 106.
2. PS 1105, Jaisingh's letter.

government of his state in his absence. Moropant Pingle, Abaji Sondeo and Annaji Datto were given full powers. Kadatoji Gujar was appointed commander-in-chief. Netaji Palkar was called but he did not attend the meeting and went to Bijapur instead. Probably this was a ruse and we are not prepared to believe that Netaji who was styled 'second Shivaji' was disloyal or was won over by Jaisingh or Adilshah, as a contemporary letter says.[1] He, however, went eventually to Northern India after Shivaji had left Rajgad.

Taking the blessings of his beloved mother, Shivaji left Rajgad on Phalgun S'. 9, S.' 1587 (15th March 1666), together with his son (J). He took with him trusted men like Tanaji, Yesaji, Sarjerao Jedhe, Trimbakji etc. and Niraji. Jaisingh had assured him on his honour that he would not be harmed and that his son Ramsingh at the Imperial Court would stand guarantee for his safety. How far Jaisingh

1. Karwar letter dated 24th April 1666 (PS 1102; ER 126, p. 111), giving a budget of news, tells that Netaji was won over by Adilshah and given a jagir of one lakh of hons. He, however, handed over the territory to the Moguls who subsequently arrested him. "Some say that he was killed, but others that he was alive". We know that he was alive, went to the north and was forcibly converted in 1667 (Maasir-i-Alamgir-Tilak). He finally returned and was reconverted on Ashad Vadya 4 S'. 1598, 19th June 1676 (J).

was honest cannot be definitely stated, though nothing which happened hereafter goes to show that he was privy to any sinister plan. Shivaji, however, got the first idea of this when at Aurangabad he was not well treated by the Mogul Subedar who did not go forward to receive him. From Aurangabad, taking the usual route via Handia, Bhopal, Sironge, Narvar, Gwalior and Dholpur, Shivaji arrived at Agra on 9th May. Aurangjeb was at Agra, Shahjahan being recently dead, and held a big Durbar to receive Shivaji. Ramsingh introduced him in this Durbar held on the 12th in the Diwan-i-Am. There was an impressive assemblage of Amirs and Rajput princes, standing with folded hands on both sides, in different compartments. On the other side of a silver railing, Aurangjeb was seated on the most brilliant and costly (peacock) throne in the world, with royal princes seated on the steps and with hundreds of armed attendants ready, behind a screen. Shivaji fearlessly entered this august Durbar held to receive him and made due obeisance from a distance. He thought he would be treated as a prince; but he was pointed out a place among third class sardars and had to stand. He was beside himself with rage at this treatment and said so to Ramsingh who had meanwhile presented the things he had brought. What actually happened there hereafter, we do not exactly know. Probably Shivaji sat down or sank down with rage and this was a transgression of the Durbar procedure, as is mentioned in a letter by Jaisingh's gumasta[1]. Aurangjeb at once dissolved the Durbar and Shivaji returned to the place of his residence where on the next day Fauladkhan Kotwal (Police Chief Officer) himself mounted guard with five thousand men by order of the emperor. The above letter from the gumasta of Jaisingh states that "the emperor has debarred Shivaji from coming to the Durbar again for some time only for transgressing ceremonial rules. It is his intention to send him back after showing him some favour and doing him honour."

The news flew to the Deccan, as swiftly as swift couriers could run and Jaisingh was apprised of it in a week. From his letter[2] he appears first not to have blamed his son, his responsibility having ceased, but he expressed sorrow at the prospect of Shivaji being kept in confinement under Ramsingh's supervision. Jaisingh advised Aurangjeb to keep Shivaji confined and not to allow him to return, as Govalkonda and Bijapur had combined and, as already stated, Shivaji might join them on return. "Shivaji should be well cared

1. PS 1129 dated June 1666, Bhandarkar Volume.
2. P 1130.

for ; otherwise his officers being enraged and believing Shivaji's life to be in danger, might think of doing so". Jaisingh also complained in this letter of Bijapur affairs lingering on and becoming more complicated.

The expected had happened and Shivaji was confined in Agra with no prospect of release. But the unexpected was soon to happen and it did happen on one day, when it was discovered to Fauladkhan's consternation and the emperor's amazement and chagrin, on August 17, that Shivaji had escaped. The mountain rat had given the slip to the cat even in the plains and in the cat's own house.

Shivaji must have foreseen this misfortune and must have made suitable provision against it even when he started. With a mind never daunted by any disaster and a resourcefulness which rose equal to any contingency, Shivaji planned a scheme for escape. He expressed no dissatisfaction at his confinement, honourable as it was; and even sent away his men and military followers, with the consent of the emperor which was naturally easily obtained. He then feigned illness and called in hakims and began to send presents in boxes to fakirs and grandees. Manuchi says that by Aurangjeb's order a separate palace was being built, suitable

1. P. 1132, Bhandarkar Com. Vol.

for Shivaji's permanent confinement, like that of his father on the fort, and Shivaji was to be removed to that palace, doomed to decadence and death, also like his father. But Shivaji forestalled Aurangjeb and one evening at about 4 p. m. he and his son went out of their guarded house, concealed in two boxes along with other boxes carrying presents. They passed the guards unchallenged. The bearers took the boxes to a place about three miles out of Agra, where Niraji, Tanaji and others were waiting with horses. They paid the bearers handsomely and sent them back pleased. Crossing the Jumna, they proceeded northwards instead of southwards and recrossing the river came to Mathura where thousands of pilgrims had gathered for the Janmashtami festival. There were already in Mathura three relatives of Moropant Peshwa who perhaps were sent there when Shivaji started for Agra with a view to assist him in the event foreseen. Mathura was a sacred place between Delhi and Agra and Shivaji would certainly visit it in any case and perform its pilgrimage. Shivaji got himself shaved; and, besmeared with ashes as a Gosavi, he, with Niraji as the leader of the party of Gosavis, started for Tirthayatra. Niraji was conversant with many tongues and led the party, doing bhajans, to Prayag and thence to Kashi and thence to Jagannath. Sambhaji was kept with the Tirthopadhyaya of Mathura to whom the secret had been divulged by Moropant Pingle's men and he was to reach him to the Deccan, when called for.

Having finished the Tirthayatra, the party travelled from Jagannath to Indur on the Godavari, through Gondvan and from thence, via Govalkonda and Bijapur, they came to Gokarna on the west coast. Thence they reached Rajgad on the 20th of November (Margashirsha S′. 5, J). Stories are told even by Kafikhan of how Shivaji was on the point of being discovered at various places, Aurangjeb having issued immediate orders to the Suba officers throughout his dominion to watch for Shivaji and arrest him. But these stories are not quite reliable and it is not necessary to relate them here. Suffice it to say that good luck favoured Shivaji and the holy cause he had undertaken; and successfully undergoing all the troubles and sufferings of a travel on foot and of the life of a Gosavi for three months, Shivaji stood before his mother on that eventful day to the greatest exultation of her and of the whole of Maharashtra. The glad tidings spread so swiftly that a Surat letter dated 24th November,[1] only four days after the event, stated that "Shivaji had escaped and would now trouble the whole country."

1. PS 1142; ER 132, p. 116.

Note : **Further details of the event.**

PS 1136, Surat letter, dated 25th September 1666, (ER 129, p. 114) states that Shivaji being placed among Umraos of lower grade fearlessly left the court in rage, not counting even the emperor. This shows that the story about Shivaji's calling for a dagger from Ramsingh to commit suicide is an absurd later suggestion. The postscript of the letter records the news of Shivaji's escaping with his son in two baskets.

PS 1139, Jaisingh's letter dated 5th November, shows that he too had sent detectives in false dresses to ferret out Shivaji. PS 1141, Surat letter dated November 1666 (ER 133, p.116), details how Jaisingh threatened to take his own life, if Aurangjeb would do harm to Shivaji's life and that consequently the latter handed Shivaji over to Ramsingh's custody. After his escape, Aurangjeb suspected Ramsingh of connivance and dismissed him from his mansab. Aurangjeb wished to send a large force again to the Deccan, but he was prevented by an invasion from the north by the king of Persia and he called back Jaisingh.

Sabhasad describes how Hiroji Farjand* (illegitimate half-brother of Shivaji and like him in appearance) slept on Shivaji's couch feigning illness, covered with a shawl, the whole night and also the next day till afternoon, how watchmen often came in and saw Shivaji still asleep, his hand coming out with a diamond ring on one finger and how Hiroji got up in the afternoon, put on his own clothes and went out, saying he was going to fetch medicine and asking the guards not to allow anybody to go in and disturb Shivaji's sleep. He

*This Persian word means a son, but in Marathi it is applied to an illegitimate son.

too thus slipped away together with the boy who had sat all the while shampooing Shivaji's feet. His name is given as Madari Mehtar by others and he was a Mahomedan. This shows how even Mahomedan servants were loyal to Shivaji and were also trusted by him. The guards, after some time, finding everything quiet, informed Fauladkhan who thereon went in and found nobody. He was aghast and immediately informed the emperor that Shivaji had disappeared, even like a magician.

J records that Trimbakpant Dabir and Raghunathpant Korde were arrested on S'ravan Amavasya, four days after Shivaji had escaped. They had taken a different route. They were confined in Agra but were released in March 1667. J also mentions strangely enough that Shivaji came to Rajgad wih Sambhaji. This is not correct, as Sambhaji could not have returned the same day as and with Shivaji[1]. But he was safely brought to Rajgad by the Deccani Brahmins Krishnajipant and others. Shivaji felt so grateful to them that he gave them one lakh of hons as reward and the title of Vishvasrao (S)[2]. Shivaji appointed Niraji Pandit, the leader of his party of Gosavis, Nyayadhish or Chief Judge and Dattajipant, Waknis of the state. Ragho Maratha, the servant, the fourth companion, was appointed head of Hujurias or private servants. Shivaji was as prompt in rewarding as in punishing. Prompt and severe punishment for serious misdeeds and immediate and generous reward for distinguished services are the *sine qua non* of the master's influence and Shivaji was thus both feared and loved by his followers.

1. See also PS 1145, dated December 1666, a letter from Udayaraj, Gumasta of Jaisingh, which speaks of Shivaji's return and of his anxiety for his son.

2. PS 1458 of S'. 1593 confirms this, but speaks of one lakh of rupees.

XXVI. CONCILIATION AND CONSOLIDATION

When Shivaji returned, Jaisingh was at Aurangabad, having retreated there successfully, from his unsuccessful attempt to conquer Bijapur which kept on attacking his rear in the guerilla fashion through Maratha sardars, at the same time keeping on talks of peace with payment of tribute. There were three enemies thus against the Moguls now, Bijapur, Govalkonda and Rajgad. The Moguls were also in difficulty on the North-Western frontier of their empire. The offer which Shivaji now made of peace was consequently acceptable to Aurangjeb. The Mogul and the Maratha were now marshalling, not armies but artifices, on the chess-board of Maharashtra to secure their own ends. Shivaji, instead of resorting to hostilities, as expected, like an escaped wounded tiger, wrote a letter to Aurangjeb that he still wished to serve the emperor and remain at peace with him[1]. Jaisingh had no doubt made provision, by appointing officers, for keeping Shivaji's territory of Poona, Supa and Indapur in imperial possession; but it was constantly harassed by Shivaji's adherents. Thus a letter of Jaisingh's gumasta[2] shows that Babaji

1. PS 1158, 22nd April 1667.
2. P 1145, December 1666, Bhand. Com. Vol.

Bhosale, probably from Khandesh, who was in charge of Supa, had to fight with Mahadji Nimbalkar, son of Shivaji's son-in-law Bajaji; he was eventually killed in a sudden raid by the latter. Jaisingh could not move against him from Aurangabad for fear of an attack by Bijapur on Mogul territory during his absence. Shivaji, taking advantage of the difficulty experienced by the Moguls in holding his territory, offered to hold it on behalf of the emperor and to keep his son with 5,000 horse with the Moguls for their service. These peace terms were eventually accepted by Aurangjeb and Shivaji's territory was returned to him, the emperor keeping, as suzerain power, as before, the two strong forts in the territory, Sinhgad and Purandar. The Konkan territory from Kalyan to Chaul was also given back with the exception of the forts of Karnala and Mahuli. This peace was made in Chaitra S′.1589 (J) which means that the above letter of Shivaji, dated 22nd April 1667, was written after his proposals had been accepted. In making these proposals, Shivaji may also have requested the release of his two men, Trimbak and Raghunath Korde, who were imprisoned in Agra and who were accordingly released at about the same time as noted in J.

Jaisingh was fighting with three enemies as best as he could and was ready to do any act of treachery against Shivaji in the interest of Aurangjeb (see his letter[1] to Jafferkhan, dated 1666, probably December-Bhand. Com. Vol.); but the emperor distrusted him, thinking him also privy to Shivaji's escape, and recalled him. Muajjam was appointed governor of the Deccan and Jaswantsingh again his sub-commander. Dilerkhan was appointed to Malwa to keep watch on both ; for Aurangjeb suspected everybody of evil designs like himself. Jaisingh gave over charge to Muajjam in May and broken-hearted proceeded towards the north ; but he died on the way at Burhanpur on 2 July 1667–a sad end indeed after such loyal service of his master !!! Shivaji sent his son in Kartik or September 1667 (J), accompanied by Prataprao (originally Kadatoji) Gujar, commander of 5,000 horse, to pay respects to the emperor's son. Sambhaji was mansabdar no doubt ; but being young he was excused personal service and he was sent back after he had paid his respects to Jaswantsingh (J). Shivaji was given a jagir in Berar for this mansab (not in Nasik or Nagar which adjoined his territory), at the time of this peace and Shivaji sent a mokasdar to take charge of it. In this conciliatory manner, Shivaji gained back his own old territory including Karyat Mawal[2]

1. PS 1152.
2. PS 1154.

and a large addition too, in Berar, which Sabhasad estimates as worth 15 lakhs of hons, probably an exaggeration.

It must have taken some time before Shivaji got his original territory back and we actually find[1] that pargana Poona was still treated as in the Sarkar of Junnar in the Suba of Aurangabad. Shivaji must, therefore, have felt it inconvenient to retain Rajgad as his chief residing fort. He also had to settle matters with his southern enemies, Bijapur and others. He appears at this time to have hence chosen Raigad as his second chief fort, it being also stronger and more extensive than Rajgad. We find from a letter[2] from the Governor of Goa to Shivaji (Pisurlekar) that Shivaji was then residing at Raigad, having removed there from Manohargad, the place of his temporary sojourn and that the Governor sent there his letter of congratulation on his escape from Agra. The Portuguese from the first were friendly to Shivaji, just as the Dutch and the English were usually unfriendly.

The Konkan territory from Chaul to Kudal remained practically with the Marathas during Shivaji's absence, though attempt was often made by Bijapur officers to attack it. Kudal was a Suba

1. PS 1163, Khand 18, No. 13, July 1667.
2. P 1160, dated 5 July 1667.

under Shivaji in September.[1] Next was Vengurla Desh mentioned in a Dutch letter dated 25th September 1667.[2] Next was Dabhol Suba with Sringarpur and Devrukh. Above the Ghats Shivaji had the territory to the south of the Nira. Krishnaji Bhaskar is mentioned as Subedar over Rohid Khore.[3] Wai and Karhad were, however, under Bijapur,[4] but Masur, which was Shahaji's jagir, appears to be under Shivaji[5]. In the Konkan territory, Bijapur officers now and then made incursions. Immediately after his return, Shivaji had thus to attack two such officers, namely Pirmiya and Tajkhan, who were in Devrukh in the Dabhol Suba and they were driven away and an elephant was captured. The entry in J of this event can be interpreted in this way only, though we have no other supporting document. In May 1668 Bahilolkhan and Ekojiraje, step-brother of Shivaji himself, surrounded the fort of Rangana which was in Shivaji's possession and Shivaji with his usual suddenness attacked and drove away the besiegers (J). The Bijapur authorities eventually saw the futility of fighting with Shivaji and in Bhadrapad (September), a peace was concluded between

1. PS 1135 of 1666.
2. PS 1170.
3. PS 1172, dated 27th October 1667.
4. PS 1167, 68, 69, dated September 1667.
5. PS 1209, dated 23rd April 1668.

Shivaji and Adilshah by which Shivaji promised to pay a yearly sum to Bijapur by way of tribute for South Konkan.[1] About this time, Bijapur also concluded a peace with Aurangjeb directly at Agra through Shah Abdul Hussein, ceding the fort of Sholapur with adjoining territory yielding 1,80,000 hons.[2] Thus there was peace in Maharashtra for a time and the three powers, Bijapur, Delhi and Rajgad, were friendly.

Shivaji was also at peace with the three European powers on the sea-coast, though the English still continued unfriendly; PS 1214, 14th August 1668 (Forrest), and PS 1216, Surat letter dated 25th August 1668, directing seizure of the ships of Shivaji in the many ports between Surat and Goa belonging to him, may be referred to. There was some disagreement between Shivaji and the Portuguese of Goa for a time, as the latter gave shelter to Lakham Sawant who had again rebelled against Shivaji and Shivaji consequently harried Bardesh with fire and sword, as many letters tell us; see PS 1221 dated 7th October 1668, which is a Dutch letter and which also states that Shivaji was the Subedar of the coast-territory and that the Dutch had, therefore, to pay tribute to him. This must have happened at the end of 1667, as PS 1192, dated 22nd January 1668, also refers to Shivaji's invasion of Bardesh. But the Portuguese remained friendly with Shivaji and on his remonstrating, drove out the Sawant from their territory (PS 1194, Portuguese letter dated 16th February 1668,

1. PS 1221, Dutch letter dated 8th Oct. 1668.
2. Duff and PS 1219, Karwar letter dated September 16.

Pisurlekar) and the Sawant again acknowledged allegiance to Shivaji.

Shivaji devoted this leisure time in his otherwise intensely active career to the consolidation of his kingdom. A short note in J refers to this fact in the sentence : "The same year the territory was divided." तेच वर्षी मुलखाची बटाई केली (Chaitra S'. 1589 or April 1668). Shivaji probably made new divisions of his state and made arrangements for the extension of cultivation. The cultivation of land had been much neglected owing to people being constantly harassed by Mogul and Adilshahi armies during the last several years. Moropant Peshwa thus in this year made arrangement for the cultivation of land in the Shirval Pargana[1]. We have already described the military system of Shivaji consisting of forts, infantry and cavalry. The forts were hill, ground and sea; infantry consisted of Mawalas and Hetkaris or of men on the Ghat and in the Konkan and cavalry consisted of Paga and Shiledari. We have also described the revenue system of Shivaji. The existing hereditary officials, Patels and Kulkarnis and Deshmukhs and Deshpandes, were not disturbed, but the actual collection of revenue was in the hands of the Karkuns, Tarafdars and Subedars. As in the military, so in the civil, the Marathas, the Brahmins and the Prabhus were given different

1. PS 1197 of 1667.

employments, thus co-ordinating all the higher classes in administration.* For the whole state he appointed new officers besides the old Peshwa and Mujumdar. Surnis was the superintendent of correspondence, the despatcher of orders, sanads etc. He examined all documents issued and marked on them Surushud (issued, from the Persian word suru meaning 'begun'). The first Surnis appointed was Annaji Datto (Duff). Waknis or the recorder of events ('wākā'-Persian-meaning event) kept the private records, journals etc. of the king and the first Waknis was Dattajipant. Dabir was the foreign minister, a new office; so also was Nyayadhisha or Chief Judge. With the extension of dominion, a high judicial official was a necessity and the first Chief Judge was, as already noted, Niraji, who had accompanied Shivaji on his incognito travel. Upto this time, judicial cases came

* We may note how the various officers connected with a fort belonge to different castes. Besides the garrison, there were several hereditary officers on every fort called Gadkaris who always resided therein and hadlands assigned to them near it. These were Brahmins, Prabhus, Marathas, Ramoshis, Mahars and Mangs. The last three were employed on outpost duties, watched the paths, brought intelligence, misled enquirers and in war time cut off enemy's stragglers. "This establishment while new was admirably suited to the genius of the people and also served in providing for old and meritorious soldiers." —Duff.

before Shivaji himself and in his absence before his mother who, like all Maratha ladies, took a share in the administration intelligently[1]. Lastly, an officer was needed for the proper performance of religious duties pertaining to the king. All these officers, except the last two, had to perform military duty often and they appointed their lieutenants, called Mutaliks (from taaluk–Persian–connection). There were other officers also such as Sabnis (from saff-line) who kept registers of the number of men in the army and other departments, Phadnis (from fard–a list) who assisted the Mujumdar or accountant, Karkhannis who kept all articles and Chitnis (from chithi–a letter) or writer of letters; also Potnis (phote-meaning purse) cash-keeper. Balaji Avaji was the first Chitnis of Shivaji himself and he served him loyally throughout his life.

1. PS 1206, dated 6 April 1668 and PS 1234.

XXVII. THE ASTONISHING ESCALADE OF SINHGAD

From April 1667, when peace was concluded with Aurangjeb, Shivaji practically remained inactive for two years and more. He no doubt led a sudden raid against Bahilolkhan at Rangana in May 1667, but that was followed by peace with Adilshah in September. He also invaded Bardesh in November 1667, but this was also followed by peace with the Portuguese[1]. (This raid is referred to in a Bombay letter[2] dated 2nd April 1668, as these letters many times mention events long passed by). He made a tour of his forts in Konkan and strengthened them with provisions etc. in November 1668 and went as far as Rajapur[3] (Karwar letter dated 12th November 1668) and it was thought that he would attack Goa with the help of a navy of the Arabs of Maskat[4]. But Shivaji did not intend to fight with Goa and returned about the end of December, as noted in Karwar letter[5] dated

1. PS 1184, dated 26th November 1667, Pisurlekar.
2. PS 1206; ER 142, p. 122.
3. PS 1228; ER 152, p. 126 and PS 1231.
4. PS 1230; ER 155, p. 128.
5. PS 123.; ER 156, p. 128.

16th December. This inactivity of Shivaji even led to the belief that he would now sink into insignificance. The English at Karwar and also at Surat thought so (see Karwar letter dated 9th March 1669),[1] as he did not issue out as usual after the rains that year. Indeed, he was at this time actually a feudatory of Aurangjeb, holding his territory under him and keeping an army at Aurangabad for service under the Mogul governor. Prataprao Gujar was there with 5,000 horse as also Niraji, as stated in a note dated August 5th, 1668 in J. Even in Kalyan which Shivaji possessed, as is proved by an order dated 25th January 1669[2], issued by Shivaji regarding the Deshpandes of Kalyan to the officers of Tal Konkan and Mamle Kalyan, there was a Mogul Subedar, as we find from a Bombay letter[3] referring to the efforts of the English to obtain the port of Pen in the territory of Shivaji, from Muajjam through Abdullakhan, Subedar of Kalyan and Bhivandi, as "Shivaji was a vassal of Aurangjeb." Shivaji also got the title of Raja from Aurangjeb in March 1668, (see his farman dated 9th March 1668)[4]. This title was not really wanted, for Shivaji was *de facto* king already and was styled so in the Portuguese treaty referred to above, dated 26th November 1667.[5] Raje was a title taken by leading Maratha

1. PS 1242; ER 160, p. 129. 2. PS 1238.
3. ER 147, p. 124. 4. PS 1200. 5. PS 1148.

families no doubt (Shahaji Raje, Shivaji Raje, etc.); but Raje prefixed would show that Raje was a title bestowed upon one or taken by one.

J mentions that "Aurangjeb destroyed the temple of Vishvanath at Benares in August 1669, and that in December the peace between the Moguls and Shivaji was at an end, and "Prataprao who was at Aurangabad with the Shahjada, returned to Rajgad with his army". Why the peace ended and who ended it, is related in Sabhasad as follows :— "Aurangjeb secretly ordered Prince Muajjam to arrest Prataprao and Niraji and to take possession of the horses of their cavalry, for the state. The Prince, however, was on good terms with Shivaji and clandestinely intimated to Prataprao that he should leave Aurangabad before the imperial order arrived." There is no contemporary record to support this statement of Sabhasad. But his account may be believed, inasmuch as the motive with which Aurangjeb had generously treated Shivaji upto this time was probably to inveigle him again into his clutches; and finding no opportunity, he attempted to destroy his power by imprisoning his commander-in-chief and acquiring his cavalry horses without any effort. Shivaji who, on his own side, had accepted the policy of conciliating Aurangjeb with the motive of gaining strength during the respite, succeeded in his game while Aurangjeb failed in his, because Shivaji's officers were trustworthy and loyal and Aurangjeb's, venal and untrustworthy, the usual cause of a nation's weakness.

It further seems to us that there is a connection between Aurangjeb's outburst of fanaticism at this time and the end of the peace between Shivaji and the Moguls. Shivaji must have felt deeply, as a devout Hindu, the affront given to the whole Hindu nation in the destruction of the Benares temple. As he had, from the first, stood forth as the champion of the Hindus, he could not have now remained at peace with Aurangjeb. This also seems probable from an English letter from Bombay, dated 23rd January 1670[1] (Garry to Lord Arlington), "The arch rebel Shivaji is again engaged in arms against Aurangjeb who out of blind zeal for reformation hath demolished many of the Gentu temples and forced many to turn Mussalmuns." We also find from a Surat letter[2], dated 22nd January 1668, that Aurangjeb's fanaticism, perhaps designed to dazzle Mahomedan orthodoxy, had become intolerable to the Hindus even in that part. "The emperor has importuned his officers to throw down the temples and build mosques on their sites as also to forcibly convert Hindus." It is probable that orders were received

1. ER 178, p. 140. 2. PS 1192; ER 139, p. 120.

in the Subas of Aurangabad and Surat and the people about Surat and Junnar might have become alarmed. Shivaji, therefore, must have resolved to declare war against the Moguls in order to relieve Hindus from religious oppression. The Portuguese also (though alone of all Western peoples who had come to India) often resorted to religious oppression through fanaticism, like Aurangjeb, and we find from a Goa letter[1], dated 30th November 1667, that the then Governor of Goa had ordered the expulsion of inhabitants who did not belong to the Roman Catholic faith and that four Padres had even advised that the Hindus should be massacred. Shivaji in his invasion of Bardesh caught hold of these Padres and on their refusing to become Hindus executed them. The Governor of Goa[2] thereupon found it necessary to cancel his order. It is possible, therefore, that Shivaji may have himself declared war against the Moguls from a religious motive. Whatever may have been the cause, the state of peace between the Moguls and the Marathas came to an end in December 1668 with the return of Prataprao Gujar to Rajgad.

It was first necessary to drive away the enemy from the forts of Sinhgad and Purandar which kept Shivaji's original home, the Poona district, under control. We will relate the story of

1. PS 1186. 2. *Ibid.*

the wonderful escalade of Sinhgad by Tanaji Malusare at this time, with the help of Sabhasad and various songs and Powadas which describe this great event, as we have no contemporary account to rely upon. The fort of Sinhgad could be seen from Rajgad and Shivaji's heroic mother asked him first to drive away the Moguls from it, as the sight of the Mahomedans in possession of it pained her. Tanaji Malusare assured her that he would soon capture it on a dark night. On Magh Vadya 9 Friday or 4th February 1670 (J), Tanaji approached, at night-fall, the perpendicular basalt rock on which the fort is built together with its strong rampart, and two Mawalas escaladed (how, it is yet a mystery) the rock and the wall at a vulnerable point. Going to the top of the wall they let down a rope-ladder and Tanaji and 300 Mawalas got on to the wall with its help. The watchmen on the fort getting a clue raised an alarm and Udebhan, a brave Rajput (probably kept there by Jaisingh), rushed to attack the Mawalas with his Rajput soldiers. A terrible hand-to-hand fight took place in the light of torches and 500 Rajputs lay dead as also many Mawalas. Tanaji and Udebhan in a duel killed each other. The remaining Mawalas were on the point of running back when Suryaji, brother of Tanaji, who had come up by this time with the help of the rope-ladder with more Mawalas, stopped them and led them back to a fresh attack and finally to victory. The fort was taken; and the Rajputs and Mahomedans who had concealed themselves were taken prisoners, while those who attempted to escape by jumping over the wall were mostly killed. A thatched horse-shed was set fire to as a signal and Shivaji saw it and knew to his intense joy that the fort had been taken. The intense joy soon changed into intense grief when he knew that Tanaji, his loyal friend and follower through life, had fallen. "A *gad* is taken," he exclaimed, "but a *gad* is lost for ever."

It is impossible to conceive how the two Mawalas "like monkeys" got up to the top of the rampart with the aid of their hands only (Sabhasad). Later accounts state that Tanaji had a ghorpad (iguana) which, as is her wont, mounted to the top and stuck there while the Mawalas with the help of a rope fastened to her tail climbed up. This is also not quite believable, though less unbelievable than the above version. The place where Tanaji and his Mawalas climbed the rock is still shown on the Sinhgad fort and it seems to us that at that spot the rock is not quite perpendicular owing to a water fissure and is climbable by those who are accustomed to climb steep mountains. The two Mawalas probably knew this weak point in their constant rambles about the fort and took advantage of it. They might even have tried it in sport in their boyhood. The defect has subsequently been removed by a second rampart.

J records that Nilopant Mujumdar took the fort of Purandar about a month after on Phalgun Vadya Dvadashi, a date proved by a sanad of Shivaji[1]. In the assault Yeso Narayan Narhekar fell. Both these were Brahmins. The other forts also were taken one by one by other officers such as Moropant Peshwa, Annaji Dabir etc. with the help of Mawalas.

Shivaji got back the forts in Konkan also, as Bombay letter, dated 30th March 1670, speaks of Shivaji as being in possession of the territory about Bombay having "recovered from the Mogul many of his castles on the Maine opposite to us." (PS 1294; ER 184, p. 144). Surat letter of the same date (PS 1295; ER 185, p. 144) speaks of Shivaji being in command of 30,000 men and moving about, "not like a thief but like a king." He was in possession of Kalyan and Bhivandi, which was preferable to their being in the hands of the Moors. The English had now a favourable opinion about Shivaji's rule. PS 1313, Bombay letter dated 11th June 1670, shows that Shivaji attacked the fort of Mahuli but was yet unable to take it. He, however, took it before June 28 as Bombay letter of that date speaks of his having taken Mahuli (PS 1314; ER 199, p. 157).

"Shivaji began his rule again after taking the forts ceded at the time of peace." Sabhasad thus curtly records the change. Indeed, it was impos-

1. PS 1303.

sible that Shivaji could remain long a feudatory of Aurangjeb and be another Jaisingh or Jaswantsingh to be employed anywhere by the emperor for his own purposes. Shivaji's good fortune was further shown at this time by the birth of his second son Rajaram on Phalgun S'uddha 15 at Rajgad (J),' after the recapture of Sinhgad and before that of Purandar. This son was destined to fight finally to the finish the war with Aurangjeb and after a long struggle, the most glorious in Indian history, to achieve the independence of the Marathas establishing the maxim of politics that the greatest power even cannot subdue a nation unitedly striving to assert its independence.

Shivaji, however, again failed against the Siddi of Janjira. He entered his territory Danda Rajpuri but could make no impression, as the English assisting the Siddi at this juncture gave protection to its people at Bombay.[1] Shivaji carried on the operations even in the rains and tried *sama* or conciliation even, as a Karwar letter dated 20 August[2] shows. But the Siddi rejected such offer. Duff records that there was a revolution in Janjira, the Siddi was wavering and was, therefore, set aside and Siddi Sumbol became the chief. He, through the governor of Surat, offered allegiance to Aurangjeb who accepted it and conferred upon him the title of Yakubkhan.

1. PS 1257 ; ER 166, p. 132, 9th June 1669. 2. PS 1327.

XXVIII. SECOND SACK OF SURAT

Having decided upon an aggressive war against the Moguls, Shivaji first provided for the safety of his state and made a new arrangement with regard to his chief ministers which is metioned in an important document[1], dated August 1670, published in Rajwade Khand 8, No. 10. These ministers often performed military duties up to this time. Shivaji asked Nilopant Mujumdar to remain henceforth at home and transact all business regarding the state, while the Peshwa Moropant would go on military duty. Shivaji offered Nilopant two per cent on all money spent on buildings etc., but he loyally declined this percentage and asked for only $\frac{4}{5}$ths of such honorarium as would be paid to the Peshwa. This Shivaji gladly accepted and gave him his word in a regular order. Nilopant asked also for power to take to task such subordinates as would act wrongly. This was also given. Nilopant further asked for non-interference from Annaji Datto, the Surnis, which was also guaranteed by Shivaji who thus showed his implicit trust in the trustworthy Mujumdar, as he was fit for the work assigned to him. Shivaji was

1. PS 1339.

thus able to enter upon the war with a free heart together with Moropant Peshwa.

Shivaji also at this time entertained, as Sabhasad mentions, a force of bodyguards for himself consisting of 2,000 select Mawalas, some armed with guns, some with swords, some with other weapons, all having the same dress and gold ear-rings. This force, like the bodyguard of Mahmud of Ghazni, was of great use when there was fierce fighting to do. The expenditure on his army, thus increased, could be met only from plunder and Shivaji soon entered upon a career of plunder more extensive than he had hitherto pursued.

Shivaji first suddenly carried a raid into Mogul Deccan territory and plundered Junnar, Ahmednagar and Parenda, as is reported in a Persian letter[1], dated 8th May 1670. He advanced even as far as Aurangabad as noted in a Surat letter, dated 2nd April 1670[2], and people thought that he would go to Surat[3], and the English at Surat entertained a Lashkar and called for a small force from Bombay for their protection. But Shivaji plundered Chandwad only and defeated a Mogul force in Tal Konkan, as stated in a Persian letter dated 7th April 1670[4]. The Moguls

1. PS 1309.
2. PS 1297; ER 187, p. 145.
3. PS 1291; ER 180, p. 141, dated 12th March 1670.
4. PS 1298.

collected a strong army near Junnar with the design of advancing against Kalyan and Bhivandi and other Konkan territory of Shivaji; but as reported in a Bombay letter, dated 11th June 1670[1], the Mogul force was not mobile and was usually idle. It took quarters for the rains below a hill near Junnar. " But Shivaji did not allow grass to grow under his feet. " " He moved about even in the rains and took Lohgad and other forts and advanced upon Mahuli " which he took before the end of June as already stated. Having taken these forts, his way to Surat was now safe and clear and the people of Surat were so terrified that money became "scarce in Surat", as noted in a Bombay letter dated July 5th[2]. But Shivaji did not go to Surat and plundered Junnar instead in Bhadrapad or August (J). Shivaji's movements were always unexpected and sudden and his spying system was also perfect. In the beginning of October, his spies reported that Surat was full and unprepared and Shivaji suddenly appeared before Surat on 3rd October 1670.

Surat, having many a time failed in its expectation of Shivaji's coming, was not ready. The Subedar of Surat had died a month before and a protecting force which had been thrown therein in expectation of Shivaji had left (Duff). A new

1. PS 1313; ER 198, p. 150. 2. PS 1315.

governor had come as stated in a Surat letter, dated 12th September[1]. There was a mud-wall around the city which Shivaji easily took and Shivaji plundered the town for two days. The first day, being Diwali day, Kartik S'udha 1st, as stated in J, the merchants must have taken out their valuable property. The English and the Dutch were not interfered with as before. The French who were on friendly terms with Shivaji allowed the Marathas to attack a Turkish prince put up in a serai. The prince had just returned from pilgrimage and had very valuable property with him (Duff). This is supported by an English letter from Surat, dated 20th November[2], which states that Shivaji got into the Tartar serai and seized much gold and silver, and a golden bed. This letter also mentions that Shivaji expressed friendship for the English and even invited them to settle in Rajapur again. They gave him a small tribute. He left a letter to the citizens on the third day to pay him a yearly tribute of twelve lakhs of rupees, if they desired exemption from future pillage. A Dutch letter, dated 4th November[3], gives the same account and shows that Shivaji observed strictly his promise to the French (as well as the Dutch) who were friendly to him not to molest them. It is express-

1. PS 1332. 2. PS 1357; ER 237, p. 175.
3. PS 1356.

ly stated in Subhasad that the plunder consisted of gold, silver, jewels, etc. but not of cloth or copper and other things difficult to be removed and it was valued at 5 crores of rupees. The plunder was put into purses and placed on horses of half the cavalry men; and Shivaji himself escorted it towards Rajgad (S).

Surat was plundered for two days only and not three or six, as is stated in some later accounts. The first was 3rd October (PS 1330 dated Swali near Surat the same day) and Shivaji did not come on the 4th, but he suddenly came on the 5th and as suddenly went away on the 6th October. Probably he received news that a Mogul force was coming upon him. He stayed at Peinth for six days while he sent away the plunder to Rajgad and remained to meet the expected Mogul force. It was hence even thought at Surat that Shivaji would come once more.[1]

The prince Muajjam apparently remained inactive. Probably he had not sufficient force. It was also rumoured that he was preparing for war with Aurangjeb; but he asked the English to assist him against Shivaji.[2] They, however, declined, deciding to remain neutral for fear of attack by Shivaji. The reinforcements which Aurangjeb

1. PS 1342; ER 222, p. 16, Sawali letter dated 12 October.
2. P 1325, Surat letter 16 August 1670; ER 210, p. 158.

sent had not yet arrived. It was also expected that the prince with the help of Shivaji would rebel against his father, as Aurangjeb had rebelled against his. Surat letter, dated August 18th[1], as also Bombay letter of 5th September[2], again speak of this rumour. This letter also mentions that Shivaji could get lead and cannon from the French at Rajapur.

Whatever the attitude of the prince, a Mogul force under Daudkhan* from Burhanpur marched against Shivaji and overtook him near Dindori. Shivaji gave him battle and defeated him, capturing an elephant, on Kartik S′ 14 or 17th October 1670 (J). Thus the plunder safely reached Rajgad though Shivaji remained at Kunjargad (J), probably, in Nasik District. It is difficult to understand the military movement detailed by Duff who says that a detachment of the Mogul force arrived between Shivaji and Nasik and Shivaji divided his army into four parts and gave battle to both the forces. There is no mention of this in contemporary letters so far as we have seen.

We must bear in mind the position of the country in order to understand Shivaji's movements

1. PS 1326. 2. PS 1630; ER 213, p. 160.

* Daudkhan appears to be the governor of Burhanpur (PS 1378 Bombay letter 6th February 1671 ER 256 p. 189).

at this time. Shivaji had gone to Surat from Kalyan through the Konkan, but he returned via Peinth and not Baglan which is a patch of fertile country, consisting of the present Kolvan and Satana Talukas, between Surat and the Desh. Tavernier mentions that the latter was the route by which the great stream of traffic between Surat and Govalkonda passed (Nasik Gazetteer). In this route there are no intervening high ranges of mountains; but Shivaji did not take this route and went from Peinth to Dindori through a mountain pass and thence southwards towards Nasik and Poona. Shivaji usually took the unexpected path and thus discomfited his enemies.

XXIX. SIGNAL MOGUL DEFEAT NEAR SALER

Taking advantage of the defeat of Daudkhan and the delay in the arrival of Mahabatkhan sent by Aurangjeb, Shivaji conquered important forts in the present Nasik District adjoining his state. Though he failed in taking Shivneri near Junnar, Moropant Peshwa took the fort of Trimbak in Kartik Vadya (November 1670), a few days after Daudkhan's defeat (J). In Margashirsha (December), Shivaji went on a plundering expedition but first secured his rear by taking the forts of Ahivant and Rawla-Jawla in the Chandor range which commanded the route through Baglan. He then plundered the country as far as Burhanpur and sacked Karanja, the richest town in Berar next to Amraoti. Moropant Peshwa took the fort of Saler to the north of Baglan which was the strongest and the highest fort in that quarter (5295 ft., Nasik Gazetteer, page 441).* It had been taken by the Moguls from the Baguls of Baglan as

* J records that Moropant took the fort of Saler by *bheda* or treachery in January 1671. It appears from PS·1378, that Daudkhan who was near Saler had left for Burhanpur at this time and thus the Marathas could easily take the fort.

stated in Parnālākhyāna which is a contemporary poem written by Jayarama and which will be referred to now and then hereafter. Aurangjeb was so perturbed with the news of the loss of Saler fort that he at once ordered Ikhlaskhan and Bahilolkhan (?), probably then in Gujerat, to take back that fort at once and Dilerkhan of Malwa to go against Ahivant and Rawla-Jawla. Dilerkhan could not, however, take these forts as Moropant sent 12,000 Mawalas to attack the besiegers. There was here a severe hand-to-hand fight in which the Moguls were worsted.

Mahabatkhan arrived at Aurangabad about February, 1671 (Bombay letter[1] dated 6th February) and proceeded to the scene of conflict, leaving only 500 horse with Prince Muajjam[2]. He was apparently invested with the chief authority in the Deccan. Bahadurkhan and Dilerkhan who were deputed also by Aurangjeb against Shivaji joined him and Dilerkhan was entrusted with the administration of the whole District except Surat city. Mahabatkhan first went towards Nasik[3] and took back the forts of Ahivant and Rawla-Jawala as also that of Markund (J). Bombay letter, dated 29th May, states that he had taken 5 forts[4]. The fort of Saler

1. PS 1378; ER 256, p. 181.
2. PS 1395; ER 262, p. 191.
3. P 1930, Bombay letter dated 8th April 1671.
4. PS 1395.

was invested in Vaishakh (May 1671) by Dilerkhan and Bahadurkhan (J). The siege continued for many months through the rainy season; but in the month of Magha or February 1672 Moropant and Prataprao were sent by Shivaji against the besiegers. A tough battle was fought near Saler between the Marathas and the Moguls, a graphic account of which is given in the Bakhars, summarized by Duff as follows:— " For the relief of Saler, Moropant and Prataprao were detached by Shivaji with 20 thousand horse and were ordered to give battle. As soon as the Mogul general (Mahabatkhan) heard of their approach, he sent the greater part of his force under Ikhlaskhan against them. Prataprao, seeing Ikhlaskhan eager to attack him, fled before him until the Mogul troops were broken in order and then turning round, supported by Moropant, he gave them a signal defeat. The Moguls no doubt recovered their order and fought to the last; but they were charged, broken and routed with prodigious slaughter. 22 officers of note were killed and several of the principal commanders wounded and taken prisoners. The Marathas lost Suryarao Kakde, a commander of five thousand horse, and had also upwards of 500 killed and wounded." We have no contemporary evidence regarding the details of this battle, but there is no doubt of the fact that the Moguls were signally defeated at Saler and they withdrew towards Aurangabad, inasmuch as Surat letter, dated 6th April 1672, speaks of the 'notable' defeat of the Moguls who were investing a fort and of their two generals who had entered Shivaji's territory retreating with shame and loss.[1]

Duff properly observes that the victory "was the most complete one achieved by Shivaji's troops in a fair fought action" with the Moguls and contributed greatly to the renown of the Marathas; for a Surat letter, dated 14th June[2], speaks of Shivaji's "recent signal success near a fort which has raised him to high dignity in the eyes of the world."

Some further facts in connection with these events are given in J. It first states that Bahadurkhan and Dilerkhan who had besieged Saler in June raised the siege in As′vin (September) and went to Aurangabad where they kept their force. This action is inexplicable, they having passed the rains at Saler. Whatever the reason, they seem to have left a sufficient force on the *machi* of Saler (lower ground); for J records tha[illegible] on the *machi* was attacked and [illegible] Moropant in Magh (February [illegible] probably after the success in the battle de[illegible]d above. J thirdly adds that Prataprao and [illegible]ndrao in that

1. PS 1463; ER 300, p. 217.
2. 1472 Oronemss 114.

battle took Bahilolkhan* prisoner as also Mohokumsingh and Darkoji Bhosale. Eleven elephants and 1700 horses were seized. Sabhasad states that these prisoners were sent back to the Moguls after their wounds had been attended to, and they were duly honoured, as was the usual humane and masterful manner of Shivaji, which advanced his cause and also increased his fame.

Moropant followed up his success by taking Jawhar in Jyeshtha and Ramnagar in Ashadha in the Konkan (J). This is mentioned also in a Surat letter, dated 21st June 1672[1], and a treasure of 17 lakhs of rupees was seized at Jawhar[2]. Its chief was the Koli Vikramshah who was a tributary of the Moguls. Surat was again afraid and the gates were closed. But Shivaji simply sent a letter demanding Chauth from Surat and saying, "Your emperor has compelled me to keep an army for the protection of my country and my people and you must make a contribution for the maintenance of that army."

Thus by the end of June 1672, Shivaji was successful in his war against the Moguls and was also master of almost the whole of the Nasik District including Baglan and of the corresponding

*This Bahilolkhan seems, from the Parnālākhyāna, to be a brother of the Bijapur Bahilol.

1. PS 1474 ; ER 308, p. 220. 2. ER 310, p. 221.

portion of the Konkan including Jawhar and Ramnagar.

It is said that Shivaji went hereafter to Bhaganagar (Duff). As the usual route from Surat to Govalkonda lay through Baglan, this is possible. But J records that Shivaji sent Nirajipant to Govalkonda and settled a tribute of one lakh of hons from that state. Niraji brought to Rajgad 66 thousand hons at this time (J). Sultan Abdulla Kutubshah had died in Jyeshtha (June 1672) and his son-in-law Tanashah had succeeded to the throne, taking the name of Abdul Hasan. A new treaty for tribute was hence necessary.

XXX. WAR WITH BIJAPUR

During these operations, fortunately for Shivaji, Bijapur was at peace with him. His power was acknowledged by all the southern states. As mentioned already, Abdul Muhammad, chief minister of Bijapur, paid tribute or Chauth to Shivaji in order to induce him to abstain from plundering Bijapur territory. Jayarama, in his Parnālākhyāna, states that even Kutubshah of Govalkonda paid tribute, as also the Portuguese and the Siddi of Janjira for similar safety (Parnā. 2, 13). Aurangjeb advised his defeated generals to unite with Bijapur and Govalkonda and make a combined attack on Shivaji. This advice succeeded, because there was a change of masters and ministers at Bijapur. Ali Adilshah died about this time (24th November 1672) and his five years old son Sikandar was placed on the throne. Abdul Muhammad, the chief minister, who had maintained friendly relations with Shivaji, lost power and Khavaskhan, an Abyssinian, acquired ascendancy again. He was inimical to Shivaji and resumed hostilities. Shivaji thereupon called back his vakil Babaji Naik Punde from Bijapur. J records shortly that " Ali Adilshah died in Margashirsha S'. 1594 and Khavaskhan becoming Karbhari, the peace between Adilshah and Shivaji came to an end and Babaji Naik returned from Bijapur." Shivaji at once took the offensive and immediately sent Anandrao on a plundering expedition both in the Mogul and Bijapur territories and asked him to take the country from Wai to Lakshmeshwar. It was necessary for this purpose to seize the fort of Panhala which was the dominant fort adjacent to this territory and Shivaji deputed Annaji Datto to take it. J records that the fort was taken on Phalgun Vadya 13, (6th March 1673) by 'bheda' or seduction of officers and through Kondaji Farjund assisted by Sathis (infantry soldiers in companies of 60, from Shivaji's bodyguard–Sabhasad). The seizure of this fort is the theme of the Parnālākhyāna of Jayarama which gives a florid account of the event, the substance being as follows:—" Shivaji sent Annaji Pandit to take the fort and deputed also Kondaji, Gunaji and Motyaji, (probably officers of the Sathis), to assist him. After three days, Annaji advanced from Rajapur with these officers, taking with him rope-ladders, iguana and iron nails. Reaching in pitch dark the bottom of the perpendicular rock on which the fort stood and placing one man on the shoulders of another, making a human ladder, they succeeded in getting on to the top of the wall. They then suddenly sounded war-drums and attacked the guardsmen who, roused from sleep, rushed to the defence. The Mahomedan commander was killed in a fight with Kondaji. Nagoji Pandit, the officer who superintended the defence-guards placed at night, fled ; and the fort with all its palaces was taken." There is no mention in this account of 'bheda' which the poet probably purposely omits and hence the difficulty remains here, as at the taking of Sinhgad, of explaining how the Marathas got on to the fort. The bravery of Kondaji, like that of Tanaji, and of the Sixties cannot, of course, be underrated.

Shivaji came to the fort after three days on 9th March 1673 (Chaitra S'udha Pratipada, J), with his ministers with great ceremony. His progress from Raigad via Poladpur and Pratapgad is described with poetical embellishments by Jayarama. Shivaji was highly pleased on finding the fort well-provisioned and well-armed with cannon etc. He stayed there for about a month In the same Chaitra or April 1673, J further records the defeat of Bahilolkhan by Prataprao and Anandrao near Bijapur, the details of which are given by Jayarama in his poem as follows:—

"Khavaskhan sent Bahilolkhan with a huge army against Shivaji and many other officers such as Siddi Masaud, Dilerkhan etc., (named in Parnālākhyāna) were asked to join him. A terrible conflict took place at Umrani* near Tikota, by the side of a tank where the Mahomedan army had encamped and where Prataprao with his cavalry attacked it. Siddi Hilal, Vithoji Sinde, Krishnaji Bhaskar, Vithal Pildeo, Viso Ballal with their contingents assisted Prataprao. Many imaginary individual fights are described in this battle by Jayarama also and one incident is that of a mad elephant of the enemy stampeding and doing havoc in its own army. Eventually Bahilolkhan was defeated; but he escaped " by a way shown by Prataprao (with his connivance ?)." J records the above incident in the short note, " An elephant was captured." Parnālākhyāna describes the mad elephant as being finally taken away by Sidhoji Nimbalkar and presented to Shivaji " calm as a Yogin." (This poem ends here. It seems Jayarama composed short poems on different incidents in Shivaji's life, but we have got this poem alone of all his compositions.)

Shivaji took advantage of this decisive victory and on Chaitra Vadya 10 (6th April 1673) he took the fort of Parali (J). He also took Satara in S'ravan (26th July 1673, J) and thus extended his dominion to the east of the Ghat-Matha over the present Kolhapur and Satara territories. Hubli was plundered by Prataprao (Annaji Datto-Duff)

* Umrani is about 36 miles to the west of Bijapur.

about the middle of April, as also appears from a Karwarl etter[1], dated 16th April 1673, and from a Kaulnama[2], dated 27th April, of Athni speaking of Shivaji's raid on that side. The English sustained loss in the plunder of Hubli for which they demanded compensation from Shivaji. A list of things taken (given at ER 346,) shows that the loss was estimated at 7894 hons. Shivaji's Vakil, however, denied that his men had plundered the English.

Sabhasad states that at this time many more forts such as Chandan Vandan and Nandgiri were taken. Shivaji himself went from Raigad to see these forts and he himself took the ground fort (Kot) of Wai and of Karhad, Shirol and Kolhapur and seized territory as far as Hukeri and Raibag.

Bijapur sent Sarjekhan again against the Marathas after the rains and J records that Vithoji Shinde fell in the battle fought with him in Kartik (October 1673). This battle was followed by another action in which another great soldier of Shivaji *viz*. Prataprao Gujar fell. It was fought on 24th February 1674. Prataprao had allowed Bahilolkhan to escape in the battle of Umrani and he came again with a sufficient force given by Khavaskhan, whereupon Shivaji again sent Prataprao against him. Sabhasad says that Shivaji sent him a letter with instruction to fight to the bitter end," as

1. PS 1524; ER 346, p. 241. 2. PS 1527.

Bahilolkhan came again and again." Prataprao did fight to the bitter end and was killed in the battle. The consequent imminent defeat was, however, changed into a victory by Hansaji Mohite who, rallying the Marathas, charged the enemy and defeated him (Duff). The Mahomedan army thus returned to Bijapur without achieving anything.

Shivaji during these years was often at war with the Siddi of Janjira also. Securely ensconced in an impregnable island-fort, the Siddi could harass Shivaji's country by land and water. He was also incited at this time by Aurangjeb whose subordination and protection he had accepted, to attack Shivaji and Aurangjeb also sent some ships from Surat and Ghogha to assist him. These ships wished to plunder Shivaji's territory near Bombay, but they were not allowed to enter the Bombay creek[1]. The English in Bombay assisted Shivaji at this time, as they detained in Bombay harbour six ships of Shivaji built in Kalyan creek with his consent and gave out that they had detained them for securing compensation demanded from him regarding their plunder at Rajapur.[2]

A naval indecisive action was, however, fought between the Mogul navy and that of Shivaji near Bombay, as reported in a letter from Bombay, dated

1. PS 1500, Bombay 31 Oct. 1672; ER 328, p. 230.
2. PS 1505, Dec. 1672; ER 333, p. 232.

9th November 1672.[1] Sabhasad, who cannot be relied on for sequence of events, though he faithfully relates all, twice mentions an unsuccessful war with the Siddi. " The Siddi who kept a navy of 40 Gurabas (ships) began to harass the Raja's country. Baji Phasalkar with 2,000 Mawalas was sent against him by land and ships also were sent by sea. 'The king saddled the sea with ships as it were' ; (and it may be added also bridled it by building forts on coast-islands). Kaya Savant came to the help of the Siddi with 5 thousand men and a tough battle was fought between him and Baji Phasalkar, in which both the leaders were killed. The two armies returned to their respective places. " Shivaji thus lost the second of the three great companions, who from boyhood had stood by him through thick and thin. The exact date of this action cannot be fixed. Shivaji, however, fortified the hill of 'Henry Kenry' in the sea to enable him easily to attack the Siddi by sea. Naquada Omed of Surat offered to prevent this if Aurangjeb paid him one lakh and twenty thousand rupees, as noted in a letter from Delhi of an English artillery officer in Mogul service, dated 26th September 1672;[2] and Aurangjeb accepted the proposal demanding security from him. Nothing came out of this apparently; and Shivaji succeeded in fortifying Khanderi, as we shall see later on.

1. PS 1501; ER 329, p. 230. 2. PS 1494; ER 321, p. 227.

XXXI. PREPARATION FOR CORONATION

The following dates and events, mostly taken from J, will show us how Shivaji had upto now defeated and plundered the Moguls and the Adilshahis and extended his dominion during the two years 1673 and 1674. In March or Chaitra 1673, Prataprao and Anandrao defeated Bahilolkhan (Abdul Karim-S) at Umrani near Bijapur and on 1st April (Chaitra Vadya 10, Tuesday), Shivaji took the fort of Parali (J). Other forts like Chandan Vandan were also taken soon after (S). On 26th July (S'ravan Vadya 9, Sunday), the fort and town of Satara were taken. This is supported by Bombay Consultation Record, dated 15th September, which states that Shivaji has recently taken the central and important fort of Satara and acquired immense booty, which was safely removed on bullocks to Raigad[1]. Bijapur sent Sarjekhan again and he fought a battle in Kartik (October) with Vithoji Shinde but could not do much though Vithoji fell in the battle (J). It is probably this battle which is mentioned in a Karwar letter, dated 17th December[2]. Shivaji on

1. PS 1563 ; ER 392, p. 283.
2. PS 1606 ; ER 431, p. 317.

Vijayadashami or Dasara day (10th October 1673) went against and plundered Bankapur, a town in the present Dharwar district (J). A Bombay letter, dated 15th December 1673, states that Shivaji was away for the last three months, plundering Bijapur Kannad territory[1]. Bahilolkhan advanced from Bijapur and in the Karwar letter above noted he is said to have defeated Shivaji. But in the greater action which was fought at Nivati (Nesari*-Sabhasad) on Magh Vadya 14.or Shivratri day (24th February 1674), although Prataprao fell, Bahilolkhan was defeated by Hansaji Mohite as already described and pursued back to Bijapur (J and Duff). Anandrao thereon went and plundered Sampgaon Peth (bazzar town) in the present Belgaum district (on 23-3-74). Sabhasad relates, however, that it was Mohite who plundered Sampgaon. He was opposed there by Husseinkhan Pathan of Bijapur. "A fierce battle was fought from noon to the next morning and Husseinkhan was signally defeated. He was taken prisoner and 4,000 horses and 12 elephants were captured. Moropant Peshwa, thereafter, carried an expedition as far as the Tungabhadra and obtained surrender of the fort of Kopal from Hussein's brother who was its Killedar, and all the territory upto Kopal came into

1. PS 1604 ; ER 429, p. 314. * In Kolhapur State.

Shivaji's possession." J states that Anandrao was intercepted by Khidarkhan, a Bijapur captain, while returning from Sampgaon; but the latter was defeated and two elephants were seized. Probably, these two fights mentioned by Sabhasad and J are one and the same. On the 24th of April 1674, Shivaji himself took Kelanja, a fort near Wai (J). The Bijapur army thus was helpless and could do nothing against Shivaji and a large part of its territory was seized by him.

The Moguls also were powerless, though Aurangjeb, recalling Mahabatkhan after his defeat at Saler and also the prince (who had left in March or February 1672–J), had sent a new commander with 70,000 horse, and he was on the border of Shivaji's country.[1] His name was Bahadurkhan, also called Koka (Sabhasad), and he was subsequently honoured by Aurangjeb with the title of Khanjahan (Duff). Bahadurkhan did not think it possible even with his large force to attack Shivaji or to take his forts and adopted a defensive policy in order to prevent the Marathas from raiding and plundering Mogul territory. But he failed even in this, as under his very eyes, Maratha raiding parties did enter Mogul territory and plundered and collected *Chauth* as far as Khandesh, Berar and Jalna. Dilerkhan, his second

1. PS 1604.

in command, was for active fighting, and he fought a battle with the Marathas but was signally defeated, as is reported in a Surat letter, dated 6th February 1674.[1] Bahadurkhan advanced as far as the Bhima, his boundary,[2] and there encamped, building a fort to defend himself, at Pedgaon. (This fort is called Bahadurgad). He also was thus helpless and remaining inactive could make no impression on Shivaji.

Shivaji had thus defeated in pitched battles the armies of the boastful Abyssinian of Bijapur and the haughty Mogul of Delhi and had plundered their territories with impunity, being the master of a powerful force of cavalry and infantry which now began to be feared for its hurricane-like movements and 'eagle-like swoops.' The English at Surat thought that Shivaji would be squeezed between the Mogul Bahadurkhan coming from the north and the Adilshahi Bahilolkhan advancing from the south, as also the Siddi moving from the west. But Shivaji rose superior to all these three, as was foreseen by the English at Bombay[3] in their letter of 15th September 1673. He had also by this time acquired a large territory which now extended on the Ghat-Matha from

1. PS 1615 ; ER 441, p. 321.
2. ER 447, p. 325, dated 19th March.
3. PS 1563 ; ER 392, p. 283.

Baglan to Banda and along an east line in the Deccan extending from Nasik in the north to Kopal in the south. He had the Konkan from Bassein to Goa and important ports on the west coast like Rajapur, Vengurla, Dabhol, Chaul and Kalyan where the English now thought it safe to open factories.

On 8th April 1674, Shivaji called together and reviewed his whole army at Chiplun (J)[1], the country above the Ghat being partially stricken with famine (Duff), a famine felt even in Bombay, as noted in the above noted letter. He appointed Mohite as his commander-in-chief or Sarnobat, Mohite having distinguished himself in the battle of Umrani, as already stated. He honoured him with the title of Hambirrao. Two other captains were also promoted at this time, having distinguished themselves in that battle, namely, Dhanaji Jadhav and Santaji Ghorpade. These were destined hereafter successfully to oppose Aurangjeb when, after the death of Shivaji, he personally came to the Deccan and with all the might of the Mogul empire vainly tried to crush the independence of Maharashtra, defended as it was, under Rajaram, by these two, then renowned veteran leaders of Maratha forces.

Having thus made arrangements for the strength and efficiency of his army, Shivaji also made

1. PS 1563.

arrangement for the civil administration of his large territory. Sabhasad relates that Shivaji divided his territory into three parts and placed them under three Sarkarkuns or commissioners. The northern division from Kalyan-Bhivandi to Saler, including Kolvan, was placed under Moropant Peshwa and it included both Konkan and the Ghat-Matha with its forts of Lohagad and Junnar. The middle division consisting of Konkan alone from Chaul, including Dabhol, Rajapur, Vengurla, Banda and Kudal territory with its commanding fort of Phonda, was entrusted to Annaji Datto. The third division consisting of the territory in the Deccan from Wai to Kopal was placed under Dattajipant Waknis who was to reside in the fort of Panhala. It was settled (Tah) that the forts in these divisions would also be under the control of the Sarkarkuns who were to appoint all officers except the killedars. These last were to be appointed, after personal inspection, by Shivaji himself, as the forts were the most important places commanding the districts and afforded shelter in times of invasion. There were four or five Subedars also in the Mogul country, presumably for realising tribute or Chauth (Sabhasad).

The only enemy unsubdued and the only weak spot left was the Siddi of Janjira. Sabhasad speaks of a second campaign against him, as he, breaking the treaty concluded with him by Raghunathpant, began to harass Shivaji's country near him. Vyankoji Datto was sent by Shivaji on this campaign against him and he defeated a Siddi force in a tough fight, though himself receiving twelve wounds. Duff speaks of Ragho Ballal being killed in this or some other action. Shivaji took all the plain territory belonging to the Siddi and confined him to his sole island fort. He then could obtain subsistence only from the coastal towns in his ships. Siddi's men sometimes cut and took away corn from fields in Shivaji's territory; but they were once seized by Shivaji's men and their heads were cut off and sent to Shivaji[1]. Shivaji for this purpose increased his navy also and the navy now consisted of Gurabas, Tarandis, Tarve, Shibade and Pagars. These several kinds of ships were kept under two commanders or Subedars, one Darya Sarang, a Mahomedan, and the other Mayanak Bhandari (Sabhasad). Ships, two hundred in number, were under each Subedar and they also led plundering expeditions against other coastal towns. (The coastal powers were seventeen in number, according to Sabhasad, including the Moguls, the Portuguese, the Dutch, the English and the Hindus). Though Shivaji could not destroy or subdue the Siddi, even after spending

1. PS 1583.

immense treasure and sacrificing about 15,000 men on Janjira,[1] he succeeded at this time, with the help of his strong navy, in confining him to his island fort. He sought the help of the English, but they remained neutral,[2] being afraid of incurring the enmity either of Shivaji or of Aurangjeb.

Shivaji had thus at this time (middle of 1674) realised the dream of his boyhood and established a Hindu independent kingdom in the western part of Maharashtra. He had a large powerful army and also a navy which inspired fear and ensured respect. He had amassed immense treasure by his plunders which were always safely conveyed either to Rajgad or Raigad. He was now a *de facto* independent king, and not a jagirdar as he was in the beginning, or a sub-ordinate chief as he was before he went to Agra; nor even a feudatory prince like Jaswantsingh or Jaisingh to be employed by an emperor on his own mission. Indeed, Shivaji as king hereafter sent sub-ordinate chiefs and commanders on expeditions,* he himself taking little part in actual fighting.

1. P 1523; ER 343, p. 240, Bombay letter dated 25th March 1673.

2. PS 1530; ER 351, p. 246, Bombay Consultation, 10th May 1673.

*The statements hereafter found that Shivaji did this thing or that have usually to be taken in the sense

(*Continued on next page*)

Shivaji was, therefore, in every way fit to be crowned as king and he resolved properly enough, as the head of Hindavi swarajya, to have the religious ceremony of coronation (राज्याभिषेक) performed to him according to Vedic rites, in order to impress his subjects with his new position as a crowned king. For this purpose, he had no doubt to spend an enormous amount of money; but his treasury was full. He had also built a palace on Raigad fort with an assembly hall resembling the Diwan-i-Am at Agra, a hall mentioned by Niccolls in his diary[1], dated 19th May to 17th June 1674. We know that an assembly hall was built for the Pandavas by Mayasura before they performed the Rajasuya or coronation sacrifice. But above all, he had to satisfy the qualms of those too orthodox Brahmins of the Deccan who believed that there were no Kshatriyas in the Kali age. The descent of the Bhosales from the Sisodia kings of Udaipur had always been accepted, as we have already shown, and there was no necessity of

that Shivaji ordered those things to be done. Thus, though Karwar letter, ER 365, p. 259, dated 14 June 1674, speaks of Shivaji's plundering Hubli, Niccoll's diary, ER 358, p. 267 shows that it was not Shivaji himself who plundered Hubli but his commander Anandrao and that Shivaji knew nothing about the affair and was waiting for the report of his commander about it.

1. ER 358, p. 252.

concocting a new Kshatriya pedigree, as has been supposed by some writers on the basis of later Bakhars. But the Brahmins had to be satisfied that a Vedic religious ceremony could be performed to the Maratha Shivaji. Fortunately Gagabhat, a renowned Deccani Pandit of Benares, learned both in Veda and Shastra, had come to see Shivaji (S) or was invited to come and see Shivaji when the former was at Paithan. The consent of this Shastri was obtained and it was settled that Shivaji should mount a specially constructed throne and have an umbrella (Chhatra) held over him, "just as Mahomedan kings ascend a throne and have an umbrella held over them" (Sabhasad). Shivaji meant to make it known to the people that he was a crowned king, as good as the Mogul Padshah or the Bijapur Sultan. The common people in India and in Maharashtra at that time believed that there were only Mahomedan sovereigns in their country, as the Mahomedan rule over N. India had extended for the last 600 and over Deccan 300 years, and it was necessary to emphasize the fact that Shivaji was now a sovereign, equal in status with the Mogul emperor as well as the king of Bijapur or of Portugal. And it was resolved in March 1674 that Shivaji should perform the ceremony of coronation and assume the title of Chhatrapati with Vedic rites; and due preparation, such as the construction of a golden throne etc., was made. It is reported in Bombay letter[1] by Narayan Shenvi, dated 4 April 1674, that "Shivaji is constructing a magnificent throne with gold and diamonds."

It seems that Shivaji had already begun to style himself Maharaj and Chhatrapati, after his return from Agra, in important state documents like sanads given to feudatary chiefs. Thus, we find that in a sanad issued to Pilaji Raje Ghatge, Shivaji styles himself Maharaj and Chhatrapati, see sanad, dated 26th January 1669[2]. It is supposed that these words are put in by the copyist in this document in the possession of the Ghatges of Kagal; but this copy has been printed in the volume of sanads issued by Government and the words are in such a place that they cannot be looked upon as put in subsequently. Again it was intended in this sanad to emphasize Shivaji's higher position than that of the grantee who was also styled Raje. This word 'Chhatrapati,' therefore, we think, cannot be looked upon as subsequently put in, though in ordinary orders issued by Shivaji to his officers or village people, he simply styles himself 'Shivaji Raje.'*

* Its seems that this title was already intended to be taken when Shivaji reserved the umbrella to himself and directed his officers and chiefs not to take umbrellas, as in Mahomedan states, but to take abdagir instead (S).

1. PS 1625; ER 451, p. 327. 2. PS 1239.

XXXII. THE IMPOSING CEREMONY

The gorgeous and imposing ceremony of Shivaji's coronation took place on the spacious fort of Raigad, in the presence of subordinate chiefs and jagirdars, military captains and civil administrators and thousands of happy villagers and village officers. The top of the fort is extensive enough to accommodate the vast concourse that had gathered there and the tanks excavated on the top contained water enough for their use. The main ceremony took place on Jyeshtha S′uddha 12, S′.1575 or 6th June 1674 (J). But it was preceded by two important ceremonies. On 26th May, the thread ceremony of Shivaji was performed, as this ceremony was necessary to enable him to be crowned with Vedic rites. The Marathas had long given up (probably since Buddhist days) this ceremony of initiation of the Vedic Aryans and it was hence that Brahmins in Maharashtra looked upon Marathas as S′udras. But as they were Kshatriyas by race and as they had restricted marriages to themselves, they were only Vrātya Kshatriyas and Gagabhat rightly held that the Upanayana ceremony; could be performed to Shivaji, even at the age of 44, with the requisite

SHIVAJI THE FOUNDER OF MARATHA SWARAJ.

Throne Platform at Raigad.

To face page 24

expiatory ceremonies performed before the initiation rite. That this controversy did take place at that time is clear from the Dutch account of the coronation, dated 3rd October 1674.[1] As the coronation ceremony required also a queen wedded with Vedic rites, on the 30th of May the marriage of Shivaji with his eldest living queen was again performed with Vedic mantras (J). It is sometimes supposed that Shivaji had a new wife on this day, but the wording in J 'समंत्रक विवाह केला' "marriage was performed with mantras," without specifying the name of the family of the bride, can only be understood in the above sense. The main coronation ceremony took place six days after on Friday, Jyestha, S'.12 (Ghati 21-14,) when the night remained only 3 ghadis, which means that the ceremony took place on the 13th, early in the morning of Saturday, an hour and twenty minutes before sunrise. These details of time are important and J gives them purposely as they belong to the most important event in the life of Shivaji and the history of Maharashtra. J gives the Mahomedan Fasli date also, namely, 10 Ravilaval, Khamas Sabain Alaf. This date and hour is also given by the Dutch letter above referred to.

At this astrologically auspicious moment, Shivaji sat on the Sinhāsan specially prepared,

1. PS 1684.

a gold-plate-covered ivory throne, (in which jewels were set in various places and gold lion-heads in the four corners), with his chief queen by his side and his eldest son Sambhaji on the step in front. The eight ministers with the insignia of royalty in their hands such as Chhatra (umbrella), Chamar (deer hair) etc., stood on the four sides by the eight pillars which supported the canopy from which hung festoons of big pearls. And Gagabhat, amidst the sounding of auspicious instruments and the boom of cannon, sprinkled on Shivaji's head the holy waters brought from the four seas and the seven sacred rivers of India specially for the occasion, chanting the Vedic mantras prescribed in the Aitareya Brahmana for Mahabhisheka, one of which is the ever-to-be-remembered blessing—

May′ thy sub′jects lo′ve thee e′ver
May′ thy ki′ngship sli′p thee n′ever.*

Shivaji then started on a triumphal procession through the streets of the city on the fort, to show himself to the thousands of his subjects who had gathered to greet him, and also to pay a visit to the temple of Mahadeva and Durgā. Led by two painted elephants decked with golden ornaments and two horses similarly decked, and seated in a car drawn by bullocks, Shivaji received the Jaya acclamations of his happy subjects, amidst showers

* विशस्त्वा सर्वा वाञ्छन्तु मा त्वद्राष्ट्रमधिभ्रशत्—ऋ.

of small gold and silver flowers sprinkled by women looking at the procession from windows. Having worshipped Mahadeva and Bhavani at the temple which he had constructed, he returned by another road amidst similar demonstrations to his palace.

On the next day, namely, the 7th of June, Shivaji held a Darbar in which officers and jagirdars made presents to him. Moropant Peshwa presented 7,000 hons which were sprinkled over Shivaji's head, thus giving him what is represented as a bath in gold. The Mujumdar similarly presented 7,000 hons and two other ministers 5,000 each, see Dutch record, dated 3rd October. Then Poshaks (garments) were presented to all including the envoys. The Portuguese, the Dutch and also the English envoys were most probably present. The eight ministers stood as follows: (with their old and new titles-S).

*1. Moropant, Peshwa or Mukhya-Pradhan (Chief Minister)	*1. Hambirrao Mohite, Sarnobat or Senapati (Commander-in-Chief)
2. Niraji Nilkanth, Mujumdar or Pant Amatya (Accountant)	2. Ramchandra Trimbak, Dabir or Sumant (Foreign Minister).
3. Annaji Datto, Surnis or Pant Sachiv (Corresponding Minister).	3. Raoji Niraji, Nyayadhisha (Chief Justice), —a new office

*This represents the place on each side in the Durbar.

4. Dattaji Trimbak, Waknis or Mantri, (Privy Purse)	4. Raghunathrao, Pandit-rao, (Ecclesiastical Minister). do.

These ministers were presented each with one lakh of hons, one elephant, one horse, garments and ornaments. Gagabhat was given one lakh of rupees for seeing the whole ceremony through. The Dakshinas granted by Shivaji on the several occasions of the coronation ceremony were very large, as was suited to the occasion. Sabhasad reports that the whole expenditure amounted to one crore and forty two lakhs of hons or 426 lakhs of rupees.

But this enormous expenditure was justified by its results. It gave a religious sanction to the new position of Shivaji as the crowned king of Hindavi Svarajya and created a sentiment of patriotic love of country in the hearts of Marathas, of such strength that it lasted one hundred years at least and weathered successfully Aurangjeb's invasion of Maharashtra after Shivaji's death and even led to the extension of Maratha power, after Aurang-jeb had passed away.

The ceremony gave the greatest gratification to one person and the greatest grief to another. Shivaji's old mother Jijabai had, with Rajput instinct, sympathised with Shivaji's sacred plan of founding Swaraj and had made him what he was by her highly spiritual life. It was a moment of supreme happiness to her, when crowned Shivaji stood before her to bow to her and receive her blessing. She felt the greatest gratification to find that she had lived to see that day; for she was very old (about 80 years), according to the Dutch letter above quoted, and she had really lived for it; for she died only 12 days after the happy event. The Dutch letter states that she left 25 lakhs of hons to Shivaji.

The greatest grief was caused to Aurangjeb. His general Bahadurkhan had done nothing to prevent this ceremony. He indeed wished to go into the Konkan; but Shivaji had taken precaution by posting strong guards at every pass. Probably, he was afraid of mountain-traps also and he was further not very keen. The Bijapur ministers were also not much pleased or grieved, nor the Sultan of Govalkonda; for the latter saw in Shivaji a strong ally against the threatening encroachment of Aurangjeb. Thus Aurangjeb alone felt real grief at this event. He had lost the game against Shivaji who, though equal to him in every art of fraud or force, had won, by God's favour, the game of politics which they were playing on the plain of Maharashtra. " God has favoured the Marathas ", he exclaimed, " and given them an independent king." (Sabhasad).

The English were good enough to send a representative on this auspicious occasion, as they were glad to see Shivaji crowned, being at the time friendly towards him. The following graphic account of his visit by Oxenden may be quoted for the curious reader:—"The next morning, he and his retinue went to court and found the Raja seated on a magnificent throne and all the nobles waiting on him in rich attire. His son Sambhaji, Peshwa Moropant and a Brahmin of great eminence were seated on the ascent under the throne, the rest, as well the officers of the army as others, standing with great respect (following the manner of the Durbar of Aurangjeb which Shivaji had seen at Agra). The English made their obeisance at a distance and Narayan Shenvi held up the ring that was to be presented. Shivaji personally took notice of it and ordered their coming to the foot of the throne where, being seated and presented with Poshaks, they were desired to retire."[1]

Oxenden further records that on the two sides of the throne there were held the Mahomedan insignia "of government and dominion" such as, on the right side on heads of gilded lances, two golden heads of fish with very large teeth (showing sovereignty of the sea) and on the left side a pair of golden scales[2] (showing justice as the sign of royalty).

1. ER 486, p. 375. 2. *Ibid.*

Oxenden also records that Shivaji signed the treaty with the English on the 11th of June, excepting the article regarding coins. Shivaji had probably delayed signing upto this day, as he intended to sign the document as a crowned king covenanting with another crowned king.

Shivaji started a new era from the day of his coronation, namely, 6th June 1674 and this era, called the Rājyābhisheka era, was used for many years after him. Unfortunately it has ceased to be used now like the coronation eras of mediæval Hindu kings such as Harsha of Kanauj, Vikramāditya of the Deccan or Kumārapāla of Gujarat. It is strange that even the Peshwas later on ceased to use this era and always mentioned the Fasli year.

Note:—**Some minor details**

(1) Dakshinas:—Sabhasad relates that 50,000 Vaidika Brahmins had collected on the occasion of Shivaji's coronation. This is clearly a mistake for 5,000. Besides these there were Jogis, Sanyasis etc., by thousands. These were fed or given corn below the fort. It is related in contemporary papers that Shivaji, before coronation, was weighed against gold and almost every other metal as well as auspicious thing. Dutch record describing the ceremony in detail on 3rd October, PS 1684, states that Shivaji weighed 17,000 hons or 160 lbs., and he was also weighed against silver, copper, iron etc., and against camphor, salt, sugar, butter, various kinds of fruit, betel-nuts etc., and the value of the whole was distributed amongst Brahmins. On the 7th of June, the day after the corona-

tion, Dakshina was given in general and every Brahmin got 3 to 5 Rs.and every one else, whether woman or child, 2 Rs. and 1 Re. In all, the Dakshina amounted to 1½ lakhs of hons in value.

Oxenden also states in his diary from 13th May to 13th June that Shivaji was weighed against gold and the weight, 16,000 hons, together with one lakh of hons in addition were distributed as Dakshina among Brahmins.

The above noted Dutch record further states that for the Vrātya ceremony 7,000 hons were given to Gagabhat and 17,000 to other Brahmins. On the 5th of June, Shivaji bathed in holy Ganges water and every Brahmin present was given 100 hons.

(2) It is reported that the ministers represented that their offices should be declared hereditary and that Shivaji granted this request on the coronation day. But this does not seem probable, as it was against the principle of Shivaji to make any office hereditary. He, however, gave to Balaji Avaji Prabhu Chitnis whose work was most satisfactory, a Sanad (PS 1654, dated 7th June 1674) conferring on him the offices of Karkhannis and Jamnis in the whole state. The sanad relates that Balaji was offered a ministership, but he declined it and asked for the above offices hereditarily in his family.

The Deshmukhs of Mawal were also rewarded. They were the first to assist Shivaji and loyally stood by him to the last. On the day when Shivaji sat on the throne, they asked for reward and they were given the right to the first place among Deshmukhs and the right to enjoy their Watans hereditarily (J).

(3) Another coronation ceremony—Obstructive and dissatisfied Brahmins there were even then as always.

They did not deem the ceremony satisfactory, though it was acclaimed by the whole of Maharashtra. A poem named Rājyābhisheka Kalpataru, a copy of which is in the Library of the Bengal Royal Asiatic Society and which has been published from it by the Itihasa S. Mandal of Poona (Quarterly Vol. X-I), embodies some objections raised against the coronation ceremony gone through. This poem is not quite contemporary, as it mentions the later idea that Shivaji was an incarnation of S'iva (not of Vishnu as represented by the earlier Shivabharata) though it is of the time of Rajaram. It gives an imaginary conversation between Nis'chalapuri, a learned Brahmin ascetic of Benares, who was an opponent of Gagabhat, and Govindbhat Barve as taking place in Konkan. It recounts the ill omens which preceded and followed the coronation, such as the death of Prataprao Gujar, the death of Kashibai, wife of Shivaji, etc. and the wound caused to Gagabhat himself on the nose by the falling of a rafter. The poem expressly says that Gagabhat engaged for the ceremony those Brahmins only who were his followers and refused to employ those recommended by Nis'chalapuri. Many defects in the ceremony itself are next mentioned. Thus when Shivaji was getting into the chariot after the ceremony of ascending the throne, Gagabhat himself first sat in the chariot and then Shivaji. After seeing the whole ceremony through, Nis'chalapuri left the fort but told Shivaji that bad events would happen on the 13th, 22nd and 55th days. On the 13th accordingly, Shivaji's mother died. Next a horse-shed was burnt at Pratapgad with good many horses in it and an elephant died on Sinhgad. These incidents induced Shivaji to call Nis'chalapuri back and through him and his Brahmins

Shivaji performed afresh the ceremony of ascending the throne, not with Vedic rites, but Tantrik or magical. This ceremony is also described in detail. There are mentioned some Vedic mantras from Sāmaveda as recited ; but the ceremony was not Vedic. It was performed on Ashvin S'uddha 5 (Lalita Panchami day, S'. 1596), as is stated at the end of the poem. This ceremony is also mentioned by J and Nis'chalapuri is also spoken of in a Mahomedan record.

Shivaji must have performed this ceremony, not because he was so bigotted as to believe that his mother's death and other evil events really were due to defects in the ceremony. He performed it because he desired to satisfy all Brahmins, both Gagabhat and his opponent, so that no one should detract from the great importance of his coronation.

(4) Wives married again with Vedic rites. Oxenden states that on the 8th of June Shivaji married without ceremony the fourth wife. This shows that Shivaji had four wives alive at the time and that they were, one by one, married again with Vedic rites to Shivaji, without, of course, any kind of celebration.

XXXIII. SHIVAJI AND RAMADAS

It would be proper to give here in brief the life and work of Ramadas who was, according to our view, a co-worker with Shivaji in the sacred cause of the deliverance of Maharashtra from the oppression of a foreign rule and religion. He was unquestionably, at this time, the spiritual guru of Shivaji and Shivaji must have gone to Ramadas after his coronation to bow to him. Ramadas resided at Sajjangad near Satara. He sent his blessings from there but, as was proper for a Sadhu, had not gone to Raigad to attend the coronation ceremony. Shivaji placed his whole kingdom at the feet of Ramadas as he bowed to him; but the latter returned it to him, asking him only to have a banner of the saintly colour (Bhagva or soiled red) in recognition of its re-gift to him. This story simply impresses the fact that Shivaji ruled Maharashtra not for his personal enjoyment and profit but solely for the good of the people. The truth of the story is doubted by some, because it is found that the banner of Maloji was also of a soiled red colour. But it is pointed out by the other side that the eye-witness Oxenden reports (?) that Shivaji's banner at the time of the coronation was white in colour.

That Shivaji placed his kingdom at the feet of Ramadas after his coronation is, however, proved by his own words in a document addressed to Ramadas, dated 1679-80[1]. Ramadas was henceforth closely associated with Shivaji in the cause of the uplift of Maharashtra. We think it, therefore, proper to give here in substance the leading facts in the life of Ramadas and show also how and when he came into contact with Shivaji and eventually became his guru.

Ramadas was born in 1608 A. D. at Jamb on the Godavari in Nizamshahi territory (now in the Nizam state). His father, a Brahmin and a Kulkarni, died early and he was brought up by his mother and brother. When twelve years of age, he ran away from his house. He was intensely religious from early childhood and did not like to be married, for which preparations were being made, according to the custom of the time, at that early age, by his loving mother and his brother. He also disliked the life of a Kulkarni for which he was born. Ramadas, thus running away, went to Nasik and there lived twelve years incognito, performing religious austerities. He then, at twenty-four, is said to have gone on a pilgrimage through India. In 1644, after about twelve years, he returned

1. PS 2237. आवरीं राज्य संपादिलें तें चरणीं अर्पून सर्वकाळ सेवा घडावी असा विचार मनीं आणला.

and settled first at Masur on the Krishna, which was then in the jagir of Shahaji. He subsequently went to Chaphal where he built a temple of Rama, his tutelary and also favourite deity, and began his mission of rousing the people to a sense of their duty to their religion and their country. He lived in this part, passing days together in the hilly gorges of the Sahyadri mountain, till the last of his days and died in the year 1681, one year after Shivaji.

The two most disputed points in connection with Ramadas's life and work are these:—(1) Did Ramadas work for the political uplift of Maharashtra or was he merely, like other Maratha saints, a religious preacher? (2) When did he come into contact with Shivaji and begin to inspire the latter's political actions? There are two schools, as usual, in Maharashtra on this question, the orthodox and the heterodox. The first, on the basis of the poetical lives of Ramadas, written after him by his disciples which resemble the Bakhars of Shivaji and which naturally exaggerate matters, believe that Ramadas inspired Shivaji's actions from the very first. The other school believes that Ramadas was never a political agitator and was only brought into contact with Shivaji, as a religious teacher, at a very late stage of his life, probably, just before Shivaji's coronation. The truth, according to our view, lies, as usual, in the golden mean. We will discuss these points in short here, relying as before only on contemporaneous documents.

The chief of these is, of course, the Dasabodha of Ramadas himself which, like the Jnyaneshvari, has immortalized the name of Ramadas and has enriched Marathi literature. Indeed, it is the greatest work in Marathi next to the Jnyaneshvari. It is an original work by Ramadas, teaching Jnyāna (philosophy), Bhakti (devotion), and what is more important, Vyavahāra (political and worldly wisdom). Ramadas composed this powerful poem, divided into twenty chapters, after he settled at Chaphal. The sixth chapter mentions its date as S'aka 1581 or 1659 A. D. The eighteenth chapter was certainly written just after the Afzalkhan affair, as is evident from its contents, apparently giving advice to Shivaji, though his name is not mentioned therein. There is also extant a letter in verse, addressed to Shivaji, which, by its glowing tribute to Shivaji and by its powerful Marathi, is undoubtedly written by Ramadas and he complains in this letter that "though he resided in Shivaji's territory, the latter had not yet visited him." Shivaji must have gone to see Ramadas immediately after and chapter XVIII contains the instructions then given. It is thus certain that Shivaji first came into contact with Ramadas in

1660 after the Afzalkhan incident. He could not have thus inspired Shivaji's actions from the very beginning, as is maintained by the admirers of Ramadas. Ramadas, when he settled at Chaphal in 1644, was thirty-six years old and Shivaji was then fourteen. Both began their political careers at one and the same time. But they did it in different parts of Maharashtra and could not have come together till after Shivaji had conquered Javali and destroyed Afzalkhan and thus become master of the mountainous country wherein Ramadas lived and preached. Shivaji, at first sight, must have marked the greatness of the saint and he eventually selected him as his guru. The sanad that he gave to Ramadas declares no doubt that by the blessing of the saint, he was successful in *every* undertaking but this expression is of the usual conventional nature and cannot justify the view that Ramadas inspired every action of Shivaji from the very beginning.

On the second point, we think that it can be conclusively proved from Ramadas's own writings that he was both a religious and a political preacher. While we cannot admit, as the orthodox party propounds, that Shivaji began his political career under inspiration from Ramadas, we cannot also admit, as the other party persistently preaches, that Ramadas never took part in politics and never inspired Shivaji's actions. Both were great men from the beginning and had thought out an identical plan for the regeneration of their country, and both began their work independently. But they, as kindred spirits working for the same end, each in his own way, came together, as they always do, and worked together for the same end. How Ramadas came to take up this political work and how he worked first in his own way, we proceed to explain.

The fact that Nizamshahi fell at the same time that Ramadas, an impressionable, highly religiously-minded young man, was performing austerities at Nasik, a town in the midst of the turmoil, has to be taken into consideration in this connection. This coincidence of time explains why Ramadas, alone of all Maratha saints, thought and spoke of the political oppression of the people. We have seen that the Nizamshahi was going to pieces from 1627 to 1633, and Ramadas at this time, in his 19th to 24th. was practising austerities at Nasik. Two Mahomedan armies had invaded the country, one from the north and the other from the south and were harassing the people. Shahaji was trying his utmost to save the kingdom. At such times, the Mahomedan excesses become frequent, almost of every-day occurrence. Women are seized and taken away into captivity and men are killed by hundreds with tortures of different kinds. These tortures are described in detail in the first part of the Dasabodha. Ramadas must have witnessed or come to know these horrible miseries round about Nasik and we even think that he left Nasik and went on a long pilgrimage for this very reason. Even in the vast Mogul empire in which he hereafter travelled, visiting different Tirthas in Northern India, he must have seen the religious oppression initiated by Shahjahan already noticed, namely old Hindu temples being destroyed and new ones not being allowed to be built. When he returned, he did not go to Jambgaon where Mogul rule had been substituted for the tolerant Nizamshahi rule and he did not also like, we think, to return to his kindred. He went to the Krishna region and that part of it which was under Hindu chieftains. His first sanads are those by Diyanatrao, Shahaji and Ghorpade and he lived in the ghalis or gorges of the Sahyadri range, because they were never visited by Mahomedans who liked to live in the plains of the Deccan. The experiences of Ramadas were thus entirely different from those of other noted saints of Maharashtra. Jnyaneshvar lived, indeed, before the Mahomedans came to the Deccan, and under the ' benign rule of the Hindu Maratha king Ramachandrarao Yadava." Ekanath, no doubt, lived under Bedarshahi Mahomedan rule at Paithan;

but the Bedar kings were tolerant and the governor of Daulatabad was the Brahmin Janardanpant, himself a saint and the guru of Ekanath. Tukaram lived under Nizamshahi and in the Poona district under the good Shahaji and Dadaji Konddev and he had no personal experience of, and nowhere speaks about, the excesses committed by Mahomedans. We can thus see why these saints did not become political preachers and why Ramadas alone devoted much of his time and energy to the cause of the political deliverance of Maharashtra.

Ramadas thought that the first thing necessary was the strengthening of the religious feelings of the Hindus. At that time, the hold of the Hindu religion on the people was evidently weak, as Ramadas complains in Dasabodha that Hindus turn Mahomedans, even of their free will, and that many go to worship Daval Malak (Daud-ul-mulk or the saint of the district). For this reason, Ramadas founded the order of Ramadasi Sadhus who preached Hindu religion along with the worship of Rama. The worships then prevalent were those of Vithoba and Dattatreya. The first was mild and the second was so tolerant that Dattatreya often appeared himself in the form of a Mahomedan fakir. Ramadas wanted a fighting god, one who had destroyed Rakshasas. Moreover, a new religious preacher cannot build on old foundations. He has to adopt a new form of worship, a new god, a new gospel and a new book of prayer, in order to make impression. He, like Jesus, did not condemn the old worships, but established a new one not inconsistent with the old. He built temples to Rama wherever possible and to Hanuman almost everywhere. He also brought his new order of Sadhus under strict discipline. In fact, he may be said to have founded an order of Hindu Jesuits who were to live by begging while preaching the worship of Rama among the common people. He got *mathas* or monasteries established in almost every important city in Maharashtra and even outside and appointed tried disciples as their heads called Mahants. The qualifications of a Mahant, given in detail in Dasabodha, are very important, as they show that Ramadas intended his Mahants to be both religious and political workers. All the Mahants were to go to the central matha at Chaphal and there report to Ramadas their year's work on the Ramanavami day. These Mahants and preachers were naturally all Brahmins, for Brahmins alone can live by begging and these preachers were not intended to be a fighting community like the Sikh community which, originally a religious one, subsequently became, under Guru Govindsingh, a fighting order. Ramadas wanted the Kshatriyas to fight and not these preachers and for this purpose, he preached to the Marathas both patriotic and religious sentiments to enable them to establish Hindavi Swaraj.

Ramadas thus did not stop at preaching religion and philosophy in his Dasabodha but also preached political sentiments and worked directly to rouse the patriotic feelings of the Marathas, even before he came into contact with Shivaji and saw his work. He knew that without a physical struggle with the Mahomedans, the political emancipation of Maharashtra could not be achieved. To wage this physical fight was the duty of the Kshatriyas or the Marathas and in his poem on Kshātradharma, Ramadas says, in immortal lines (which even the English repeated when they called upon the Marathas to enlist for the last European war), " Enlist each and every Maratha and fight for Dharma of Maharashtra (मराठा तितुका मेळवावा । महाराष्ट्र-धर्म वाढवावा). Those who call themselves high-born Marathas should at once join while it is time. If they do not do so, they will hereafter suffer heavily." The following verse is even more explicit : "All those dogs who hate the gods should be beaten and sent back. The servants of gods will always conquer. There is no doubt about it. When *all* rise, the army of the enemy will not count; but fight cautiously and keep the people pleased." Ramadas points out the extreme length to which they would have to go, " In the name of God and for Him, beat the whole country, even destroy it for establishing Dharma."

These lines could not have been uttered after the success of Shivaji over Afzalkhan; for there was then no need of such powerful preaching. Marathas were then joining Shivaji's cause in hundreds. This shows us what Ramadas did directly, politically, for rousing the Marathas before he saw Shivaji.* The further fact that he *invited* Shivaji after the Afzalkhan incident to see him shows that he had found at last the man he was looking after and he wished to support him with all his power. For no purely religious preacher invites any devotee, however great he may be.

In the remarkable letter in verse addressed by him to Shivaji, evidently after the Afzalkhan

* Two letters are very important, in determining dates of Ramadas's activity and his meeting with Shivaji. PS 1039, dated 18th December 1654, a letter of Divakar Gosavi, says that Ramadas has gone into Shivthar ghal (gorge) and has begun his work (Dasabodha), resolving not to move from there for ten years. The second is from Bhaskar Gosavi and is dated 13th February 1658. It states that when he went to Shivaji to ask for alms, he enquired who Ramadas was and where he lived and when told that he was a saint originally of Jamb but now settled at Chaphal in his math with the temple of Rama, Shivaji ordered the payment of 200 hons yearly for the Utsava of the Mandir. (PS 1040)

incident, Ramadas says, "God has blessed you. Indeed Tuljabhavani stands at your back in every fight. But act cautiously all the same; for the Mlechchas are terribly bad men and they have prospered here long.* Persistent effort, brave action at the right time and astonishing deeds, these spring from God. Those who strive to establish religion are incarnations of the deity. God has inspired your heart to undertake this righteous work." These words show how Ramadas sympathised with Shivaji and found in him the man he had wanted. And Ramadas having got his Kshatriya warrior instructs him in this very way. The sanad granted by Shivaji to Ramadas expressly states how Ramadas at the first interview desired him to do the work of a Kshatriya. In this sanad[1] Shivaji says, "'Your duty is to establish kingship and protect religion, Brahmins, deities and subjects. Remove their oppression. You will succeed in this by the favour of God.' Thus advised Ramadas and under this advice, in whatever efforts I made to destroy the Mahomedans, to build strong forts with money obtained in plunder and to do other things, I was successful through his blessings." These words of Shivaji show that Ramadas assigned him the Kshatriya's part and gave him blessings in all his subsequent undertakings.

* म्लेन्छ दुर्जन उदंड । बहुतां दिवसांचें माजलें बंड ॥ 1. PS 2237, 1679.

And finally, when Shivaji succeeded in founding a Hindavi Svarajya and got himself crowned with Vedic rites, the exultation of Ramadas knew no bounds. It is expressed by him in a poem which can only come from the exultant heart of one who had succeeded in his life-long desire. "The sinful Aurangya has been drowned (defeated). The Mlechchas have been destroyed. The sacred places which had been broken have been set up again in this land of joy (Maharashtra)."* This epithet itself (आनंदवनभुवन) shows how Ramadas dearly loved Maharashtra. These words of intense joy clearly prove that Ramadas had worked for the political uplift of the country. Shivaji firmly believed so, as in a letter of Dattaji of 1677 to Dinkar Gosavi, agent of Ramadas, Dattaji says that "Shivaji has given eleven more villages as inam, though Ramadas wants nothing and is indifferent, and that the ornaments which Shivaji had put on at the time of his coronation have been sent as present to Shri (Ramadas or Rama), as was at that time intended and declared."[1]

Shivaji respected Ramadas highly and carried out his wishes willingly till the last day of his life, (e. g. see his order dated 2nd September 1675[2].)

* बुडाला औरंग्या पापी । म्लेंच्छ संहार जाहला ।
मोडली मांडली क्षेत्रें । आनंदवनभूवनीं ॥

1. P 2022. 2. PS 1777.

XXXIV. FRESH FIGHTS AND FURTHER ACQUISITIONS IN 1675-76

It was impossible that Shivaji, having "assumed the insignia of royalty" (Duff), would take rest for the rest of his life. Nor was it possible that his two neighbours who were unable to prevent him from proclaiming independence would allow him to take rest. Delhi was still at war with him though the war languished. Bijapur was apparently at peace with him but it was not quite sincere.[1] Bijapur did not pay Chauth (tribute) and the Mahomedan Subedar of Phonda arrested a rich merchant living at Narsa in Shivaji's territory about this time[2]. Shivaji, therefore, after the rains, invaded the Karwar territory of Bijapur. He first sent an army to besiege the fort of Phonda which commanded the passage to that district and which was then in the possession of Bijapur. Phonda, like Sinhgad and Panhala, frequently changed hands and was always kept by the suzerain power. After having performed the thread ceremony of his son Sambhaji with Vedic rites on Magh Vadya 5 (J), as he now recognised the importance of this

1. PS 1666; ER II 5, Surat, 6th August 1674.
2. PS 1695; ER II 18, Karwar, 2nd September 1674.

initiation ceremony. Shivaji, on 6th March 1675, marched against Bijapur Southern Konkan territory and on Chaitra Vadya 5 or April 5 (J), he deputed Annaji Datto Pandit to invest Phonda[1] with a further force of two thousand horse and seven thousand foot.[2] The killedar who was a Mahomedan sent for provision from Bijapur and also Goa and held out bravely, though no provisions were received either from Goa or from Bijapur. But the fort was mined by the Marathas and taken on 17th April (J). Bahilolkhan advanced from Bijapur for its relief as far as Miraj, but, finding it taken, returned. Some said that he was given[3] 50 thousand pagodas to return. But Shivaji had also obstructed his coming on by blocking the passes of the Sahyadri with felled trees.[4] After taking the fort of Phonda, Shivaji immediately took possession of the Konkan tract including Karwar[5] which town he plundered, though he treated the English there with consideration. Shivaji also took other forts in the district like Shiveshwar and Ankola.[6] This change of masters in the district was disliked by the English at Karwar, as they complain

1. PS 1724; ER II 60, p. 33, Rajapur, 6th February 1675.
2. PS 1741; ER II 80, p. 41, Karwar 13th April 1675.
3. PS 1757; ER II 95, p. 55, Karwar, 9th June 1675.
4. & 5. PS 1753; ER II 91, p. 50, Rajapur, 31st May 1675.
6. PS 1751; ER II 88, p. 52, and PS 1753.

in a letter[1] that the new masters of Karwar were more troublesome than the Mahomedans.

Before and while operating in this Konkan district, Shivaji as usual sent an army on a plundering expedition in the corresponding Deccan of Bijapur and it plundered Aitgiri and two other towns even near Bhaganagar and brought the plunder safely to Phonda[2]. Two Portuguese towns were also plundered[2], as the Portuguese were in league with the killedar of Phonda.[2] Another army of Shivaji had plundered Hospet even before this and had obtained two lakhs of hons.[3] Dattaji with two thousand cavalry also levied tribute from Kolhapur and Raibag.[4] Shivaji eventually took this territory including Kolhapur with a force consisting of 16,000 cavalry and 14,000 infantry.[5] In the next fighting season, (November 1675 to June 1676), Shivaji was really ill. Moreover, he was highly displeased with the conduct of his son and heir, Sambhaji, as will be related later on.[6] He, therefore, remained at Panhala for a long time

1. Karwar, 1st July 1675; PS 1761; FR II 102, p. 59.
2. Karwar, 22nd April 1675; PS 1743; ER 82, p. 48.
3. Kochin, Dutch, 6th December 1674 ; PS 1709.
4. Rajapur, 6th February 1675 ; PS 1724.
5. Rajapur, 1st April 1675; PS 1740; ER II 79, p. 41.
6. PS 1811; ER II 139, Bombay, 17th January 1676.

apparently quiet.[1] But his army again plundered Bijapur territory including Athni, from the merchants of which place three lakhs of hons were obtained.[2]

While Shivaji was thus fighting with Bijapur in Konkan and the corresponding Deccan, his Peshwa, commissioner of Northern division, successfully fought with the Moguls during the two years 1675-1676. Fighting was going on between the Moguls and the Marathas in Kalyan Prant till Jan. 1675; the Moguls were defeated and they could not take Kalyan.[3] Moropant took possession of Ramnagar and from thence, like Shivaji in the south, he sent a plundering expedition into Aurangabad territory. Kutubkhan, a Mogul commander, opposed it; but his army was almost destroyed.[4] The Marathas then plundered as far as Dangaon and Burhanpur[5] and southwards as far as Mahur[6]. Dilerkhan advanced against this plundering force, but he was badly defeated, one thousand Pathans being killed in the battle[7]. Consequently, it was rumoured that a peace was being arranged by which Shivaji, for his son

1. & 2. PS 1833; ER II 150, p. 83; Rajapur, 13th March 1676, also PS 1853 Dag Register.

3. PS 1711; ER II 50, p.23 and PS 1715; ER II 53, p. 25.

4. Surat, 9th January 1675, PS 1716; ER II 55, p. 25.

5. Surat, 20th January; PS 1719; ER II 56, p. 26.

6. Sabhasad and Duff.

7. Bombay, 5th February 1675; PS 1723; ER II 59, p. 26.

Sambhaji as Mansabdar of five thousand horses, would be given the Mogul territory of Aurangabad up to the Bhima[1]. But this was too flattering to be true and the war between Shivaji and the Moguls continued.

Next year, Moropant Peshwa was below Mahuli with a large force in January 1676[2]. He moved towards Ramanagar and took Pindol and Paineka[3]. A force of ten thousand cavalry sent by Shivaji from Panhala came to Kalyan and passing through the Portuguese territory of Bassein, joined Moropant. Thus reinforced, he appeared before and demanded tribute from Surat. A sum of nine lakhs of rupees was demanded as tribute, besides the regular Chauth. But the Mogul subedar resisted and closed the gates. The Marathas eventually retired owing to the coming of the rainy[4] season. Friar records, however, that Shivaji got his usual Peshkash[5]. Moropant kept four thousand men to garrison Pindol and returned to Rajgad[6].

In order to understand why the Moguls and the Bijapuris were thus unable to make headway

1. Surat, 13th February 1675; PS 1725; ER II 65, p.34.
2. Bombay, 26th April 1676; PS 1839.
3. Surat, 27th May; PS 1848; ER II 164, p. 89.
4. Surat, 22nd Sept. 1676 ; PS 1871; ER II 182, p. 97.
5. PS 1904.
6. Surat, 4th July 1676; PS 1859; ER II 173, p. 94.

against Shivaji, we must remember the circumstances, favourable to him, which subsisted at Delhi and Bijapur in these two years. "Aurangjeb was occupied in establishing his authority and in suppressing revolt in the north" (Duff). He, therefore, did no more than urge Bahadurkhan who, though formally recalled, was still in the Deccan. Aurangjeb had, however, never given up his design of annexing the whole of the Deccan. "In fact his ambassadors were employed to create dissensions in Bijapur and Govalkonda by bribing every man in power and stirring up factions in their internal government" (Duff). He, therefore, did not dislike the activities of Shivaji in the Konkan and the corresponding portions of the Deccan as these disabled and weakened Bijapur, which thus became the more fitted for being swallowed. Shivaji was, no doubt, growing strong; but Aurangjeb always thought that he could crush his state, small as it was, at any time. He could employ factions and force even ag[illegible] Marathas as against Bijapur. He sca[illegible]ed that Shivaji was developing a powerful sentiment of nationality among the people of Maharashtra or that Shivaji's officers would never fall a prey to corruption or be ready to destroy their own nation, for their individual gain. Sambhaji, however, proved a vulnerable point

Aurangjeb, kept on remonstrating with and even scolding Bahadurkhan for doing nothing. Bahadurkhan, therefore, advanced against Bijapur and Khavaskhan, not being ready or willing to fight, offered terms of peace, namely, holding the Bijapur kingdom as a dependency of the Mogul empire and offering the king's sister in marriage to a son of Aurangjeb. But these terms were distasteful to the nobles of Bijapur and Khavaskhan was one day murdered. J records that Bahilolkhan seized Khavaskhan and became Karbhari on 3 Ramjan (19th Nov. 1675). The quarrels at Bijapur between the two opposing parties, namely, the Abyssinian and the Pathan, increased and there were even skirmishes between their followers, the former led by Sarjekhan and the latter by Bahilolkhan, as is reported in a Rajapur letter of 9th May 1676,[1] as also Dutch record, dated 21st May[2]. Taking advantage of this state of affairs, Bahadurkhan moved against Bijapur; see Surat letter, dated 1st May.[3] Bahilolkhan had, however, in the meanwhile, somehow become strong and issuing out, gave a crushing defeat to the Moguls at Halgi on 1st June 1675 (J).

Two contemporary English letters mention these events. Bombay letter, dated 26th November (PS 1798) states that Bahadurkhan who was scolded by Aurangjeb for his

1. PS 1844; ER II 101, p. 88. 2. PS 1846.
3. PS 1842.

inactivity, formed a marriage relation with Khavaskhan, 'the protector' and induced him to send a large army against Shivaji, instead of making a treaty with Shivaji which was most imminent. The Siddi with his navy and with two thousand newly enlisted men was also giving trouble on the sea, " and had even burnt Vengurla". This letter also expresses concern for Shivaji, beset as he was with these many difficulties. He was also ill at this time and it was rumoured that he had even died. But the whole scene changed. The factions at Bijapur terminated in a manner favourable to Shivaji. Rajapur letter dated 11th January 1676 (PS 1805) which mentions the rumour about Shivaji's death, states that Bahilolkhan has seized and confined Khavaskhan and taking possession of the boy king has himself become the regent. " It was also rumoured that he had put Khavaskhan to death ".

The defeat of the Moguls is reported in a late Dutch letter, dated 6th November 1676 (PS 1881), which also states that Shivaji was extending his dominion towards Surat without opposition. Another Dutch record of 18th November (PS 1882) gives more details of this defeat, namely, that " four thousand men and four well-known captains on the Mogul side fell in the battle " (J records that Islamkhan Rumi on the Mogul side fell). The Dutch record also reports that Bahilolkhan subsequently opened negotiations for peace and the matter was referred to Aurangjeb. Bahadurkhan appears at this time to have received offers of peace from Shivaji also and rumours of a peace concluded with Shivaji reached Surat and Bombay about December 5, 1676. The terms were as before, four lakhs of hons for territory to be given to Sambhaji for his mansab and it was even reported that Niraji on behalf of Sambhaji had gone with five thousand horse to the Moguls for service (PS 1885). But, as before, these terms were too good to be accepted and on 20th December, Bombay wrote that the peace negotiations were broken off (PS 1893). Bahadurkhan was thus still at war with Shivaji at the end of 1674.

Bahilolkhan was unwilling to fight with two powers at the same time and was willing to make peace with Shivaji so that they both might oppose the Moguls. Rajapur letter to Surat, dated 24th July 1676[1] states that this peace was brought about by the mediation of Govalkonda so that the three might unitedly oppose Aurangjeb. It was settled that Shivaji should keep the territory east of Kolhapur upto the Krishna, paying three lakhs of rupees as Peshkash (present) and one lakh of hons as yearly rent. This method of retaining conquered territory under a lease paying a small rent, by which the minds of the people and the powerless suzerain are gradually reconciled to the new conditions seems thus to have been first started by Shivaji. It was copied by the English when they leased the Divani of Bengal from Shahalum. Shivaji had, we have seen, similarly taken his own Poona district on lease from Aurangjeb in Jaisingh's time; but after a second fight subsequent to his escape from Agra, the lease ended of itself and

1. PS 1863; ER III 175, p. 95.

Shivaji became full master. In this way, a new rule is quietly substituted for an old one without causing disturbance of the public sentiment.

About this time Netaji Palkar who had been converted to Mahomedanism was reconverted and admitted to caste privileges by Shivaji's order (11th June 1676)[1]. We have seen how Netaji was won over by Jaisingh and sent to the north and how he was there converted. He was a bold captain and was even styled 'Second Shivaji'. But it was difficult to be Shivaji himself. He probably found no opportunity to establish a kingdom like Shivaji or even a feudatory lordship under Aurangjeb. He, therefore, returned from the north and was probably at this time in the Mogul army, or he may have come directly to Shivaji and joined him after reconversion.

1. J and PS 1863, Rajapur, 24 July 1676; ER II 175, p. 95.

XXXV. DARING EXPEDITION INTO DISTANT KARNATAK (1677-78)

Shivaji was at peace with Bijapur and had secured his new conquests above the Ghats upto the Krishna, including Kolhapur[1] and both Satara[2] and Wai[3]. There was thus no room for extending his dominion in this direction. Shivaji, therefore, while he resided at Panhala in the rainy season of 1676, conceived in his mind a plan for acquiring territory in another direction. Ekoji, his half-brother, had fought against him in the Bijapur army on several occasions, on the ground that he held the jagir inherited from Shahaji under Bijapur. Why should he not claim and acquire half of this jagir? Ekoji was also acquiring new territory, as he had just conquered the Nayak of Tanjore. (The Nayak of Tanjore quarelled with the Nayak of Madura and the latter appealed to Bijapur Durbar for help. They commissioned Ekoji to subdue the former. Ekoji not only subdued him but annexed his territory to his

1. Also noted in Surat 10th January 1677; PS 1907; ER II 198, p. 106.

2. Sanad, 28th June 1676; PS 1856–57.

3. PS 1889 of December 1676.

Shivaji on an Expedition into the Karnatak.

From a painting in the Louvre, Paris.

To face page 278.

possessions[1]). Ekoji thus became full master of the Tanjore district on the Coromandel coast, as is reported in a Dutch record dated 22nd July, 1676[2]. Why should he not also acquire territory on that coast and if necessary hold it under Bijapur as his brother did, indeed, as he himself held his own Kolhapur territory? Bahilolkhan was fickle and might declare war against him at any time. But Shivaji could conquer even Bijapur if its Karnatak province were in his possession and if he could attack Bijapur from the south as well as from the west. Considerations like these must have occurred to Shivaji when he revolved in his mind this daring expedition into distant Karnatak. He finally decided in its favour and silently made preparations for it. Shivaji's motive in this distant expedition was not mere plunder, but extension of his territory as Mr. Sen has properly pointed out in his article on this expedition (S N. 1, pp. 57-60) on the basis of French testimony from Pondichery.

The motive of Shivaji was even higher, as may be gathered from his remarkable long letter to Maloji Raje Ghorpade written from Hyderabad in March 1677[3] while Shivaji was there on this expedition. "Adilshahi has been seized by Bahilol-

1. Historical Miscellany, Tanjore and Venkoji, PS 1906.

2. PS 1862.

3. Saraswati Mandir; PS 1901.

khan Pathan. It is not good that the Deccani Padshahi should be in the hands of a Pathan (a Northerner). The Padshahi of the Deccan belongs to us, the Deccanis. (It is note-worthy that Shivaji includes in this word the Deccani Mahomedans). Our castemen, the Marathas, should go over to Kutubshahi which is a Deccani state. I forget all that your father, Baji Ghorpade, did to my father and I did to Baji and he did to me. Let the past be past. We will combine. Adilshahi can subsist no longer. You are a Maratha and in order that you may be benefited, come to Kutubshahi. My father Shahaji, when he became supreme in Adilshahi, raised to dignity many Marathas and your father Baji, among them. I swear by God, you should give up all doubt and send your *vakil*." This extract is long but we can gather from it the high motives of Shivaji in undertaking this expedition, as indeed in all the activities of his whole life.

As expected, Bahilolkhan changed his mind and made peace with Bahadurkhan, subedar of the Moguls. Shivaji, therefore, strengthened his relations with Kutubshah who was for Deccanis fighting with the Northerners. Akanna and Madanna, his Brahmin ministers, were also favourable to Shivaji, who now sent Pralhad Niraji to settle a fresh treaty with Kutubshah, so that he might allow

Shivaji to pass through his territory to Karnatak, on condition that the former might share in Shivaji's conquests there. As usual Shivaji gave out that he was preparing for an expedition against towns on the west coast. Malwerer writes from Bombay on 2nd October, 1676 that Shivaji has started with a large army on an expedition against Kannad, especially the territory adjoining Barcelore and Honavar.[1]

We may note here that the word 'Kannad' or Karnatak then meant the whole of South India between the Coromandel and the Malabar coasts, as it formed part of the kingdom of Vijayanagar which was the real Kannad land where Kanarese was spoken. The eastern coast territory was really Tamil land and was called Cholamandala (corrupted into Coromandel) meaning the kingdom of the Cholas and the people there spoke and speak even now Tamil. After the conquest of the Vijayanagar empire by the five Mahomedan kingdoms of the Deccan in the battle of Talikot, the several tributary local chiefs called Nayaks became practically independent. They were subdued one by one by Bijapur generals, assisted by Shahaji, in the first half of the seventeenth century. Shahaji got for his services a big jagir *viz*. Bangalore and the adjoining parts, as we have already seen. Bijapur

1. PS 1873; ER II 185, p. 99

subedars holding different divisions of Karnatak, however, repeated the old order of things and were either practically independent or in revolt against Bijapur. And Bijapur kings, who valued these possessions as they were rich, were constantly engaged in subduing these insubordinate subedars.

As Shivaji resolved to start on this distant expedition, which would take many months, he made adequate arrangements for the safety of his kingdom. Sabhasad states that he sent large presents to Bahadurkhan and induced him to promise secretly not to molest Shivaji's territory. Bahadurkhan was ready to accept a bribe; for he was not really in a position to take the offensive against the Marathas, and skirmishes only now and then took place.[1] Moropant Peshwa, Annaji Surnis and Dattaji Waknis, the three veteran commanders and commissioners of the three divisions of Shivaji's state, were left to oppose him. Shivaji also built new forts from Tattora (Phaltan) to Panhala to strengthen his hold on the Deccan region about Kolhapur (Duff). Thus securing his possessions. Shivaji started, taking with him twenty-five thousand horse and Raghunath Narayan and Janardan

1. Bombay, 24th Jan. 1677; PS 1910; ER II 201, p. 110.

Bombay, 19th March 1677; P 1918 speaks of trustworthy news being received of a peace between the Moguls and Shivaji.

Narayan Hanmante who were the sons of the Secretary of Shahaji and who were fully acquainted with things and affairs in Karnatak. Hambirrao Mohite, his commander-in-chief, probably took a southern route while Shivaji himself went by the one due east after passing through the Vengurla Ghat. For J mentions a battle between Hambirrao and Husseinkhan Mayena, a Bijapur captain, near Gadag in which the latter was signally defeated and was himself taken prisoner (January, 1677).

Shivaji on arrival at Hyderabad or Govalkonda was royally received by Akanna and Madanna outside the city and by the Sultan in his palace. Shivaji as a crowned king was treated as an equal. J records that this visit took place in Phalgun S′ 1598 (March 1677) and that with Shivaji were Sarjerao Jedhe and Yesaji Kank who was Sarnobat or commander-in-chief of infantry. The Sultan gave a large sum of money to Shivaji, as the latter had scrupulously abstained from plundering Govalkonda territory. Sabhasad states that Shivaji maintained strict discipline on the march and even put to death some plunderers. Akanna and Madanna, the two brothers, also entertained Shivaji at their house and gave him large presents.

Joined by a strong contingent from Govalkonda (J and S), Shivaji marched towards the south and at once succeeded in capturing the impregnable fort of Jinji[1]. It was held by some Abyssinian captains who were opposed to the Bijapur Pathan party and they are said to have been bribed and they easily handed over the fort to Shivaji. Sabhasad also states that Rupalkhan and Nasarkhan, sons of Khavaskhan, the Vazir of Bijapur, who were in the fort, were induced to leave it on an assurance given them (of patronage). But Dag Register 1677, dated 16th July, states that the Bijapur captain Nasirkhan with seven thousand men held the fort and defended it against Shivaji who had 16 thousand cavalry and 15 thousand infantry.[2] Shivaji took possession of the territory about the fort of Jinji and repaired and strengthened its fortifications. " New walls and towers were built which appeared as if they were built by Europeans. Tanks and houses were also built so that they might be of use in times of war." The Jesuit record also states that Shivaji made preparations "for future fighting with the combined Mahomedan powers." These words written in Jesuit letters in 1677 are almost prophetic; but it is not strange if Shivaji with his now advanced political wisdom and high military genius foresaw that a life and death struggle with Aurang-

1. PS 1920. His. Mis. Jesuit letter, p. 11.
2. PS 1920 and PS 1954,

jeb was inevitable and that a strong extensive fort like Jinji in the distant south would afford him a last stand if Panhala and Raigad were lost.

There was one captain Sherkhan Lodi Pathan, a partisan of Bahilolkhan who, however, opposed Shivaji in this district with 5 thousand hors and many elephants. He was totally defeated and taken prisoner. Five hundred horses and 17 elephants were captured and incalculable wealth was seized and " the Mahal (territory) of Trimul was conquered " (Sabhasad). But from a Madras letter, dated 16th July, it appears that Sherkhan escaped and was being pursued by Shivaji's men near Punamali. The writer of this letter Ramanna, envoy of the English, saw Shivaji encamped at Trimul Vada on the Kaveri[1]. The fort of Vellore in that district was another important and strong fort. It was laid siege to, but it held out for over a year before it eventually fell, being taken by Hambirrao and Raghunathpant on 22 June 1678 after Shivaji's return (J). Sabhasad says that it had a moat full of deep and natural water with alligators in it and the rampart was so broad that two bullock-carts side by side might run on it. Eventually territory of 20 lakhs of hons revenue with Jinji as capital came into the possession of Shivaji who appointed Ramchandra Narayan as its sube-

1. PS 1953; ER II 240, p. 130.

dar with the office of Majmu bestowed upon him (Sabhasad). These events are shortly given by J as follows: "Shivaji took Jinji and the whole of Karnatak in Chaitra S'uddha S' 1599 (April 1677). In Ashadh (June to July) he seized Sherkhan near Tirupati with ten elephants. Bahilolkhan could not do anything to check Shivaji, as Bahadurkhan the Mogul advanced against him and took Lal Darga Kot (ground fort) and in June took Naladurg through Ranamastakhan." We get confirmation of this fact in letters from Fort St. George. Thus on 9th May the 1677, the English speak of Shivaji with 20 thousand horse and 40 thousand infantry advancing on Jinji, a portion of his army passing by Madras and Tirupati[1]. Shivaji remained friendly with the English and even called for some medicines from them[2] for which he sent a complimentary reply from Vellore on 25th May[3].

Ekoji came to see his half-brother Shivaji and he was well received. After eight days of stay he, however, suddenly left Shivaji's camp as Shivaji asked for $\frac{3}{4}$ share in his father's estate and also jewels and emblems enjoyed by his father as he was the elder son[4]. Shivaji did not pursue

1. PS 1932; ER II 241, p. 132.
2. PS 1934; ER II 222, p. 117.
3. PS 1937; ER II 224, p. 118.
4. Supported by Madras letter PS 1957 ; ER II 240, p.130.

Ekoji; but allowing him to enjoy his new acquisition, namely Tanjore, he passed through the Ghats and seized Kolar, Bangalore and other parts which were in the jagir of his father. He had left Hambirrao Mohite Senapati for the protection of the province of Jinji with Raghunathpant. The district of Kolar was next entrusted to Rango Narayan as subedar to work under Raghunathpant and Shivaji kept with him a strong force under Manaji More. He then turned towards the north accompanied by a force under Anandrao and came to Panhala via Kopal, Lakshmeshwar and Sampgaon (S). There was an insignificant fracas with the heroic lady Desain of Velvad, the ground fort of which was taken and the Desain was punished (S). She probably was compelled to pay a fine. A Rajapur letter,[1] however, speaks of this incident as the most ignominious defeat inflicted on Shivaji: " He who had conquered so many kingdoms was not able to reduce a woman."

J records these subsequent events with dates as follows: " In S'ravan (July 1677), Shivaji Raje and Ekoji Raje met; but the latter fled owing to disagreement, whereupon his vilayat (ancestral jagir) was seized, namely Chidambar, Bangalore, etc. Shivaji laid siege to Kolar in As'vin (September). Shivaji appointed Raghunath Narayan to the

1. PS 2019; ER II 285, p. 157, 28th Feb. 1678.

Majmu and made him subedar of Jinji giving him one lakh of hons as reward. In Kartik (October) Shivaji returned from Karnatak to Gadag and besieged Velvandi (of the Desain). Taking possession of the whole of Gadag, Shivaji returned to Raigad in Jyeshtha (May 1678).

An interesting letter from the English Hindu envoy in Shivaji's camp to Fort St. George, dated 27th July 1677,[1] supports the above account and date of the meeting of Ekoji with Shivaji. "Shivaji accepted six lakhs of hons", it first states, "as present from the Nayak of Madura, as settled by Raghunathpant for not molesting him. Ekoji came to meet Shivaji at Trimalvadi and was well received; but Shivaji demanded his share in the father's property, both moveable as also territory. Ekoji consequently left; but his Brahmin ministers were seized by Shivaji."

Surat wrote on 31st October 1677 that Shivaji had plundered Shrirangpattan and acquired immense wealth. He also levied tributes from those polygars who submitted and punished those who opposed him.[2] Thirdly, a letter from Madras dated 28th November, reported that Shivaji had left Karnatak with four thousand horse[3].

1. PS 1957; ER II 241, p. 132.
2. PS 1992; ER II 264, p. 145.
3. PS 1995; ER II 264, p. 146.

The daring distant expedition led by Shivaji into Karnatak was thus a complete success like all his other undertakings. Indeed, it was the climax of Shivaji's wonderfully successful career. The English at Bombay wondered how Shivaji constantly got success over the powerful kingdoms of both north and south.[1] Surat people feared that he would become master of the whole country from Surat to Cape Camorin.[2] His celerity of movement and consummate generalship were so fully displayed that the English compared his Karnatak expedition to that of Cæsar into Spain, " veni, vidi, vici, he came, he saw, he conquered."[3] The facility with which he took forts was compared to the ease of Alexander in taking strongholds. He impressed the Mahomedans so much that Mahomedan Killedars evacuated forts and fled in fear, on hearing of his approach. In fact, Shivaji and his army had become a terror to all.

This expedition brought to Shivaji further acquisition of territory of the yearly income of nearly forty lakhs of hons and secured to him two strong forts, Jinji and Vellore, in a distant part of the country, where he might retire in the last resort. Nearly half of this territory was that of his father

1. PS 2006 of 15 January 1678; ER II 269, p. 148.
2. PS 1992, 31 October 1677; ER II 263, p. 146.
3. PS 2007, Bombay 16 Jan. 1678; ER II 272, p. 150.

taken from Ekoji's servants. He was justified in seizing this territory in the upper Karnatak. He was justified in demanding it of Ekoji as he was the elder son of Shahaji. Jagirs were generally descendable in the elder line. Even if it be supposed that some jagirs are partitionable, Ekoji, being a jagirdar under Bijapur, had fought against Shivaji and if Shivaji had a right to seize Bijapur territory, being at war with it, he had also a right to seize the half portion of Ekoji in the ancestral jagir. It cannot, therefore, be contended that Shivaji treated his brother unjustly.

It may, however, be said that Shivaji was now extending his dominion over other lands than Maharashtra and was not there establishing Swaraj. He established in fact Maratha rule in Karnatak. But it may be said it was a Hindvi Swaraj all the same. Hindu Marathas had a better right than Mahomedans or the English to establish their rule in Karnatak. Karnatak unfortunately was at this time parcelled out into small kingdoms or chiefdoms ruled by petty nayaks who constantly fought with one another and who thus were unable to establish a Hindvi Swaraj of their own. Indeed, after the fall of Vijayanagar, Karnatak was an open field for any outsider strong enough to seize it. The Mahomedans, the English, the French and the Dutch were actually striving at this time to pounce upon such parts of it as they could. Shivaji was thus, according to the political ideas of the time, justified in carving out a kingdom for himself in Karnatak. His rule may also be properly called Hindvi Swaraj, as the population there was chiefly Hindu.

Shivaji, a devout Hindu that he was, visited every sacred place in Karnatak and observed all the formalities of pilgrimage at each. Thus English letter, dated 2nd August, 1677, mentions Shivaji's going to see the god at Hirudachalam, keeping his army at Yelvanarasor[1]. We, however, doubt the story recorded even by Sabhasad that Shivaji was so overpowered with the religious sentiment of renunciation at the temple of S′risailam that he wished to cut his head and place it on the altar before Mahadeva. He was, we know, a true disciple of Ramadas and he would scarcely have thought of doing so. Ramadas had already told him in the beginning that his highest duty and devotion to God was to establish Hindvi Swaraj and protect Hindus, especially Brahmins, cows and the sacred idols in temples.

Finally, it may be stated that after Shivaji departed, Ekoji tried to destroy Hambirrao by attacking him with an overwhelming force of his own and of local polygars; but he was signally de-

1. PS 1964, from Ramanna; ER II 244, p. 133.

feated by Hambirrao, even with his smaller force and four thousand horses and some elephants with incalculable wealth were seized by him (S). Raghunathpant and Hambirrao thereon invaded Tanjore, the new jagir of Ekoji, and brought him to his senses. Shivaji sent word that Ekoji, though he had erred, was after all his brother and might be left in the possession of Tanjore. The date and place of this battle was November 1677 (Kartik) and Ahiri (J). Ekoji concluded peace, agreeing to give up his claim to the Kolar ancestral jagir.[1]

Fort St. George letter, dated 20th Nov., states that Santaji, another captain of Shivaji, was attacked by Ekoji's men and defeated. His force fled; but like Ashvatthama of the Mahabharata, he returned at mid-night and massacred Ekoji's men as they lay asleep in the glee of victory.

Shivaji at the conclusion of this most successful expedition into Karnatak went to Sajjangad to pay his respects to Ramadas and there asked permission to rebuild the temple of Rama at Chaphal after the fashion of the great temples he had seen in Karnatak. This permission Ramadas did not give; perhaps he was against having splendidly built temples, but he allowed Shivaji to build a Math for him at Sajjangad itself and to give further inam lands for the Utsava at Chaphal.[2]

1. PS 1995; ER II 204, p. 146. 2. PS 2022.

XXXVI. DOUBLE SUCCESS OF DILERKHAN'S DIPLOMACY

From the two notes in J, namely, " Shivaji passed from Karnatak (country beyond the Tungabhadra) into Gadag prant, in November, 1677 " and " after having captured Gadag prant, Shivaji came to Raigad in June, 1678," it is clear that Shivaji remained in Gadag territory during the whole of the fighting season of 1678, *i. e.* from November 1677 to June 1678. The heroic Desain of Velvad (near Bellary) could not have detained him so long. He seems to have remained in this part near Bijapur, carefully watching the events happening there and ready to attack that city if necessary. We have seen that Bahilolkhan offered terms of peace to Bahadurkhan even before Shivaji started on his Karnatak expedition. A peace was eventually concluded and it was settled that "the latter should forbear the tribute due from Bijapur (Nalbandi) for eight years " and the two joining their forces should march against Govalkonda, and then against Shivaji.[1] They accordingly took Gulburga in August, 1677. Aurangjeb, however, was not satisfied with this as Gulburga had originally belonged to Bijapur and he asked

1. PS 1965, Surat, 3rd August 1677; ER II 245, p. 134.

Bahadurkhan to recover one crore of rupees from Govalkonda for allowing Shivaji to pass through its territory and even for assisting him[1]. Govalkonda, of course, refused this exhorbitant demand and prepared to fight. It was aided by the Siddi party at Bijapur which was opposed to Bahilolkhan. An indecisive battle was fought in which, however, the Moguls suffered great loss. Bahadurkhan was suspected of having been bribed by Govalkonda[2] and he was hastily sent for from Delhi.[3] Dilerkhan, his fighting and energetic second, was made the Suba of the Deccan in Bhadrapad (J) and he gave a battle to the three combined combatants, Sarjekhan, Masaudkhan and the Bhaganagar Sarlashkar, in Ashvin at Malekhind; but he also was defeated and he had to retire to Naldurg (J). Thus while Shivaji was operating in Karnatak, Bijapur and the Moguls were unitedly but unsuccessfully fighting with Govalkonda and the Siddi party in Bijapur who were its friends. Shivaji thus easily plundered Gadag and Lakshmeshwar in October, as reported in a Bombay letter, dated 29th October[4]. A Govalkonda English

1. PS 1973, Govalkonda English letter, 19th September, 1677; ER II 250, p. 136.
2. PS 1973; ER II 250, p. 137.
3. PS 1979, Swali, 1st October, 1677; ER II 254, p. 139.
4. PS 1990; ER II 262, p. 145.

letter[1] speaks of further fights at about the same time between the Moguls assisted by Bahilolkhan on one side and the Sarlashkar of Govalkonda on the other. Shivaji held himself ready to move on Bijapur as reported in a letter from Fort St. George, dated 20th November.[2] But in the next month there was a sudden change at Bijapur. Bahilolkhan Pathan died of wounds received in battle. Rajapur letter stated on 8th December[3] that Dilerkhan was also in a sad plight. J also notes that in December, Pathan Bahilolkhan died and he was succeeded by Masaudkhan (of the Deccan party) in the regency. It seems that Bahilolkhan before his death set about effecting reconciliation with the Deccani party so that both might fight Shivaji.[4] Shivaji was at this time at Hubli demanding *chauth* from the subedar, which he eventually paid by levying contributions from the inhabitants. The English refused to pay and their property was confiscated.[5] Masaudkhan obtained possession of the fort of Bijapur by a stratagem and thought of combining with Govalkonda and driving out Dilerkhan from the Deccan. Shivaji,

1. PS 1989, dated 28th October ; ER II 261, p. 144.
2. PS 1995 ; ER II 264, p. 146.
3. PS 1998 ; ER II 266.
4. PS 2000, Karwar, 13th December ; also PS 2013.
5. PS 2038, Karwar, 5th May 1678; ER II 296, p. 162.

therefore, retired to Panhala after taking the fort of Bankapur, as reported in Rajapur letter, dated 3rd April.[1] Dilerkhan had already retired towards Pedgaon, as reported in Rajapur letter of 28th February, 1678.[2]

Dilerkhan, however, was strong in diplomacy also and during the rainy season he set about creating a change of opinion both in Bijapur and at Panhala. While Masaudkhan was upto this time friendly towards Shivaji, he was induced by Dilerkhan to consent to terms originally settled with Khavaskhan and to give the Sultan's sister in marriage to a son of Aurangjeb. Hostilities, therefore, again began between Bijapur and Shivaji and Sarjekhan took Athni and Raibag and drove away Shivaji's men from there, in June 1678[3]. We may shortly relate the subsequent events at Bijapur from Duff. The Afghan party there had a dislike to the Deccani party, but a still greater dislike to the Moguls. The Mogul envoy demanded Padshah Begum as the only means of avoiding an immediate advance on and siege of Bijapur. A battle between the opposing factions in the centre of the city was imminent, when the king's sister herself repaired to the spot and declared

1. PS 2030 ; ER II 292, p. 160.
2. PS 2019 ; ER II 283, p. 157.
3. PS 2046, Rajapur, 20th June 78; ER II 303, p. 165.

her intention of proceeding to the Mogul camp "vainly but generously imagining that by this sacrifice, her brother and his kingdom might be saved." She reached Dilerkhan's camp and a fitting escort was furnished her to conduct her to Aurangabad. This event happened about February, 1679.

Dilerkhan succeeded in another direction also in creating a defection. Sambhaji had been confined at Panhala as a punishment for attempting "to violate the person of the wife of a Brahmin." (Duff). This is also referred to in a Bombay letter already noted. Shivaji was so strict and strong in his respect for women that, like Mahmud of Ghazni, he would not spare even his son if he offended in this respect. Sambhaji was put in confinement at Panhala and though subsequently released from Panhala he was kept under strict surveillance at Parali. Dilerkhan succeeded in approaching Sambhaji at this place and induced him to come over to him and accept a mansab under Delhi. J records that Sambhaji escaped from Parali on Pausha S'uddha 10, S' 1600 (13th December 1678), and went to Dilerkhan who honourably received him and made him a mansabdar of 7,000 horse. This must have been a kind of sword-thrust into Shivaji's heart. The ill omens which occurred after this event are recorded by J in three notes. The energetic Dattajipant Waknis died fifteen days after and there was an earthquake on Magh Vadya 10, *i. e.* 25th January 1679. On Phalgun Vadya 10 or 25th February 1679, Ajmer was invested by Aurangjeb in person and a campaign was launched against the Rana of Udaipur. Dilerkhan, with the help of Sambhaji, according to Duff, advanced against Bhopalgad and took that fort in Vais'akh S'2 (2nd April 1679, J). These successes of Dilerkhan were, however, not eventually fruitful, as we shall see in the next chapter.

Shivaji's personal movements in the fighting season of 1679 (November 1678 to June 1679) cannot be determined. Probably, he was too pained at Sambhaji's defection to himself move about; but he was undaunted and his generals were on the alert. J records that Moropant Peshwa took the fort of Kopal (which had probably revolted against Shivaji in the new state of things at Bijapur), with the help of Husseinkhan Mayena's son and set at liberty Husseinkhan himself (who had probably been confined there) on Chaitra S'. Pratipada S' 1601 or 3rd March 1679. So also Balapur was taken by Anandrao the senior, on Ramanavmi day or 11th March.

Contemporary corroborating evidence may be finally noticed. The change of front at Bijapur against Shivaji is noted in a letter of the English from Athni, dated 31st

August 1678, in which it is stated that Shivaji would be attacked by Bijapur within a month or two (ER II 325, p. 178). So also Karwar wrote on 12th November that Jamsherkhan was at Bankapur with a large army, but Shivaji had assembled his army at Panhala (estimated at 20,000 foot and 15,000 horse). Jamsherkhan was waiting for reinforcements from Bijapur before attacking Shivaji (PS 2084; ER II 343, p. 189). Bombay wrote on December 18, that Shivaji had surrounded the Siddi in Danda Rajapuri both by land and water. (PS 2087; ER II 348, p. 191). The Siddi was unable to move out. Swali Consultation Record, dated 24th January 1679, states that the Adilshahi people sought the help of the English for taking Shivaji's forts, but they declined as they intended to remain neutral. (PS 2090; ER II 357, p. 193). Surat, on 17th February 1679, reported that the eldest son of Aurangjeb had arrived near Aurangabad with a large force to fight with Shivaji and that Adilshahi had obtained a victory over Shivaji. (PS 2092; ER II 352, p. 113). But it adds that the greatest thing that has disheartened him is that his son Sambhaji had gone to Dilerkhan. But Bombay wrote on 10th March 1679 that Shivaji remained undaunted at Panhala and cared not for either the Shahjada or Sambhaji and defied both the Mogul and the king of Bijapur. (PS 2099; ER II 355, p. 195). Bombay wrote on 4th April 1679 that Shivaji himself plundered Shahapur near Bijapur; probably Shivaji had only sent one of his captains (PS 2101; ER II 356, p. 175). Masulipattan wrote on 11th May that Bijapur and the Moguls were going to attack Shivaji. (PS 2108; ER II 362, p. 198). So also did Bombay on 29th July. It appears from Bombay 21st May that Sambhaji and the Deccani army had besieged Panhala (which is a mistake for Bhopalgad). (PS 2110).

XXXVII. THE LAST GREAT EXPLOIT OF SHIVAJI

Masaudkhan and Sambhaji became the enemies of Shivaji through the diplomacy of Dilerkhan. They soon became his friends through the treachery of Aurangjeb. Aurangjeb was not satisfied with the generous self-sacrifice of the princess of Bijapur, and directed Dilerkhan to bring the kingdom under full subjection. Perhaps, he would not forego tribute for eight years. Similarly, in his suspicion of everybody, he thought that Sambhaji would do harm and he thus asked Dilerkhan to send Sambhaji as prisoner to Delhi. We have seen that he had on a previous occasion similarly ordered the arrest of Niraji and his horsemen who were serving the Moguls at Aurangabad in behalf of Sambhaji himself, when he had previously been made a mansabdar at the request of Shivaji. But, as on that occasion Niraji was forewarned, so was Sambhaji given a hint by Dilerkhan and allowed to escape.

At the conclusion of the rainy season, Dilerkhan thus under orders from Delhi advanced upon Bijapur and laid siege to that city in As'vin, S'. 1601 or October 1679 (J). Dag Register, dated 21 November, speaks of Dilerkhan's having crossed the Bhima (he was encamped at Pedgaon on the north bank of the Bhima) and advancing on Bijapur reaching a spot about 9 miles from it.[1] Masaudkhan sought the help of Shivaji against this impending invasion and the latter sent his vakil Shamji Naik Punde to Bijapur on Bhadrapada S'uddha 1st or 26th August 1679 (J) to settle a treaty. A treaty was accordingly settled in Kartik (November) and Shivaji started on a long plundering expedition in Mogul territory in order to create a diversion. Rajapur reported on 16th October 1679 that Shivaji had concluded a peace with the Deccanis (at Bijapur) and gone somewhere with his whole army.[2] Shivaji crossing the Bhima carried fire and sword in the Mogul dominion in November (J), " leaving inhabitants houseless and the villages in ashes" (Duff). He went as far as Jalna and plundered that prosperous town (J) leisurely for four days (Duff). Laden with booty Shivaji was returning, when Ranamastakhan with ten thousand horse overtook him under orders of prince Muajjam who remained at Aurangabad. A fierce battle was fought near Sangamner (J) in which, " by the impetuosity of Santaji Ghorpade, confusion was caused" (Duff) and Sidhoji Nimbalkar was killed by a bullet (J). But Shivaji himself led a charge and by personal exertion retrieved

1. PS 2181. 2. PS 2142; ER II 793, p. 207.

the day. This may be looked upon as the last great exploit of Shivaji himself in a pitched battle against the Moguls, 'who were signally defeated' (Duff). Shivaji continued his march, but he was again intercepted by a second and more powerful army sent by prince Muajjam under Kishansingh (a son of Ramsingh and grandson of Jaisingh), at the foot of a pass through which Shivaji had to go. Sabhasad gives an interesting account of how Shivaji succeeded in safely reaching Raigad with all his treasure without a fight. "The Mogul force led by Kishansingh, Sardarkhan and other captains was at a distance of six or seven miles and Shivaji thought of making two divisions of his army, one to come slowly with the treasure after the other, led by himself. But Bahirji Jasud (messenger), who was the most intelligent and well-informed scout in Shivaji's service, promised to take Shivaji by another pass, avoiding the Moguls altogether. Strenuously marching for three nights, he took Shivaji to Pattagad. Bombay letter of 29th November[1] speaks of Shivaji's being at Patta about five days' journey from Bombay (60 miles), but adds wrongly that he had been defeated by Dilerkhan at Bijapur. Perhaps this was a defeat of a section of Hambirrao's force which was engaged in cutting off the supplies of Dilerkhan.

1. PS 2185; ER II 447, p. 262.

During the two months of October and November 1679, while Shivaji was plundering the east, his general Moropant Peshwa was laying waste Khandesh and thus distracting the attention of prince Muajjam in the north. Surat wrote on 8th December, that Shivaji had burnt and plundered Dharangaon, Chopda and other neighbouring places.[1] The English writing from Dharangaon itself on 12th December mention Shivaji's force as consisting of 12,000 horse and state that though the Company's property was saved, the town was plundered and burnt. The army went towards Burhanpur but turning southwards, it went towards Malkapur to join Shivaji who was there with a force of 20 thousand horse.[2] The English even report that the prince intended to rebel against his father Aurangjeb with the help of Shivaji.

While at Raigad, Shivaji was glad to learn in the beginning of January 1680 that Sambhaji had returned and was at Panhala. We find already in the Rajapur letter noted in the last chapter, dated 16th October, 1679, a report that Dilerkhan and Sambhaji had together plundered the town of Athni and taken many citizens as prisoners and that while returning, there was a disagreement between them on the question of releasing

1. PS 2190 ; ER II 447, p. 262.
2. PS 2194 ; ER II 460, p. 271.

the men arrested, whereupon Sambhaji with three hundred horse and one thousand foot went towards Kolhapur. This was probably the pretext put forth by him for leaving Dilerkhan. After some days, Sambhaji finding his opportunity appeared at Panhala in Margashirsh or December (J). Shivaji saw his son at Panhala on Paush Vaidya 7 or 13th January 1680 (J) and was glad to see him safely come out from the jaws of Aurangjeb. Sabhasad gives in detail the conversation which took place between the son and the father which, however, seems to us to be imaginary.

In spite of the miseries which Shivaji was inflicting on the Mogul Deccan territory, Dilerkhan did not relinquish the siege of Bijapur but pressed it on, though his supplies were constantly cut off by Hambirrao. Bijapur was hard pressed and sent for help from Govalkonda asking it to attack the besiegers; but Dilerkhan threatened Govalkonda which, thereupon, desisted. But it secretly sent money to Shivaji and asked him to assist Bijapur with men. Shivaji did it so well that Bijapur was enabled to successfully resist the siege. Eventually Dilerkhan had to make peace with Bijapur and raised the siege in Magh or the end of January (J).

Duff relates that Shivaji, as the price of his help to Bijapur, asked for the cession of the tract around Kopal and Bellary (a tract conquered by himself and by Hambirrao and Janardanpant, as related already). He also demanded the cession of all claims to sovereignty on his conquered territory in Dravid (Jinji) and to Tanjore and the jagir districts of Shahaji (Kolar, Bangalore etc.). These requests were conceded by Bijapur, and Shivaji became the independent master of a large tract about Kopal and beyond the Tungabhadra, of Jinji and the neighbouring territory of Tanjore, and of Kolar and Bangalore, in all of territory probably worth fifty lakhs of hons yearly. Duff states that Shivaji then went to the neighbourhood of the city of Bijapur and had an interview and secret consultation with Masaudkhan.

It is related by Duff that Dilerkhan after raising the siege of Bijapur crossed the Krishna and laid the territory about Gadag under fire and sword. This was probably in retaliation for what Shivaji had done to the Mogul territory. He was, however, signally defeated by Hambirrao and Janardanpant who were kept by Shivaji in charge of Karnatak, and who crossing the Tungabhadra attacked him in the Gadag Prant. We find a confirmation of this invasion in a Karwar letter dated 18th March, 1680,[1] which states that a Mogul force 15,000 strong assisted by Sarjekhan, head of the Bijapur army, has come to take back all the places seized by Shivaji and the forts of Kopal and other places have been besieged.

1. PS 2235 ; ER II 496, p. 308.

It is interesting to find a corroboration of the above whole account in a letter of Shivaji himself written to his brother Vyankoji, presumably to inform him that he was now the master of all the acquired territory in Karnatak Prant, and Vyankoji now held Tanjore under Shivaji. The substance of this long letter is as follows:—
" Dilerkhan seeing Bijapur weak advanced against it. Crossing the Bhima, he approached Bijapur within eight miles. Khan Alishan Masaudkhan asked for help from us and we immediately came to Panhala and assembling all the available forces went towards Bijapur. We thought, however, that the enemy was obstinate and a Pathan besides, and that he must be routed by artifice. We, therefore, left Dilerkhan at a distance of three villages (three marches), crossed the Bhima and went as far as Jalna laying the country waste. The bazar of Jalnapur was plundered for four days in spite of the fact that the prince was at Aurangabad only four villages distant (four marches). Gold, silver, elephants and horses were seized. We then came to Patta. Ranamastakhan, Asafkhan, Jabitakhan, with other Umraos and with eight or ten thousand horse, came to oppose us; but they were adequately punished. We then sent an army again to harass Mogul territory. Moropant Peshwa was asked to take the 27 forts of the Moguls in Baglan and Khandesh. In the meanwhile, Khan Alishan (Masaudkhan) wrote from Bijapur that he was still pressed by Dilerkhan who had even reached the *kot* and that we should help him at once in order to preserve the Padshahi. We came again to Panhala and helped him with men and money. After calling together the dispersed forces, we sent them against Dilerkhan. These cut off stragglers and the supplies

of Dilerkhan. Ranamastakhan and others started from Aurangabad to help Dilerkhan; but they were beaten and levelled to dust and pursued back to Aurangabad. Our forces then again surrounded Dilerkhan. Moropant meanwhile took Ahivantgad which is a fort as big as Panhala and also Nahavagad in Baglan. Aurangjeb heard this as also the account how we plundered Jalna and defeated Ranamastakhan. He, therefore, being enraged sent orders upon orders to Dilerkhan; but Dilerkhan eventually had to raise the siege. Khan Alishan fought bravely to defend the fort of Bijapur. We have made peace with him by which Hoskot, Bangalore, Arani, Chanjaur (Tanjore) etc. have been ceded to us and your connection is now with us. Hereafter Dilerkhan went towards Adavani and Karaval, but our general Janardanpant in that Prant having punished many polygars therein, next opposed Dilerkhan who with Sarjekhan and Husseinkhan had come with five thousand horse and beat them back. Dilerkhan has at present gone to his place, namely, Pedgaon. Sambhaji who had gone to the Moguls has returned as he has come to know that he would get nothing from either the Padshah or Bijapur. We hope you are all well; with many blessings" (PS 2236).

Thus successful everywhere and happy in every respect, Shivaji celebrated the marriage ceremony of his second son Rajaram at Raigad on Phalgun Vadya, 10, S'. 1601 or 13th March, 1680 (J). Eight days before marriage, the *munja* or initiation ceremony of Rajaram was performed. He was married to a daughter of Prataprao Gujar, the late commander-in-chief of Shivaji, whose loss was greatly mourned by him and whose services were thus appreciated and rewarded by him after his death.

After this joyous event, Shivaji lived only twenty days. He was seized with a deadly malady reported as blood diarrhœa in a Bombay letter,[1] and he expired after twelve days' illness on Chaitra S'udha 15, S'. 1602, Saturday (3rd April 1680) at Raigad about noon, Surusan-samanin. J records naturally enough, in detail, this date and time of the most important but mournful event in the history of the Marathas. Thus passed away this great hero in the 51st year of his age (50 years and 2 months), and after 35 years of strenuous exertions which were always successful and which never met with any disaster, fulfilling fully the mission of his life, namely, the establishment of a Hindu independent kingdom.

1. PS 2253; ER II 504, p. 311. "Shivaji died, it is said, of a bloody flux, being sick 12 days".

XXXVIII. SHIVAJI'S CHARACTER: ASPERSIONS ANSWERED

Now that we are at the end of our treatise, we will draw the attention of the reader to what we said about Shivaji in the beginning. "Shivaji was one of the greatest heroes of the world, by his exploits, his intrepidity, his resourcefulness, his undaunted courage in difficult positions, his continuous success and, last but not least, his unique moral greatness as a respecter of women and places of worship in an age when temples were being demolished everywhere and women were being constantly seized and sold as slaves by Mahomedans." Every one of these qualities of this great hero of Maharashtra has been brought out in the foregoing pages. These qualities are rarely found together in one man and it is but natural that Shivaji should be looked upon by Marathas as an incarnation of Vishnu or S'iva. The three accepted characteristics of an Avatara are great exploits, high morality and full success in the Avatara's mission. These three are found in the life of Shivaji and the belief of the common people in Maharashtra was thus natural.

The mission of Shivaji's life was not an ordinary one but one of the highest, namely, freeing his countrymen from bondage to a foreign foe and faith. It is this which gives the greater glow to the achievement of Shivaji and necessarily to the story of his life. The story of a nation's struggle for independence carried to success is ever thrilling and ennobling; for freedom is the most precious possession of a people and the spectacle of the struggle of a people striving to attain freedom from slavery is a sacred sight.

While thus the inspiring aim of Shivaji's life is holy, the many incidents in it are so varied that they might be looked upon as forming the continuous episode of a romance. We have often said that Shivaji derived his inspiration from the Mahabharata and it is interesting to note that his life also, full as it is of thrilling incidents, resembles the Mahabharata, which narrates the struggle of the Pandavas to get back their Swaraj from the wily and powerful Kauravas. It is still more interesting to note that many actions of Shivaji, like many actions of the Pandavas, have formed the subject of adverse criticism. Indeed, the Mahabharata contains several incidents which strike us at first sight as condemnable, but which are really justifiable, if we examine their character from the deeper principles of ethics. It is in fact the merit of the Mahabharata that, unlike the Ramayana, it illustrates the exceptional rules of moral conduct which we, in this world, full of both good and bad men, are justified in observing. Shivaji, like Shrikrishna, has suffered in the estimation of many, for this very reason and it is first necessary, before we praise Shivaji, to explain the propriety of Shivaji's apparently wrong conduct, influenced as it was by the maxims of the Mahabharata itself and to show that the charges often brought against him cannot be sustained.

Duff, for example, while acknowledging all the good points in Shivaji's character observes:– "Shivaji was patient and thoughtful in his plans; ardent, resolute and persevering in their execution; but duplicity and meanness are intermixed with his schemes. Superstition, cruelty and treachery are justly alleged against him and he always preferred deceit to open force when both were in his power." Deceit and treachery are the usual charges brought against Shivaji by many other writers also and we will examine these charges in the light of what has been said in the preceding chapters.

We must, however, first point out that these charges have, in many cases, no foundation in fact and are based on statements in later accounts. The later Bakhars thus have multiplied instances of Shivaji's use of deceit, from their natural predilection to exaggerate. Indeed, Shivaji has suffered, as well from friends as from foes. We must, therefore, first ascertain and make sure that our criticism is based on authentic facts. For example, take the story that Shivaji, in order to seize the jagir of Javali, sent an emissary to Chandrarao More to ask for his daughter in marriage and the envoy, while conversing with Chandrarao, stabbed and murdered him. This story of the Bakharkars is now proved to be a myth, as we have shown in our chapter, "The Supposed More Murders." In fact, Chandrarao had no daughter and Chandrarao was not murdered.

In cases where Shivaji used deceit, as recorded in the above pages, he was certainly justified in doing it; for he always used deceit against an enemy and when at war with him. Deceit and the consequent surprise have always been used with effect in every war and by almost every commander in western as well as eastern countries. The maxim that an enemy may be killed either by deceit or open attack is preached in hundreds of places in the Mahabharata itself.* When Duff says that Shivaji used deceit in preference to open force where hoth were in his power, he seems to condemn Shivaji. But this view is not correct. Deceit in such cases is not

* अच्छद्मना छद्मना वा मृगाणां वध इष्यते ।
शत्रूणां या वधे वृत्तिः मृगाणां सा वधे स्मृता ॥ आ. १५.

condemnable, as it involves less toil and less spilling of blood. No doubt, the ancient Aryans of India disdained the use of deceit in fighting. There was then what was called "Dharmayuddha" or righteous fighting. They even declined to take advantage of the enemy being in a bad plight, *e. g.* when he had broken his weapon or had got down from his chariot or had lost his armour and so on. But these ancient ideas were first set aside by Shrikrishna who set the example of using deceit in fighting. By his advice, Bhishma was killed by Arjuna by the artifice of placing S'ikhandi before him. Drona was next killed by Dhristadyumna while he had laid down his arms in meditation. Since these examples, it has become a maxim accepted in India as in the west and followed by all people and at all times, that 'everything is fair in war.' It is strange that Duff, himself a military officer, makes a charge against Shivaji for using deceit in war in preference to open force.

It may be noted that deceit develops into treachery when used in times of peace and against friends or when a truce has been settled or a white flag has been shown. So far as we have seen, no instance can be found in Shivaji's life where deceit had thus developed into treachery. In the case of Afzalkhan, both he and Shivaji were using deceit as enemies and both were talking of peace.

Indeed, Shivaji was on his defensive and the matter would have ended quite differently, had Afzalkhan not first thrust his dagger into Shivaji's side. We have contemporary evidence to show that Afzalkhan had received secret orders from Bijapur to seize Shivaji dead or alive.[1] Shivaji's success in that tussle was due to his caution, as he had an armour on and Afzalkhan in his overweening confidence had none. It is not a case of treachery, therefore, when Afzalkhan was killed by Shivaji. Historians ought to use the words deceit and treachery carefully. A similar mistake is committed when the word 'murder' is carelessly used sometimes like the word 'treachery'. For murder is different from 'killing' or 'putting to death', 'killing' being used when death ensues in a fight, and 'putting to death' when an order of superior authority is given, either judicial or political.

Furthermore, deceit is not only justifiable but recommendable when the adversary is stronger and is himself doing an act of aggression. We are often apt to forget that when Shivaji, by some deceit, entered at mid-night Shaistekhan's camp, the latter with an overwhelming force had taken possession of Shivaji's country and of his town and even palace. This act of Shaistekhan was an

1. Dag Register A. Selections from Dutch Records, Wadekar, S. N. III, 1.

act of gross injustice ; but we forget it and we are tempted to complain of Shivaji's action only as deceit or even treachery. Open aggression by an enemy, simply because he is strong and has a powerful army, is not excusable;* is indeed more reprehensible than the adversary's entering enemy's camp by deceit and inflicting injuries on him.

Further still, it must be remembered that the Mahomedans, in their dealings with Hindu kingdoms, freely used deceipt. Indeed, both Bijapur and Delhi often used deceipt, even at this time, with success against polygars in Karnatak and Rajput chiefs in Northern India, not to speak of Shivaji. The history of the Mahomedan conquest of India contains many instances of the use of deceit with success by the Mahomedans. It was an item of Mahomedan belief at the time that a covenant with a Hindu was not binding and that rules of morality might be set at naught in dealings with the Kafirs. We know how Bakhtyarkhan Khilji, with only 18 horsemen, entered the town of Nadia, capital of Bengal, alleging that he was a dealer in horses, and reaching the palace without challenge, suddenly attacked and killed the guards-men there. Lakshmansena the king had to flee and the city was taken. We also know how Allauddin Khilji, with a small force only, took the city of Deogiri

* नेशे बळस्येति चरेदधर्मम् । Mbh.

deceitfully and compelled Ramchandrarao Jadhav to pay tribute. If deceit can be used against an innocent enemy, it cannot be wrong to use deceit against an enemy using deceit. The Mahabharata* properly teaches that those who use deceit may be met with deceit and it follows that deceit may be used against open aggression. One is reminded here of the popular story of a Pathan and a Hindu. The Pathan who is usually a dacoit, meeting a Hindu alone in a jungle, suddenly attacked him and threw him down. The Hindu fell as if dead; but when the Pathan was pilfering him, he suddenly took out a hidden dagger and stabbed the Pathan. The latter, as he fell, cried, 'Oh, the treacherous Kafir!' Morally speaking the Pathan is the really condemnable person of the two. Pilfering cannot be excused because it is open nor can a clandestine attack on a pilferer be condemned. Deceit, therefore, is lawful when used in self-defence against deceit or open aggression and cannot be treated as treachery.

Duff is unquestionably wrong when he charges Shivaji with treachery or duplicity. When Shivaji gave out that he was proceeding against the western coast, while he really intended to go against the eastern coast, he is no doubt using deceit, but deceit which is justifiable, as it secures a surprise attack on an enemy. Shivaji

* 'मायाचारो मायया बाधितव्यः ॥' Mbh.

often gave out that he was going against Surat and in fact went against some other town and effectively surprised it. The use of deceit by Shivaji in this manner with great success on several occasions strikes us strongly and leads us to think wrongly that Shivaji used duplicity. Neither treachery nor duplicity can be charged against Shivaji according to the accepted maxims of war, on all such occasions.

The idea that Shivaji was superstitious is based on the accounts in Bakhars, as to how Shivaji would fall in a trance while praying and would utter words unconsciously, indicating that his future action was sanctioned by the goddess Durga, his tutelary deity. This, however, is not corroborated by any contemporary document and must, therefore, be rejected. This would even amount to deceit, according to present-day notions. But Shivaji was incapable of any such mean deception. He was, no doubt, a devout Hindu and believed that Durga was behind him; and in times of difficulty he might have often prayed to her, as Mahmud did to God when about to engage in action. But this cannot be called superstition. The charge of meanness has still less foundation. Shivaji no doubt exacted full rendering of account regarding plunder, as plunder was one of the means of keeping a large army and was treated as a regular business for it. But Shivaji was not also slow to reward. He gave a lakh of rupees to Gagabhat at the coronation and one lakh of hons to Raghunathpant at the conclusion of his Karnatak expedition. Generous reward along with stern punishment is a necessary qualification of a successful leader and Shivaji was always generous when necessary. Lastly, the charge of cruelty is quite unfounded. We have already refuted it when speaking of the sack of Surat. Even the Historians' History of the World admits that Shivaji was never cruel for cruelty's sake. Shivaji was never cruel to the subjects of other territories whom he plundered and to his own subjects he was always kind, though he had often to deal stern justice to delinquents.

This brings us to the heavier and apparently well-founded charge against Shivaji, namely, constantly plundering towns and villages in Mogul and Bijapur territories and thus inflicting undeserved misery on the innocent people of those kingdoms. They no doubt suffered for no fault of their own; and this earned for Shivaji bad epithets, even in his own time in contemporary letters such as 'the accursed dacoit' and so on. Modern historians also have usually stigmatised Shivaji not only as a murderer, but also as a marauder. We have already refuted the charge of murder against Shivaji as being entirely unfounded. Afzalkhan was not murdered but was killed in a personal conflict. Chandrarao More was never murdered. He was killed in battle. His two sons were 'put to death' for treason; having accepted pardon and service under Shivaji they should not have secretly sought the help of Bijapur. The charge of murder against Shivaji thus fails altogether; but the charge of plunder cannot be thus refuted; for it is true that Shivaji did constantly plunder and did continuously harass the people under Delhi and Bijapur. Indeed, every year Shivaji had a plundering expedition in their territories and his large army was chiefly maintained by plunder. It was even a regular business for it in the fighting season when actual fighting was not on hand.

But even here Shivaji's conduct cannot be condemned, if we consider it from the accepted principles or laws of war. It must be remembered that Shivaji always plundered enemies only and when he was at war with them. Plunder and devastation are the *sine qua non* of war at all times and among all nations. The right of the stronger to plunder the enemy people has always been conceded. In modern times, it is considered properly to be the right of the people to declare war; for they have to suffer its consequences as well as to enjoy its fruits. But in former times and under despotic governments, the kings declared war according to their will, being considered the masters of their territory and even of the people. The people had consequently to suffer for the wrong acts of their kings. But as the kings represented the people, the people had no real right to complain. Moreover, it was then a maxim that a strong nation can attack and destroy a weak neighbour. It is only since the last great European war that the right of a weak nation to enjoy independence has been recognised and no strong nation can now attack a weak neighbour, at least in Europe. We must, therefore, first remember that the Mogul Shahjahan or the Bijapur Adilshah had, morally speaking, no right to attack Shivaji's territory and if they did, Shivaji had a right to plunder their territory and people in return. These are plain positions and were understood even in those days when political philosophy had not been fully propounded. Shivaji understood them well enough when he said to the people of Surat, as already noted, "Your king has compelled me to keep a large army by constantly invading my country and you must pay for the upkeep of that army." It is really strange that an invasion of a foreign country and its temporary occupation by a foe do not strike us as reprehensible, while plundering does.

Regular occupation of a territory by an enemy is, however, an organised and systematic spoliation and is as reprehensible, if not more, as plundering which is only a sporadic evil in which people are not subjected to continuous harassment or drain of resources. We ought not, therefore, to forget that Shivaji plundered only when he was at war with the Moguls or the Bijapuris and levied fine from their people for the aggressions of their sovereigns. Indeed, the system of *chauth* introduced by Shivaji, as a substitute for plunder, was only the exaction of one fourth of the revenue to be paid to the king and thus it was a fine on the sovereign and not on the people.

Shivaji's plundering strikes us forcibly, also because it was constant and always successful, and we are thus tempted to call him a dacoit. The following observations in our History of Mediæval Hind India, Vol. III (p. 108), are worth quoting here in this connection :—

"Two persons have suffered much in this way in being called bandits by historians. Mahmud and Shivaji have usually been called bandits and plunderers, in consequence of the large number of their plundering expeditions and their uniform success. But we forget that, correctly speaking, neither Mahmud nor Shivaji can be called a bandit or dacoit. The right of belligerents to plunder the enemy has been recognised even in the west. Plundering weakens the weaker nation's power of defence and increases the stronger's power of offence. England herself has plundered enemies many a time. Drake and Hawkins plundered the ships of Spain carrying gold from America to Spain, when England was at war with the latter country. Drake even plundered the cities of Chili and Peru without the excuse of war and he has not been stigmatized by English historians as a bandit. The British have plundered the French at Pondicherry* in Indian History and have both massacred and plundered the townspeople of Jhansi when that city fought and stood a siege in the mutiny of 1857. And yet these acts cannot legally and even morally be described or denounced as dacoities or murders. Mahmud or Shivaji never plundered their own subjects. Shivaji so far recognised his duty as a king that he recompensed his subjects, whenever his own soldiers or even the soldiers of an enemy plundered them."

The Historians' History of the World is candid enough to remark that it "is just to state that this

* Of this plunder H. H. of W. observes, "And plunder enough was received by the ravaging of the neighbouring settlements to pay the expenses of the expedition." (XXVIII, p. 187). The usual object in plundering is here plainly given.

extraordinary man, while devastating other lands, was not unmindful of the duty he owed to his own subjects." Thus Duff records that when Ghatge and Nimbalkar entered the Panhala district and laid it waste, plundering it and retiring towards Karhad, a detachment of Shivaji's army under Niloji Katkar overtook them at Korlie and dispersed them, recovering much valuable property. "As it belonged to his own subjects, Shivaji scrupulously restored it to his people."

Some historians attempt to extenuate Shivaji's plundering and even his supposed murdering, by the maxim, "The end justifies the means." The high purpose of establishing Swaraj justified, they think, even murder; and some look upon plundering as a kind of taking forced loans. But even the highest purpose, we think, cannot justify what is undoubtedly illegal and immoral. Political assassinations are always to be deprecated. In ancient times a sentence of death on an obnoxious person was no doubt pronounced, but it was openly pronounced by the people in public meeting assembled. Forced loans again had to be returned. Shivaji's actions cannot, we think, be excused on this maxim.

It is more proper to argue that Shivaji, even though he plundered incessantly, was justified in doing so by the laws of war sanctioned by all people and in all ages, as he only plundered enemy territories and when at war and he went further than all his compeers when he observed strictly the humane rule that cows, cultivators and women were to be exempt from plunder, as recorded by even the Historians' History of the World, Vol. XXIII. That this was Shivaji's own view also is proved by an English letter from Surat dated 21 June 1673[1]. When the English complained of, and asked compensation for, their being plundered at Hubli, he declared that "he prosecuted a *just* war in his enemy's country and if his army in plundering enemy's towns doth, unknown to him, meddle with any English people, or the country people did it, he was in no way liable to answer." As a friend, he even advised the English that they should trade as little as possible in the Deccan, as he was going to make a sharp war there as soon as the rains were over. Shivaji thus knew well his rights and his duties when he plundered people in enemy country.

1. PS 1545; ER 366, p. 266.

XXXIX. SHIVAJI'S GREATNESS

Having thus far shown how Shivaji is wrongly charged with deceit or treachery and is improperly dubbed a dacoit, we proceed to detail his brilliant capacities, physical, mental and moral. Shivaji resembled Mahmud in several virtues and one may say of him what Gibbon has said of Mahmud: "Turning from accounts of bloodshed of which unfortunately history is too full, it is pleasant to stop a while and appreciate the good qualities of Shivaji, undoubtedly one of the greatest kings of the world. His name is revered in Maharashtra, his subjects enjoyed peace and prosperity and examples are recorded of his justice and magnanimity." Shivaji, we know, punished his own son Sambhaji for an atrocious crime, much as Mahmud was ready to do, but fortunately had not to do. In the words of Lanepoole again, we may say that "Shivaji was a great soldier, a man of infinite courage and indefatigable energy of body and mind." Mainwaring says of him, "His talents as a soldier place him above the heroes of the East; his personal activity was astonishing." Indeed, Shivaji, as a soldier, was never afraid to go into the thickest fight; and, as a general, he was never despondent under the most adverse circumstances. Shivaji was again capable of continuous physical as well as mental exertion. He knew no rest and always moved about from hills to plains, from hill-forts to ground-forts, from Maharashtra to Karnatak. In his long incognito travel through Northern and Middle India, after his escape from Agra, he showed of what stuff he was made and what habits of hard toil he had acquired from his boyhood.

A devout religious Hindu that he was, Shivaji loved and revered his mother, his father and his guru. Like Mahmud he was a respecter of women and we do not read in any account of his plunders that women were molested, much less seized or dishonoured. Like Mahmud also, Shivaji was a loyal husband and pure in his married life. This is the greatest glory of a man's character that, rising to the highest power and prosperity, he remains pure in his private life.*

* The story related in later Bakhars may be given here regarding the beautiful daughter-in-law of the Mahomedan Subedar of Kalyan, taken prisoner and sent to Shivaji by Abaji Sondeva. It may be mentioned here though not yet confirmed by a contemporary document. Shivaji not only treated her as his sister and sent her back to her relatives with presents, but by this act he set an example to his generals which guided their conduct in future and which impressed all with his high spiritual character. If the story is untrue (which is likely) it at least shows what the people of Maharashtra thought of him.

Shivaji loved his own religion intensely as Mahmud did his own, but unlike the latter, he was not intolerant. The only blemish in Mahmud's character was (as we have shown in our history M. H. I. Vol. III) his intolerance which led him to destroy hundreds of Hindu temples and forcibly to convert thousands of Hindu inhabitants. Shivaji, having firm faith in his own religion, still respected the religions of others, for he not only continued old grants but made new ones also to fakirs and mosques throughout his territory. Even contemporary Europeans recognised this greatness. Mr. Dello (Dutch), writing on 6th Jan. 1670, observes " Shivaji allows all religions to prosper though himself an idolator."[1] He thus in this respect stands above Mahmud.*

Going on to his talents, we find Shivaji was a great administrator like Mahmud. Like the latter he rose from the jagirdarship of a small tract to the kingship of an extensive kingdom he conquered by his military achievements and he made [illegible] by his just and popular administratio[illegible] territory he introduced at once a careful system of administration which though somewhat copied from the previous Mahomedan system was his own and

1. PS 1279.

* The case was the reverse under Mahomedan and Portuguese rules. PS 2006; ER II 271

conduced to the prosperity of the people as well as of the state. His system of Ashtapradhans was also his own and his revenue system was also new, as we shall show in detail in the Appendix. Of course his greater achievement was his army which was a creation of his own from materials, insignificant as compared with the material which Mahmud had, as will be detailed later on. Every ambitious hero creates a powerful army and acquires dominion with its help. Alexander, Cæsar, Frederick the Great and others in the west, and Mahmud, Rajaraj Chola and Shivaji in the east are examples of great heroes, creating invincible armies and acquiring power and dominion. Shivaji like Mahmud also created a special force of body-guards under himself which was composed of select men with greater pay and position. This force was used for fierce fighting at the opportune moment.

But greater than this was the keeping of this powerful force under control. Powerful armies become a terror sometimes to their master as to the enemy. Only a great soldier, a consummate commander and a man of unquestioned moral superiority can command influence over an army, influence so great that every soldier is ready to lay down his life for the master. One important reason which kept the soldiers under control was the great care which Shivaji took for their punctual payment and their housing. His soldiers were regularly paid so that their pay was never in arrears. From the days of the Mahabharata, in Hindu states the pay of the soldier was fixed in coin and corn and Shivaji saw to it that these were regularly given directly and not by way of assignments on districts. The Mahabharata itself declares that an army whose pay is in arrears creates great turmoil and inflicts untold miseries on the master and the people. Shivaji knew it not only from the Mahabharata, but from the examples of it in Mahomedan states of his own time. We know how in the later decadence of Maratha power, Arab soldiers whose pay was in arrears created serious disturbances both at Poona and at Baroda. Shivaji's military administration thus deserves praise especially as such administration is so rare in Indian history. Modern armies are regularly paid and their system of administration certainly deserves the highest praise in this connection.

Shivaji's military foresight is also evident in his building of new forts and strengthening of old ones. In the hilly country over which he ruled, forts especially were a power. Forts, whether hill, ground or island, were useful for defence as well as offence. Shivaji expended lakhs of hons on his forts and made them impregnable. Shivaji knew how to save money*, but he also knew how to

* नार्थमल्पमपि परिभवेत्—स. सभा.

spend it. Whenever any weak points were discovered in the fortifications, Shivaji built further strengthening walls as at Sinhgad and Raigad. Shivaji's fortifications have been praised by contemporary European visitors. Mahomedan armies always found it difficult to attack these forts and usually avoided the hilly regions.

Shivaji also saw the necessity of creating a navy of his own and he actually succeeded in creating a strong navy. His perseverance in this respect is proved by the fact that he eventually succeeded in building a fort on the island of Khanderi. The English were afraid of Shivaji's fortifying this island which commanded the entrance to the harbour of Bombay. The Siddi of Janjira (who must be given the credit of obstinately maintaining his position and his small state against the continuous effort of Shivaji to subdue or destroy him) built a fort on Hunderi and he was connived at in this by the English in Bombay. The Siddi tried to prevent, with the aid of the English, Shivaji's attempt to fortify Khanderi. But as reported in a Bombay record dated March 1680,[1] Shivaji eventually succeeded in defeating the English and fortifying Khanderi, a few months before his death.

Shivaji, himself an educated man, was a patron of learned men like his father Shahaji.

1. PS 2229; ER II 489, p. 301.

He had no doubt little leisure to converse with pandits or hear musicians as his father did, but his patronage was always extended to learned men.* Like Mahmud his compeer at whose direction we know that the Shahanama was completed by Fardusi, Shivaji asked Paramanand to write a Sanskrit poem on his doings and the *Shiva-Bharata*, as stated in the beginning, was composed by Paramanand during Shivaji's own life. There is another poem on the taking of the fort of Panhala composed by Jayarama, a court-poet. Further Bhushan, the writer of Hindi Savais or heroic verses on Shivaji, is a well-known author and he was entertained at Shivaji's court. Then again at the suggestion of Shivaji himself, the Persian-Sanskrit Kosha or dictionary of political Persian words ordinarily used in Marathi was composed which shows Shivaji's national spirit and even the names of ministers were changed by him into corresponding Sanskrit equivalents. It is really a pity that these facts, now well-known, should have been forgotten for a

* Indeed from Shahaji's time, there was a tradition of learning and literacy which came down even to Shivaji. Shahaji had learned Pandits about him always and even took part in their disputations (see राधामाधवचम्पू). Shahaji was also fond of music and himself composed a work on music (Sangita-Saramrita). South India is well-known for Sanskrit learning and music, and these flourished at Tanjore down to the time of Ekoji and his successors.

time after Shivaji and some historians consequently represented Shivaji as illiterate.

It is somewhat strange that Shivaji's genius failed to recognise the necessity of studying the manufacture of powder and guns while he built forts and ships. The importance of cannon both for forts and ships must have been recognised by him; but he remained, like the Mahomedans, content to buy powder and guns from the western peoples who were settled as traders on the west or east coast. Shivaji should have seen that eventually these western nations would conquer India by the power of their superior weapons. Why did he not set men to study natural sciences and to found factories in his own country for the manufacture of guns and powder, even as the Japanese did immediately after they saw and felt their power?* Even accurate gunners could not be found among Mahomedans or Hindus. It is possible to explain this failure by the fact that the European nations were never aggressive at this time, like the Americans in Japan, though they had seized upon

* We have the mention of a factory of guns at Purandar; probably the Portuguese were employed for this. PS 1975, 22nd September 1677; ER II 251, p. 138. In this letter of Shivaji to Madras he asks the English to send men for making even carriages for guns and for laying mines.

patches of territory on the east and west coasts and had begun to fortify them. It is also true that Brahmins, the intelligent class among Hindus have been from the first averse to the study of the natural sciences. Even in the west, until Bacon arose, the intelligentsia was engrossed in sciences of words rather than in sciences of things. It is as difficult to foretell in the future as to speculate in the past; but the historical theoriser cannot help remarking that if the study of the natural sciences had been suggested at this time to Shivaji and if Shivaji had got his men qualified for the manufacture of guns and powder as a department of state, the subsequent history of India might have had to be written differently from what it is. Brahmins again feared religiously to go beyond India and were thus also handicapped in this matter. All the same, it was their duty, at least in Peshwa times, to look to this, so that artillery need not have been entrusted to Frenchmen or Englishmen by Bhausaheb or Mahadji Scindia.

XL. SHIVAJI'S GREATEST ACHIEVEMENT

The greatest achievement of Shivaji was the establishment of Swaraj in Maharashtra and the consequent raising of the Marathas to greatness, political as well as moral. Shivaji founded an independent Maratha kingdom in spite of the efforts of two prosperous Mahomedan empires or powers to crush him and yet the means which Shivaji had were absolutely inadequate and insignificant. This almost impossible work was, therefore, accomplished, we think, by the energy of soul, mind and body of one single individual. We note sometimes how, in history, a single individual arising among a people raises them to power and position. A single Shivaji thus raised the Marathas to the rank of rulers for at least a century and a half and established their reputation for bravery and statesmanship for all time. A single Bajirao raised the Chitpavan Brahmins to the position of emperors of India and established their reputation for intelligence also. Yet centuries before Bajirao, they were unknown and unnoticed and lived in a small tract in Konkan, going out, if they ever did, as begging Vaidikas. The Marathas were similarly insignificant before Shivaji, though not equally with the Chitpavans, and were usually looked down upon as Bargis (?) by the Mahomedan conquerors of the Deccan.

Let us see what the condition of the Marathas was before Shivaji. Except a few leading jagirdar families which claimed descent from Northern India Rajputs, the original Maratha gentry in Konkan, Ghat-Matha or the Deccan consisted chiefly of Deshmukhs and Patels. They were war-like no doubt and good riders; but they were divided and they always fought among themselves. They were also not stubborn fighters; for they had no national sentiment which alone enables soldiers to fight stubbornly. They were ready to serve any master, whether this Mahomedan king or that, who entertained them in service. The ordinary Kshatriya population in Maharashtra thus was of no capacity or strength physically or morally. The causes of the fall of Maharashtra before the Mahomedans about 1300 A. D. are nearly the same as those of the fall of Northern India about 1200. The absence of the sentiment of nationality and the want of unity among the Maratha gentry and Patels made the conquest of Maharashtra by the Mahomedans easy and three hundred years of Mahomedan rule thereafter made Maratha Kshatriyas not only content with their lot but also loyal to their foreign rulers.

The lower population of the Deccan and especially of the Ghat-Matha and Konkan was weaker still, being entirely unwarlike. In stature and strength, the ordinary Mawalas and Konkanis were insignificant, compared with the Pathans, the Moguls or the Siddis who mostly formed the Mahomedan army. Man to man, with or without arms, a Mawala could not have faced a Pathan. But nationality, self-confidence and unity can make heroes even of Mawalas as of the Japanese and the former easily defeated the Mahomedans in Shivaji's war for independence as the latter defeated the Russians in the Russo-Japanese war. When Shivaji formed his plan of founding Hindwi Swaraj in order to free Maharashtra from the oppression of a foreign rule and religion, he had only the Mawalas before him as his instrument; but he rightly thought that even these weaklings, if trained, disciplined and inspired with the feelings of unity and nationality, could be trusted to achieve wonders. Shivaji drew his inspiration from the Mahabharata as usual in this connection as it preached "how a people trodden down by Dasyus can rise and how even one thousand horsemen, if of one mind, were enough to conquer the world." Shivaji resolved, thus, to work even with these men and he enlisted them by thousands. For there was the advantage of numbers on the side of the Mawalas and

Konkanis. They were thousands as opposed to hundreds and if one thousand horsemen of one mind could conquer the world, surely a hundred thousand could easily do so. Shivaji, therefore, finally formed his plan and began his mission, ignoring the high class Marathas, the Ghorpades and the Ghatges, the Mores and the Savants and relying upon the Mawalas and the middle class Deshmukhs and Patels.

It may, perhaps, be doubted here if Shivaji at the age of 15 had in his immature mind these various thoughts and reasonings. But we believe that old age is never capable of forming high plans or carrying them out, nor probably even middle age. It is only in youth when imagination is strong, mind undaunted and body supple that such high plans are formed and an optimistic view taken of everything. We know great men have done great things only in youth. Shankaracharya formed the plan of conquering Buddhism and Jainism by his new philosophy which he had thought out even at the age of 16 and carried out his plan before the age of 32. It is, therefore, no wonder if Shivaji formed his high plan and resolved to carry it out even at 15 with such insignificant materials. It must also be remembered that Shivaji in his fifth year had seen Shahaji become almost the master of Nizamshahi with the help of his Maratha cavalry, and that he must have also marked at Bangalore with his precocious faculties from his tenth year how Shahaji had acquired extensive dominion with the help of the same cavalry. He inspired such courage, such self-reliance and such spirit of unity and nationality in his middle-class Maratha followers and the lower class Mawalas and Konkanis that they eventually formed an invincible army and fearlessly attacked armies of Pathans, Moguls and Siddis, and even defeated them in pitched battles.

This spirit of nationality which we find in the Marathas and the Mawalas at this time was a creation wholly of Shivaji and partly of Ramadas. Nationality, not to speak of patriotism, has never existed in India. The duty of Kshatriyas was always supposed to be to fight for the master and not the country, the king and not the people. Country and people indeed had no existence then. A king ruled not by the consent of the people but by his success in battle or by his descent in a particular kingly family. Hindus, therefore, fought even in the army of Mahmud against their own countrymen. Europeans have marked this defect in Hindu character. Thus, Friar states that "Every Hindu prizes the salt he eats more than the independence of his country and therefore fights even for the Mahomedans."[1]

1. PS 1823, dated 1675.

The Marathas similarly fought against Shivaji in the armies of Bijapur or Delhi. That it was the duty of the Marathas to join Shivaji in establishing Swaraj was a new idea altogether. It was first preached by Shivaji and by Ramadas and it gradually grew under the teaching of the latter. The word was a little different. It was for the Maharashtra Dharma that Marathas ought to fight. This word is no doubt older than Shivaji, but it had no political import then. This was added later in Shivaji's time and Ramadas uses it in this sense when he says of Shivaji:* "महाराष्ट्रधर्म राहिला कांहीं । तुम्हां-कारणें." The sentiment of nationality grew stronger and stronger with Shivaji's successes and when he was crowned as the king of Maharashtra, it was firmly fixed in the minds of the Marathas throughout his dominion. The crowning of Shivaji was the crowning of a Maratha, the declaration of the independence of the Marathas; and the national sentiment, thus strengthened, was put to the test and it worked wonders, when Aurangjeb after Shivaji's death vainly tried to crush the independence of Maharashtra. For the Marathas stood up against him as one man and gathered around the person of Rajaram as the representative of Maharashtra

* Jedhe, a Deshmukh of Mawal, thus said, "This is Maharashtra State and for it I will sacrifice myself and my five sons."

Dharma, in spite of nameless miseries suffered for several years, throughout their country.

The word 'Maratha' gradually extended in meaning. It originally applied to the Kshatriyas who settled in Maharashtra in ancient days, probably about the sixth century B. C. (Bhandarkar). And even the Rajput families which came later in Mahomedan times, adopted the same name, having married, naturally enough, among these older families. The other people in Maharashtra, Brahmins and S'udras, were not called Marathas in Mediæval or Mahomedan times. But when the whole people were united under the rule of Shivaji and when they became a nation so to speak, they all came to be called Marathas. Differentiated among themselves, they were called Brahmins and S'udras, while, when the word 'Maratha' was singly used, it meant and even now means the Kshatriya Marathas. But they had all become Kshatriyas or soldiers, whether they were Brahmins, S'udras or Kshatriyas, according to the maxim of the Manusmriti that every one should take up arms when religion is in danger. They had all fought with valour in the armies of Shivaji and they had all thus become Marathas or the Maratha nation.

The reputation of Marathas as soldiers was thus established for ever. The spirit of unity and nationality infused by Shivaji among the Marathas gradually waned in later times, but their renown as soldiers and as statesmen continued. Brahmins distinguished themselves as leaders of armies, even in Shivaji's time and hundreds of Brahmins enlisted in the cavalry. The British in India later on enlisted and still enlist Marathas, though not Brahmins, in cavalry and infantry, those from the Ghat-Matha and Deccan gentry being enlisted in the cavalry and the Konkanis especially in the infantry. Maratha soldiers were and are further distinguished by their simple living and abstemious habits and are capable of hard work, even on small fare, a capacity which has been developed since Shivaji led his plundering expeditions, carrying as little paraphernalia as possible and subsisting on whatever food was available. This capacity of the Marathas was found to be of great use in Mesopotamia in the last great European War as we read from published accounts.

It might be contended that favourable circumstances enabled Shivaji to found an independent kingdom. Because Muhammad Adilshah died at an opportune moment, because Aurangjeb was called away from the Deccan at a critical time, because Mogul officers like Bahadurkhan were corrupt and because Pathans and Siddis fought among themselves for power at Bijapur during the minority of Ali's son, Shivaji succeeded in his plan of founding Swaraj. This is partly true. But favourable and unfavourable circumstances arise at all times. The man of genius takes advantage of the former and conquers the latter. Absence of the sense of nationality characterised the Indian people from ancient times. The Mahabharata in the Sabhaparva advises kings to send presents secretly to the 18 Tirthas or high officers of other states and keep three spies, unknown to each, on fifteen officers in their own states; for officers were always open to corruption and Bheda has always been one of the four means of conquering an enemy. But we must remember that Shivaji succeeded not because Bijapur or Mogul officers were divided or corrupt, but because his own officers, military and civil, were not venal or divided and this was due to the great sense of nationality generated by Shivaji's great personality and his high spiritual purpose.*

Whether circumstances create heroes or heroes create circumstances is a much contested philosophical question. Our view is that circumstances always exist but great men are born by the will of

* Shivaji's emergence without injury from his tussle with Afzalkhan and his escape without detection from confinement at Agra also strike us as strokes of good fortune. But at the same time his foresight in providing for all contingencies and his resourcefulness in sudden situations cannot but be admired.

God. Apples were always falling from their stalks but the law of gravitation remained undiscovered till a Newton was born by the will of God. All people are capable of great things, but heroes come and raise them to their full height. One such great hero was Shivaji who founded an independent state of the Marathas, welded them into a nation and raised the Marathas to everlasting renown as soldiers and statesmen.

The liberation of Maharashtra in the seventeenth century somewhat the liberation of Italy in the nineteenth; hut it was even higher and more difficult. " The problem before Cavour was how a country of 37 millions could outwit and confront a nation of 230 millions." The problem before Shivaji was indeed simpler, being exactly the opposite, namely, how Maharashtra having a population of three hundred lakhs could confront three lakhs. However, as Lord Palmerston said, " Italy only *seemed* dead and Italy has arisen to a new vigorous life, breaking the spell which had bound it and showing itself worthy of a new destiny. " Maharashtra, however, was *actually* dead politically and had to be brought to life again. Hence the number of its people as compared with that of the Mahomedans had no value. Secondly, unlike the Italians, they had to be brought to life again by the sentiment of nationality and unity. Shivaji united Maharashtra under the new impulse of Swarajya and Swadharma. Thirdly, unlike the Italians, the Mawalas and the Marathas were unwarlike and had to be trained to fighting. Lastly, Italy was backed by England and the rest of Europe stood aloof. Maharashtra, on the other hand, had to fight alone, not only against its own people but against the rest of India. Thus, the liberation of Maharashtra by Shivaji was a far more difficult task than the liberation of Italy from the yoke of Austria. And further, Shivaji had not only to be his own general, his own statesman, but his own propagandist and it may be said that Shivaji was Victor Emanuel, Count Cavour and Garribaldi put together, the general, the statesman and the teacher.

APPENDIX

I. Shivaji's Personal Appearance

Escaliot writing on 28th Jan. 1664 (ER 79, p. 73) says " His person described by those who have seen him is as follows :—He is of a mean stature, erect and of an excellent proportion. He is active in exercise; and whenever he speaks he seems to smile. He has a quick and piercing eye. He is whiter than any of his peoples.

II. Shivaji's Wives and Children

Mr. S. K. Oka of Dhar has written a detailed paper on this topic, bringing together and discussing all the authorities on the subject, published in Shivaji Nibandhavali 2. We give in this note the information given in this paper, stating our view wherever we differ from Mr. Oka.

Shivaji, it is generally stated, had eight wives, but we find authority for six only. The most senior of them was Saibai, a daughter of the Nimbalkar family. She was married in Bijapur. When Shahaji finally entered Bijapur service, it is natural that the Adilshah should bring about a marriage between his son Shivaji and a daughter of the Nimbalkars who were one of the most loyal jagirdars of his kingdom. This marriage took place in April 1640, when Shivaji was about ten years of age and not in 1641, as Shivadigvijaya states. This later account of Shivaji states that the first marriage of Shivaji took place at Poona and was performed by Dadaji Konddeo and that " when Shahaji wished to see the married couple, he had them brought to Bijapur when the Padshah insisted that a second marriage must take place and in his presence." This is an absurdity. The first marriage could not have taken place at Poona and in the absence of Shahaji. For according to *Shiva-Bharata*, Shivaji went to Poona in his twelfth year, *i. e.* in 1642 or 1641 at the earliest. The first marriage of Shivaji in 1640, therefore, must have taken place at Bijapur and with the Nimbalkar family, as the Kaifiyat of that family mentions. After being taken to Poona, Jijabai probably wished that a second wife should be given to her son, as he had become now an independent jagirdar, as already stated; and Dadaji Konddeo might have brought about the second marriage with the Shirke family. This wife of Shivaji was named Soyarabai. The difficulty which Mr. Oak mentions here how Saibai could be treated as the eldest queen is solved in our view in this way.

The third queen of Shivaji was Putalabai from the Mohite family. When exactly she was married cannot be determined; but she could not have been married at Raigad in 1653 as held by Mr. Oka, as Raigad was not in Shivaji's possession till 1659 and Shivaji himself was not then sufficiently great. It seems to be a tradition among the Maratha high-born families that a girl from the Mohite family should be taken and it is possible that Jijabai got this third girl married to Shivaji.

When after the conquest of Javali, Shivaji became a powerful jagirdar and when he wished to collect friends and supporters for his Hindvi Swaraj by strengthening his position by marriage relations in important Maratha families, he married three more wives. J records that in S'. 1578 Magh (February 1658), Shivaji formed marriage relation with the Gaikwads. The name of this fourth queen appears to be Sakwarbai. Three months later, on Vaishakh S'. 5 (May 1658), he married a lady from the Jadhav family and again on Dwadashi from the Ingle family. Thus, these three important families, Gaikwad, Jadhav and Ingle, were enlisted in his cause. Mr. Oka gives Kashibai as the name of the lady from the Jadhav family. We know from the Rajyabhisheka Kalpataru that Kashibai died a few days before Shivaji's coronation and her death, according to Nis'chalapuri, was an evil omen. In an English letter also, there is a reference to a queen of Shivaji dying at this time. We are not certain as to whether the queen from the Jadhav family was named Kashibai, the one from the Gaikwads, Sakwarbai, and the one from the Ingles, Sagunabai, as Mr. Oka holds.

It is mentioned by Oxenden and Friar that Shivaji had four queens at the time of the coronation and that they were again married at the time. Their marriages were again performed with Vedic rites in order to enable them to take part in the Vedic coronation ceremony. These were not new queens married at this time, as is wrongly supposed by some. They were Soyarabai, Putalabai, Sakwarbai, and Sagunabai, Saibai having died long before in 1659 A. D.

Lastly may be noticed the controversy over the question whether Shivaji had two concubines besides his queens. Mr. Oka, accepting the testimony of a life of Ramadas which mentions two more *married* women, maintains that they were not concubines but married women, the word used in this life of Ramadas being " Lavaris lagna kelelya. " (Lavaris, a Persian word meaning la, without and varis, heir). But we hold that this life of Ramadas, full of absurdities as it is, about miracles wrought by Ramadas, must be set aside altogether and we believe that Shivaji had no concubines as some thought, or no married wives from among foundlings (Lavaris) as Mr. Oka thinks. Shivaji was so pure in his marriage relations and had such proper notions of his own dignity that he could not have condescended to marry foundlings even though they might have been very, very beautiful. It is really distressing to see how later writers add events and things and persons from their imagination, suggested to them by their surroundings. They forget that certain high persons tower above the common run of people. Ordinary kings and jagirdars might have had many wives and concubines even in ancient days; but one is pained to find that even the last recaster of Valmiki's Ramayana mentions that there were many beautiful women in Rama's seraglio (रामस्य परमाः स्त्रियः-अयो.). We reject such stories altogether and hold that there were no concubines either of Rama or of Shivaji. Shivaji, no doubt, married many queens; but he had to form a party of his own and collect high Maratha families about himself as relatives. And we think that a Hindu king may marry more than one wife rather than keep concubines or mar the purity of married life. The purity of Shivaji's married life has not been questioned anywhere.

Shivaji had a son and three daughters from the eldest queen Saibai. The son Sambhaji was born in 1657 (J) and his mother died in 1659 (J). One of the daughters was married to Mahadji, son of Bajaji Nimbalkar, who had been converted to Mahomedanism, but who was reconverted at the instance of Jijabai. From Soyarabai, Shivaji had a son and a daughter. This son Rajaram was born in S' 1591 Phalguna S'uddha 15, Thursday, 14th February 1670 (B. I. S. M. Quarterly IV, p. 21) and the daughter Dipabai was married into the family of Vishwasrao. Shivaji had a daughter from Sakwarbai and one from Sagunabai. The former was married into the Palkar family and the latter into the Shirke family. Putlabai had no issue and she burnt herself with Shivaji, properly enough.

III. Shivaji's Power and Possessions

Sabhasad closes his excellent life of Shivaji with a detailed description of Shivaji's power and possessions skilfully introduced in Shivaji's consoling conversation with Sambhaji. Shivaji proposed to divide his wealth and kingdom into two parts and give them to his two sons Sambhaji and Rajaram. As this whole scene and conversation is imaginary, we think that Sambhaji's reply is also imaginary in which he said he only wished to serve his father and remain quiet. Shivaji knew his bad and good qualities, his vices and his merits, his impetuosity and his bravery. The only thing that must have vexed Shivaji at the time of his death was, we think, the thought that Sambhaji would create a turmoil in his kingdom after his death. He had, no doubt, kept Sambhaji practically a prisoner at Panhala after his coming back and reconciliation. But he foresaw that Sambhaji's position as the elder son would go far with the army, though not with the civil officers or Sarkarkuns. Perhaps, we are here anticipating, as certainly Sabhasad does, when he gives the conversation between Shivaji and Sambhaji and also later on that between Shivaji and his officers at his death-bed.

But Sabhasad's description of the power and possessions of Shivaji at the time of his death is practically correct and worth being given here for the curious reader.

After enumerating the eighteen Karkhanas of a Maratha state copied from Mahomedan states, Sabhasad gives the twelve Mahals or departments of state and the first of them was the *pota* or treasury. Shivaji's treasury was certainly full, as the treasury of every strong and fighting king ought to be. The amount mentioned by Sabhasad is not incredible. The treasury contained one lakh of Gambars (gold coin not recognisable but heavier no doubt than a Mohor which always weighed one tola), two lakhs of Mohors, three lakhs of Putalis (half a tola) and many lakhs of hons. The current coin was hon. It was struck at several mints and it had several names accordingly. The weight, however, was generally the same, though with slight variations, being one-fourth of a tola. The total* of all the different kinds of hons given by Sabhasad comes to 72-28 lakhs and these at the rate of three rupees per hon, would be worth 226-84 lakhs or 2¼ crores of rupees. There was silver coin also, namely rupees struck in different mints. The Moguls used silver coin, called the rupee, weighing one tola and the English at Bombay also struck rupees which passed even in Shivaji's territory. The total of rupees of different mints given by Sabhasad comes to 57 lakhs. There was besides, gold and silver in bars, the former weighing 12½ khandis and the latter 50, worth respectively one crore twenty eight lakhs and thirtytwo

* Shivaji had a mint of his own and the coin struck there was called Shivrai. The treasury had 4 lakhs of Shivrai hons.

lakhs of rupees approximately. The total of all these comes to about four crores and fortythree lakhs. There were valuable jewels, diamonds, etc., and pearls also, the value of which is not given by Sabhasad. There was cloth, silk, brocade, etc., which was worth about one crore of hons. The whole thus would be about 10 crores of rupees; compared with the riches possessed by some rich men and the British Government in the Bombay Presidency alone at this time, Shivaji's treasury cannot be said to have been extraordinarily full.

Shivaji began, Sabhasad says, with the Poona jagir worth 40 thousand hons yearly and left a kingdom, the income of which was about one crore of hons or three crores of rupees which is somewhat an exaggeration. The territory consisted of two parts, the first extending "from Saler fort in the north along the Godavari to Kopal on the Tungabhadra in the south and the other from the Tungabhadra to the Kaveri," which was territory recently conquered. The former may be called Maharashtra and the latter Karnatak. The former consisted of territory above and below the Western Ghats, namely, the Deccan and the Konkan bounded on the west by the Arabian Sea from Bassein to Ankola; and the latter consisted also of territory above and below the Eastern Ghats bounded on the east by the Bay of Bengal. Shivaji proposed to give Karnatak to Sambhaji, as Sabhasad mentions, and Maharashtra to Rajaram. This, if true, must also have displeased Sambhaji.

Shivaji increased his army slowly as his territory and income increased. It was at the time of his death a very large force indeed, consisting, as it did, of one lakh and five thousand cavalry and one lakh infantry, besides artillery and a considerable navy. The cavalry consisted of two parts as stated already, the Paga and the Shiledars. The Paga or household cavalry had 45 thousand horse and at its head was Hambirrao Mohite and under him were captains whose names deserve to be recorded here. They are given by Sabhasad as follows :—

1. Santaji Ghorpade, 2. Manaji More, 3. Yesaji Katkar, 4. Santaji Jagtap, 5. Nimbaji Patole, 6. Santaji Katkar, 7. Parsoji Bhosle, 8. Ganoji Shirke, 9. Baloji Katkar, 10. Niloji Kate, 11. Nathoji Palkar, 12. Tukoji Nimbalkar, 13. Gondaji Jagtap, 14. Sambhaji Hambirrao, 15. Dhanaji Jadhav, 16. Shamakhan, 17. Waghoji Shirke 18. Haraji Nimbalkar, 19. Bhavanrao, 20. Anandrao Hapthajari, 21. Telangrao, 22. Rupaji Bhosle, 23. Vyankatrao Khandkar, 24. Khandoji Jagtap, 25. Udaji Pawar, 26. Ramaji Kakade, 27. Krishnaji Ghadge, 28. Savji Mohite. It may be noted that there was one Mahomedan captain among these.

The Shiledars (and the Subedars), we find, were both Brahmins and Marathas and they brought their own contingents which totalled 60 thousand horse. The names of the Brahmin Shiledars were : Ramaji Bhaskar and others and of the Maratha Shiledars, Nemaji Shinde, Khandoji Atole, Bahirji Ghorpade, Keloji Pawar, Narsoji Shitole, etc. In all they were 38.

There were besides elephants, small and great, in number 1260.

The infantry consisted of Mawalas and others and its commander-in-chief was Yesaji Kank and under him were captains like Suryaji Malusare, Ganoji Darekar, Vithoji Lad, etc., in all about 36.

Shivaji possessed hundreds of strong forts throughout his dominions, forts which he had either repaired or newly built at great cost. He properly held that forts were the strength of his kingdom; and they really were so in his time, indeed in modern also, till aeroplanes were invented. The names of these forts are given in detail by Sabhasad and they were of three sorts as stated already, gads, kots and janjiras. The most important of these were: in Maharashtra, Sinhgad (Kondhana), Prasiddhagad (Rangana), Vishalgad (Khelna), Satara, Parali (Sajjanagad), Kot Phonda, Kopalgad, Panhala, Purandar, Pali (Sudhagad,) Raigad, Trimbak, Saleri, etc., in number 49 old forts and 108 new ones like Rajgad, Pratapgad and so on. Besides these forts in Maharashtra, there were 79 forts in Karnatak, 38 above the Ghats like Kolar, Bangalore and others and 41 below like Jinji, Vellore and others.

Sabhasad mentions some important young civil officers who were towers of strength, so to speak, in administration, such as 1. Nilopant, son of Moropant Peshwa, 2. Pralhadpant, 3. Gangadharpant, son of Janardan Narayan, who himself was kept with Sambhaji at Panhala to watch over him, 4. Ramchandra Nilkanth, 5. Raoji, and 6. Abaji Mahadev and 7. Balaji Avaji Prabhu, Chitnis.

The eastern boundary of Shivaji's dominion from Saler to Kopal cannot be exactly determined from the evidence yet discovered. But the land-marks are as follows: Saler and Ahivantagad were in his possession, but Moropant had not yet taken Mulher (PS 2224, Surat letter dated 24th Feb. 1880). Nasik and Junnar were apparently not in his possession though Trimbakgad had been taken. Then Karhad was in his possession (PS 2238) as also Kolhapur; but Miraj was not (PS 2240). Athni and Gadag probably were (PS 2227, dated 28th Feb. 1680), as also Meskra Kot and Kopal (PS 2235; ER 11 496, p. 308), but Hubli and Dharwar were not. With regard to Karnatak territory we do not know the exact boundaries and the map hereto annexed gives them from surmise. But it must have been a large territory as Shivaji gave yearly one lakh of hons to Bijapur for sovereignty.

IV. Shivaji's Ministers : Their Names and Functions

Whence did Shivaji take the new names he assigned to his eight Ministers? They were not the names current in Mediæval Hindu times. "The Mahomedans so completely changed the whole system of administration that nothing remained from mediæval nomenclature." (History of Mediæval Hindu India, Vol. III, p. 455). Down to the villages, revenue administration names were changed, names which survive to the present times through the Maratha rule. Mr. Shejavalkar in his paper on this subject (B. I. S. M. Quarterly, IV, 1924) points out that the names were taken from S'ukranītisāra, a work on Hindu Politics. The number eight is also taken from it (अष्टप्रकृतिभिर्युक्तः). These are given as follows सुमंत्रः पंडितो मंत्री प्रधानः सचिवस्तथा। अमात्यः प्राड्विवाकश्च तथा प्रतिनिधिः स्मृतः॥ SNS II. 73. Shivaji may have been guided by this work; but he, as usual, formed his own system. Not only are some ministers different, but even their functions are different from those given by SNS. We have a Jabta issued soon after Shivaji's coronation (Jyeshth Vadya 13 R. year one), published in the first number of 'Itihasa and Aitihasika' which details the duties of the eight ministers and we can compare these with those given by SNS. On looking into this work we find that the ministers are further assigned the following order viz: 1 Purodha or preceptor, the highest of all, next 2 Pratinidhi, next 3 Pradhan, 4 Sachiva, 5 Mantri, 6 Pradvivaka, 7 Pandita, 8 Sumantra, 9 Amatya and 10 Duta. And yet it is strange that SNS lays down that the eight are to receive the same pay, (भृतिसमाः). We know that Shivaji paid his Peshwa 7,000 hons yearly and others 5,000. It would be interesting to compare the functions assigned by the Jabta and by SNS as also those appertaining to the offices in mediæval times.

There was no room for the first two in Shivaji's system; the Purohita was most powerful in ancient days (even the king feared him–SNS) being supposed to be able to destroy enemies by magical sacrifices. Next was the Pratinidhi who was to act for the king in his absence. Shivaji had no occasion for the services of either, being self-reliant and nearly always present in his state. A Pratinidhi was required and was actually created in the time of Rajaram when he went to Jinji. We will detail the duties of the eight ministers remaining as given in SNS, the Jabta and mediæval inscriptions.

1. **Pradhana**—Shivaji called him Mukhya Pradhana. His duty was to look to all work (सर्वदर्शी प्रधानस्तु SNS.) The Jabta also states: " He should do all state business, should lead armies and should act with the consent of all." The mediæval name of the Prime Minister was Amatya or Mahāmatya. In a Thana inscription he is described as राज्यचिन्ताभारसमुद्वाहन " one who bears the burden of the care of the state" (H. M. H. I., Vol. III, p. 248). His Mahomedan name Peshwa, however, was too strong to be ousted and continued to the last.

2. **Sachiva**—War Minister (सेनावित् SNS). It is strange that he was not called Senapati. This name was introduced by Shivaji. His Sachiva was sender of letters (the Persian name being Surnis). Sachiva is not a mediæval name, the keeper of the seal being called महामुद्राधिकृत (do. p. 453). The Jabta gives the duty of the Sachiva as follows: "Every royal letter should be examined and corrected where necessary by him. He should also fight."

3. **Mantri**—Foreign Minister (मंत्री तु नीतिकुशलः SNS II. 85). With Shivaji he was house-hold officer called **Waknis** in Persian. The mediæval name of this officer was Antahpurika or Pratihāra (do. p. 454).

4. **Pradvivaka**—Chief Judge (लोकशास्त्रनयज्ञ SNS). Shivaji changed this name (given in Smritis also) into Nyāyādhis'a, which was more understandable. The mediæval inscriptions do not mention him, because the king himself, with the aid of assessors and ministers, disposed of cases which came before him (do. p. 466). For the districts there were Dandanayakas.

5. **Pandita**—The Ecclesiastical Minister (पंडितो धर्मतत्त्ववित् SNS). Shivaji created this new minister and also retained his name which shows that he had probably SNS before him. His mediæval name was Dharmādhyaksha.

6. **Sumantra**—Accountant or Finance minister. (आयव्ययप्रविज्ञाता SNS II. 86). With Shivaji, he was foreign minister called Dabir in Persian (परराज्यांतलि विचार करावा. त्याचे वकील येतील त्यांचा सत्कार करावा-जाबता.). The mediæval name of the foreign minister was Sandhivigrahika.

7. **Amatya**-Writer of letters etc. (देशलेखप्रविज्ञाता SNS II. 86). With Shivaji he was the most important minister next to the Pradhan. He was both Accountant and Revenue

Minister (his Persian name being Mujumdar). (राज्यांतील जमाखर्चाची चौकशी दफ्तरदार फडनीस यांचे स्वाधीन असावे—जाबता). He had also to fight and administer conquered territory (युद्धप्रसंग करावे. तालुका जतन करून आज्ञेत चालावे-जाबता).

8. **Senapati**—This was a new office created by Shivaji—(युद्धप्रसंग स्वारी करावी, तालुका स्वाधीन होईल तो रक्षून हिशेब हुजूर करावे—जाबता).

A Duta or ambassador (Persian Hejib) was not with Shivaji a special minister. Different persons were sent as Hejib and not one man.

The above will show to us how Shivaji borrowed the idea of 8 ministers from S'ukranītisāra, but made changes in names and functions suited to his own requirements.

Of other officers the Jabta mentions first the Chitnis and then, Sabnis and Bakshi (फौजेची हाजरी घेऊन रोजमुरा वांटावा), Sena-Dhurandhar (the Vanguard officer of an army), then Subedar, Mamledar, Talukedar (of districts), Havaldar, Subedar, Karkhannis, Sabnis, Sarnobat and Tata-sarnobat (of forts) and Potnis or treasurer (नजरपेशकसी जमा करावी. पारख करावी).

V. Shivaji's Revenue Administration

The whole state was divided into Subas, the Subas into Perganas or Talukas* and the latter into Tarafs or Karyats. These are all Mahomedan names and the original meanings of the first two are not known. Taraf, however, means 'sides' and Taluka means 'connected' from Persian Taaluk-connection. There were other smaller divisions called Tappas, (tappa—Persian, meaning-a place of halting). A revenue-paying territory was general-

*The word pergana was used chiefly in the Deccan.

ly called Mahal.* The villages were called Maujas and smaller attached villages Majras. For each village there was a Patil and a Kulkarni (these names alone survive from mediæval times). They collected the revenue. There were some other village officers such as Chaughula etc. These were all hereditary. They were collectively called Mukadams (a Persian word, meaning-forward) and orders were issued in the name of Mukadams.

The revenue was paid in kind and also cash (small taxes of different kinds). The Malik Ambari system prevailed; the Mogul Todarmal system of cash payments fixed on the basis of the produce of several years had yet to come. It came when Aurangjeb occupied the country for years after the death of Sambhaji. The government share of the produce was apparently different in different places; but generally it appears to be two-fifths. The corn was collected at the head-quarters of the Mahal and thence sold or distributed to civil and military servants by the state authorities.

For each division there were Deshmukhs and Deshpandes, Sanskrit words introduced by the first Bahamani kings (in lieu of the northern Chaudhari and Kanungo); and these were generally Marathas and Brahmins respectively. They were held responsible for the revenue collection of the Taluka or division. The revenue for each division appears to have been formerly, chiefly under Moguls, fixed in money and was called Tankha to be paid into the Diwan by the Deshmukhs. These officers were together called Jamedars. But Shivaji introduced a

* e. g. महाकामिहाय. Mahal Persian means a hall and denoted here the Diwan Hall where revenue business of the division was transacted.

change and held the village Patils and Kulkarnis responsible under Karkuns or government heads of the division. The Deshmukhs merely assisted and were paid in cash for their rights.

The government officers for the divisions were generally called Karkuns. There was a Subedar for the Suba and a Talukedar for the Taluka or Pergana (The word Mamledar is not yet used, though 'mamla' for a division is found; it is derived from 'amal' or rule and Maamla means 'the territory ruled'. There were twelve Subas, it is somewhere recorded, in Shivaji's Maharashtra. These were put into three prants, as noted already and the prants were under Sarkarkuns or Sarsubedars. (Thus, PS 1238 is an order by Shivaji, dated 15th Jan. 1669 to Subedars and Karkuns सरकार महालहाय तळकोकण व देशमुख व देसपांडे कल्याण मामले.) Above these three, there was the Mujumdar or Amatya of the whole state. The Karnatak territory conquered by Shivaji in 1677 was probably one Suba placed under *Subedar* Raghunathpant Hanmante and he was also Mujumdar directly under Shivaji.

The subedar was the chief responsible officer and he was to survey and settle the Dhara (assessment) from time to time. Thus, PS 1982, dated 12th October 1677, is an order from Annaji Datto, the Sarkarkun to the सुभेदार व कारकून in सुबे सातारा stating "सालमजकुरी देशाची मसाती करून धारा देण्याचा तह केला आहे. तरी श्रीचे इनामाची मोजणी अगर पाहणी न करणें." Thus, the word मसाती meant मोजणी व पहाणी-survey and settlement and the Subedar was to do it and settle धारा or rents. Survey and settlement was necessary from time to time owing to constant war operations and the consequent reduction or extension of cultivation. As soon as a territory was acquired by conquest or even nominal lease, arrangement was at once made for its revenue administration, by the appointment of officers who looked to the cultivation of land and the encouragement of trade. Shivaji never farmed out the revenue of any territory, which was realised directly by the Patil and Kulkarnis under the supervision of officers. The system of giving Mokasa of tracts was current before his time. What the word Mokasa means originally, cannot be ascertained; but a mokasi was practically a farmer of revenue. He collected the revenue and paid into the state treasury a fixed amount. He was also responsible for the safety of travellers and had to compensate for thefts. He thus had to keep a police force. Mokasas were constantly changed as we find from papers. They were often given to captains of armies and important personages like ministers as a kind of reward. So far as we have ascertained, there were no Mokasas under Shivaji's rule.

VI. Shivaji's Judicial Administration

The bane of British rule in India is both excessive legislation and enormous litigation. Under native government, in past times. Hindu and Mahomedan law, as laid down in the sacred books, was administered and litigation was very limited. Where local conciliation was unable to settle disputes, then only parties went before officers of the state such as the Subedar and the cases were usually or almost always decided through Panchayats. Jagirdars and Mokasdars had no judicial powers apparently; for cases came before Dadaji Konddeo as Subedar of kile Kondhana (each tract had its fort) and not as the Karbhari of Shahaji. But after Dadaji's death, Shivaji became independent and cases came before him or his mother as administrator or regent.

There appear to be very few civil cases relating to debts, as we find no records practically about such cases. Probably such disputes were usually settled out of court or by Dharanā. It is also true that under the modern Civil Procedure, recalcitrant debtors are rather encouraged than otherwise. We have, however, many mahjars relating to disputes regarding Watans (Patilki, Deshmukhi etc.). They came before the Subedars and often before Shivaji himself. They were always settled by Panchayats held on the spot wherein, Patils, Mukadams etc. of adjoining villages were called together. Witnesses were examined on oath and documents also inspected. Decisions given by the Panchas are detailed in their mahjars (from *hajir* present in court) signed by all the persons taking part as assessors. This involved great trouble, the Panchayat staying in the village for days together. Hence the word 'Panchayat' in Marathi has come to mean 'trouble and difficulty.' Where there was extreme doubt, the decision was given by resort to ordeal. The ordeals were of different kinds as described in Smritis; but the one usually resorted to in Shivaji's time was that of *Rava*. It was the taking out of a piece (रवा) of gold from boiling oil. Resort to ordeal was always made with the consent of the parties. Care was taken that no trick was played. The day before the ordeal, the hand of him who offered himself was washed and then placed in bags which were sealed. The next day the ordeal was gone through before some deity in a temple and if the hand was burnt in taking out the Rava, the man was declared to have lost his case. How the hand was not burnt in some cases may be a mystery*; for care was taken as above that no medicine was applied to prevent burning of the hand. Shivaji was present personally at one such ordeal as is stated in PS 1816, dated Feb. 1, 1676. It was a dispute regarding the Mokadami (Patilki) of Pali between Kharade and Kalabhor and the former lost the case. Shivaji was present with Harji Raje Mahadik, Raghunath Narayan, Moro Trimal, Niraji Raoji, Moro Nilkanth, Prataprao &c. This Mahjar is important and the ordeal took place at Pali itself. Cases came before Shivaji himself not in appeal. For appeals had no existence then. Where parties were dissatisfied and came before the king himself, the case was tried *de novo* if it was thought proper.

Suits began with personal appearance before the officer and oral complaint. There were no stamped papers, nor, of course, pleaders. The party which was proved to be in the wrong had to pay a proportionate fine, called Harki. Security was taken for such Harki before enquiry was instituted.

In criminal cases, sentences inflicted were severe and involved chopping of hands or legs for theft; murder, treason and dacoity were punished with death. Punishments are more humane in modern times. So far as can be ascertained, we do not find mention of jails. High class delinquents were kept in confinement in forts and ordinary person in Thanas. Fines were often imposed.

* It is possible to explain it by the power of the mind supported by the consciousness of being in the right. Indeed, Chhandogya Upanishad explains an ordeal in this very way सत्येनात्मानमभिधाय न दह्यतेऽथ मुच्यते.

It shows Shivaji's anxiety for the proper administration of justice according to divine law, that he appointed a special minister among his Ashtapradhan, for justice. His name is new and it has survived to this day, *viz.*, Nyāyādhish. He was a Brahmin versed in Dharmas'astra.

VII. Shivaji's Military Administration

1. Army

We have already described the army of Shivaji consisting of infantry and cavalry. We may note here some further facts. Friar records that in the cavalry of Shivaji, Mahomedans were mostly employed (PS 1893, dated 1675). This seems strange, as Marathas were known since long as skilful riders, Friar also records that in the infantry, the matchlock men were mostly Hindus. This may be true, not because Shivaji distrusted Mahomedans, but because his infantry was composed of Mavalas and Hetkaris of the Ghat-Matha and Konkan and these are all Hindus. Friar rightly remarks that both Hindus and Mahomedans had no feeling of nationality. They were bound by the sentiment of loyalty (for salt eaten) and hence Hindus served Mahomedans and Mahomedans served Hindus faithfully.

2. Ganimi Kava

The Ganimi method of fighting for which the Marathas became famous began long before Shivaji. But Shivaji used it with advantage when he had to fight with large armies encumbered with artillery. A small active cavalry force can attack large armies by this method. This method seems to have been borrowed from the Mahomedans themselves. For Hiuen-Tsiang describes the Marathas of the 7th century as giving notice to the enemy before attack and as fighting stubbornly, never turning their backs. The first mention of this method we find in Mahmud of Ghazni's history. He used this method against the Afghans of Ghor (see our History of Mediæval Hindu India, Vol. III, p. 53) and also against the contingent from Kashmir under Tung, come to assist Trilochanapal, in the battle of the Tausi (ditto, p. 61). Shivaji must have seen Turkish cavalry in Bijapur army using this method and hence it was called Ganimi Kava (the enemy trick). The trick consisted in showing as if one's cavalry detachment is defeated and is running away and then turning round suddenly, when the enemy pursues and becomes disorganised, and attacking him.

3. Forts

Shivaji saw the value of keeping his forts in good condition and hence in 1671 A. D. gave an order for the expenditure of 175 thousand hons yearly on them for repairs &c., distributed as follows (PS 1459): 1. Raigad 50, including houses and tank, 2. Sinhgad, 3. Sindhudurga, 4. Vijayadurga, 5. Suvarnadurga, 6. Pratapgad, 7. Purandar, 8. Rajgad, each 10, and 9. Prachandgad (Torana), 10. Prasidhagad, 11. Vishalgad, 12. Mahipatgad, 13. Sudhagad, 14. Lohgad, 15. Shrivardhangad and 16. Manranjan, each 5, and for others 7, total 175.

In view of a sudden Mogul invasion, as a precaution, when money was most urgently required and could not be had elsewhere, it was settled (Tah) that the following places should maintain a reserve fund of 125 thousand hons, to be drawn upon only on the occasion of Mogul investment of forts, *viz.*, Kudal, Rajapur, Kole each 20, Dabhol 15, Poona 13, Jawli, Kalyan, Bhivandi, Indapur each 5, Supa 2,

Krishnaji Bhaskar 5 and Nagoji Govinda 1, in all 125. This also shows what towns were rich and in what order. (PS 1456, dated 1671)

4. Navy

Mr. Surendranath Sen has written an interesting detailed chapter on this subject in his "Military System of the Marathas." He rightly rejects the opinion of D. Gaarda, that Shivaji turned his attention to the sea, when he could not extend his kingdom further on land. Mr. Sen is also right when he says that Shivaji began to raise a navy about 1659, when we get the earliest reference to Shivaji's navy in a letter of the Governor of Goa, dated 16th August 1659, stating that "Shivaji has constructed some ships of war at Bhivandi, Kalyan and Panwel" (PS. 777). Shivaji with his all-embracing genius must have seen the necessity of having a navy both for fighting and trading, when he took possession of North Konkan in 1657. The importance of the acquisition of Konkan is not adequately realised. It is not realised that Konkan, especially in the north, is productive being free from famine ; and there is a very large income from the export and import trade of its ports. The country was vulnerable to attack from the forts on the mountains and *Shiva-Bharata* rightly says that whoever has Jawali has the corresponding coast line. But Konkan is also at the mercy of any power which has a strong navy and hence the necessity of a navy to Shivaji.

The Moguls, it is strange, having the Gujarat coast under them, did not raise a strong navy; but they as well as the Persians, the Turks and the Afghans in their armies were not a naval people. Nor were the Mahomedans of

Ahmednagar who had North Konkan under them, a maritime people. At Bijapur, the Siddis and the Arabs were numerous and they were accustomed to move on the sea. They held South Konkan, from the ports of which there was a large traffic of pilgrims to Mecca, besides there being centres of brisk export and import trade. Bijapur should, therefore, have been able to equip a strong navy, but it too failed to do it. The result was that the western nations, *viz.*, the Portuguese, the Dutch and the English (the French to a less degree) established their power on the west coast, especially the Portuguese who claimed the sovereignty of the sea. A Siddi had, no doubt, established himself in an island on the South Konkan coast and become strong; but he had not sufficient navy and no artillery practically. To fight with, at least to cope with, these and especially with the Siddi who unlike the Western nations constantly harassed Shivaji's Konkan possessions, Shivaji found it necessary to raise a navy and he at once made arrangements for it when he became master of the territory from Kalyan to Chaul. There was plenty of good wood in the Sahyadri mountains; and the building of ships for coastal trade was a prosperous profession already on the west coast. There was again no lack of good sailors, for the Kolis and the Bhandaris of the west coast were good sailors, being accustomed to the profession for centuries. Strong and active, they could easily be trained to fighting. The Marathas as such never took to the sea, being horsemen generally; with the exception of the Angres and the Dhulaps, we find no Maratha captains of the sea in Maratha history. Mahomedans of the west coast, being converted Kolis, were also fit to be sailors and soldiers, and they already used to go to Arabia and Zanjibar. Shivaji, therefore, was able to raise a strong navy soon, having built ships in the creeks of Kalyan, Pen and Panvel and manned them with Kolis, Bhandaris and Mahomedans. We have already seen that Shivaji had two squadrons of 250 ships each, one under Daryasarang, a Mahomedan, and the other under Maynak Bhandari, towards the close of his reign.

We cannot for want of expert knowledge enter into details about the nature of the ships in Shivaji's navy. There were, as stated already, Gurabas, Galbats, Muchwas, manned with sailors and soldiers, and minor craft manned with sailors only. We cannot state their differences of construction nor their special use in fighting. The number of fighting ships increased from time to time as 160 large ships are mentioned already in 1670 in Bombay letter, dated 24th Nov. (PS 1360).

Shivaji used his navy for industrial and trading purposes also. He even aspired to trade with Arabia and the western countries, without European agency. It is also recorded that his navy protected the conveying of salt from Konkan ports. Thus, salt is mentioned as taken from the island of Bombay in boats protected by Shivaji's navy in PS 1558 of 1673 and 1302 of 1670. The value of Konkan again in this respect is not always remembered. Salt was largely produced in coastal places only and was taken in boats to inland places on creeks, like Pen or Kalyan. And in these days of railways, we have entirely forgotten that in those days, this precious commodity was taken thence on bullocks to the up-country. There was a special Sarkarkun appointed by Shivaji to superintend coastal industrial traffic.

5. Artillery

But Shivaji's strong navy was handicapped for want of cannon. As already stated, the only point where Shivaji's intelligence failed was the manufacture of cannon and gunpowder. To cope with the navy of the western peoples, his navy required to be armed with cannon and these and even expert gunners could only be had from them. For expert gunners could not be made out of Kolis, Bhandaris or Mahomedans, much less out of Brahmins and Marathas. It must be admitted that in the Deccan and the Sahyadri mountains there are no iron mines. The art of smelting iron and other metals is not much practised there. Even with this drawback, Shivaji tried to manufacture guns and gunpowder at Purandar with the aid of foreigners. We know from the Governor of Goa's letter to Jaising (PS 1044), dated 1665, that there were some Portuguese in the employ of Shivaji as of other kings. Again PS 1053 (Jaising's letter to Aurangjeb) states that Ambaji Kharkuli and his two brothers who were manufacturing powder at Purandar were being seduced from Shivaji's service, by offers of mansabdaris. It does not seem clear whether these men were Hindus or Mahomedans and if these men could manufacture guns also. In any case, this work did not prosper and Shivaji had to depend for cannon and gun on the western peoples. Being in possession of Konkan and also their neighbour, Shivaji usually got firearms, especially from the Portuguese, 'and often from the French at Rajapur. (ER 213, dated 5 Sept. 1670 speaks of Shivaji obtaining lead and guns from the French). But these weapons must have been inferior to those used by the Westerners. Moreover Shivaji depended upon them also for expert gunners. Hence, as Sen has observed, " Shivaji's fleet, though numerically superior to the fleets of European nations or that of the Siddi, was inferior to them in artillery and the art of navigation."

We cannot say if the cannon and guns of Shivaji were superior to those of the Mahomedans who also depended upon Europeans for these arms and also for gunners. But Mr. K. P. Khadilkar thinks that the possession of Konkan was useful to Shivaji in another respect, *viz.*, the obtaining of better swords than the Moguls possessed. Good swords also came from the west; they were manufactured in Damascus and other western countries and were hence called 'Firangs' in those days. It is possible, however, that the Moguls could also obtain them from Gujarat ports. We have already shown how iron industry was not much known in Maharashtra and hence even good swords were not locally manufactured.

VIII. Currency in Shivaji's Time and Country

The most prominent fact with regard to currency in Shivaji's time and country is that the authorized money was the hon. In fact, in the whole of South India the currency was in gold hons. This was so not only from Mahomedan times but from Hindu times. Indeed, throughout Hindu times, the currency was in gold. In Vedic and Epic days, the gold coin used, called nishka, was only a piece of gold of a fixed weight. We do not know its value; but Vedic works extol a sacrifice where a Nishka was given as Dakshina to each Brahmin. It seems that gold was then plentiful both in Northern and Southern India. Ceylon was known as golden Lanka. It is no wonder, therefore, that throughout ancient, mediæval and Mahomedan times, gold coin was used in the south. It was called hon or gold, hon being the Prakrit form of Suvarna. Suvarna itself also meant a gold coin. In Mahomedan days, we find it sometimes called Lari, the name being derived from Lada or Lata (Konkan Gujarat).

When the Mahomedans of Northern India introduced silver coin cannot be stated. But I have shown in my 'History of Mediæval Hindu India,' Vol. II (page 463, and Vol. III, p. 261) that the rupee was known and used even before the Mahomedans, in Kathiawar.-(द्रम्ममेकं करी दद्यात् तुरगा रूपकद्वयम्-Bhavnagar Inscriptions). The word 'rupee' like 'hon' also means the metal, namely silver. When the Moguls conquered Nijamshahi, rupee currency was introduced into Berar, Aurangabad and Ahmednagar prants. The English at Surat had to use the Mogul rupee and they naturally introduced it in Bombay from whence it spread into Konkan and Maharashtra. They even struck rupees of their own, as appears from their letters. They traded in Shivaji's Maharashtra and hence rupees had begun to circulate in Deccan bazaars. But the government authorized coin was the hon. We can, thus, understand how Sabhasad and other contemporary writers always mention the revenue from villages, districts and prants as so many hons. Sabhasad also gives the total cost of the coronation ceremony in hons, namely, one crore and forty-two lakhs. The Peshwa and other ministers were given one lakh of hons each, as present though Gagabhat who lived in Benares is said to have been given one lakh of rupees as Dakshina.

The value of current hons in rupees varied according to the relative value of gold and silver in the market, just as even now in England the rupee value of the pound varies. It seems, however, that in the Mogul Maharashtra territory, the value of a hon was fixed at three rupees. The rupee is one tola in weight and the hon was $\frac{1}{4}$ tola. Taking the mediæval value of gold as sixteen times that of silver, we expect the hon to be taken as equal to four rupees. But the ratio of silver and gold values varied. Silver was not plentiful then as now and thus sometimes the ratio came down to 14 or even less. Then again government fixes the ratio sometimes in its own favour and sometimes in favour of the ryot. Hence we find in some old documents of revenue from Taluka Sangamner (shown to me by Mr. Shankarrao Joshi) that assessment originally in hons was converted, under Mogul rule, into rupees at the rate of three per hon. But in Jaisingh's letter to Aurangjeb of June 1665, we find Jaisingh taking the hon as five rupees (PS 1066): "Shivaji offers to pay 40 lakhs of hons as Peshkash and this represents a sum equal to two crores of rupees." This is, of course, its greatest value.

Hons being of gold contained some alloy and different mints turned out hons of different alloys. This also led to the value of the hon being taken differently for different mints. In the list of coins in Shivaji's treasury at the time of his death given by Sabhasad, there were, besides Padshahi hons, Ibrahimi, Shivrai (struck by Shivaji), Kaveri pak, Achyutarai, Devarai, Ramchandrarai (these three were Vajayanagar coins), Gutti, Dharwadi, Malkhatti, Advani, Tadpatri (these were places where mints coined hons in the South) Again the tendency to depreciate coin naturally led to old hons being prized more than new ones. Thus, we find from Dag register, dated 28th November 1663 (PS 1863) a report that the Moguls who first took tribute from Govalkonda in rupees insisted on having it in *old* hons, as the *new* ones of Govalkonda were depreciated (128 new ones being equal to 100 old).

Shivaji, of course, struck hons in his own name after he was crowned. But there is evidence that he coined money even before from 1664, especially after his return from Agra. We have not yet seen a Shivrai hon though it is understood that some have been found.

The Westerners called hons Pagodas. It is said that Pagoda means a temple and on the hons, the sign of a temple was always imprinted. The art of coining was borrowed by the Hindus from the Greeks, as shown elsewhere. But on the Hindu coin, we do not find imprinted faces of kings who struck them. Various signs, chiefly religious, were impressed along with a letter or two from the name of the king who struck the coin. Where Shvaji coined and whether the men employed where Hindu goldsmiths has not yet been ascertained.

The English in their treaty with Shivaji settled at the time of the coronation wished to insert a term regarding currency, but this was not allowed by Shivaji. We find from Oxenden's diary (ER 486, p. 376) that Shivaji accepted all the articles of the treaty proposed except the money article which was to this effect : "All manner of coins made and used in the island of Bombay should go current in Shivaji's dominions and all sort of coins made in Shivaji's dominions shall pass freely in the island." (ER 475, p. 354). Shivaji deemed this article unnecessary and said that he did not wish to force his subjects. He well understood the powers and limitations of an independent ruler.

The rupee currency, however, supplanted the whole gold currency after Shivaji's death, probably in the days of the occupation of Maharashtra by Aurangjeb for several years. Shahu's policy was one of conciliation and his acceptance of a farman from Delhi of Chauth and Sardeshmukhi perhaps induced him not to revert to the old gold currency.

The real difficulty which besets the subject is, however, the value and nature of the coins below the hon. They were named Taka and Rukka. We are, for the last two hundred years and more, accustomed to speak of rupees, annas and pies and have forgotton that 300 years ago, we spoke of hons, Takas and Rukkas. We cannot hence now tell the value and even the nature of these two inferior coins. We are thrown on guess to be made from old papers. Several papers thus of the Deshpandes of Shirval published in Rajwade Khand XX give the income of the Desh-Kulkarnis in Takas and hons. They used to take a percentage of the total income of villages and this is given in Takas, the share of one partner being stated as much as 815 Takas. For Gaon-Kulkarni work, the claimant got cash in Takas and grain. These old papers from S'. 1565 (1643 A. D.) thus speak in hons and Takas. But the question first is how many Takas formed a hon and what metal was used for the Taka coin.

Prof. Kale in a paper on this subject published in B. I. S. M. Quarterly XI-3, considers Taka as merely a money of account and that it meant money generally. (In Bengal Taka means even now a rupee.) But Taka is derived from Tanka (striking) and originally must have meant coin struck. The coin has now gone out of use; but it has remained in some Marathi phrases like the following :—१ टके मोजावे लागतात, २ टका शेर भाजा टका शेर खाजा, ३ कोण म्हणतो टका घेतला &c.

Unfortunately, no Taka coin has yet been found by researchers and hence the belief probably that it is a coin of account. Prof. Kale, however, properly holds that it was higher in value than the Dam of Northern India or the Dhabbu Paisa of Deccan which was plainly a Mahomedan copper coin. Prof. Kale has actually found an old paper dated 1694 A. D. which shows the ratios between these coins from the following :—"Daily wage $25\frac{1}{2}$ Rukkas for a year of 364 days; this means 188 Takas equal to 15·2/3 hons." This clearly shows that while 48 Rukkas formed a Taka, 12 Takas formed a hon. This was its normal ratio ; but other papers noted by him give the ratio from 10 to $9\frac{3}{4}$. In our view, the Taka could not be a money of account, for the ratio could not have then fluctuated. The ratio fluctuates owing to the changing ratio of the values of silver and gold and the above figures show that the Taka was a silver coin of about 4 annas in value, hon being equal to 3 rupees or 12 Takas.

With regard to the Rukka, we have another paper from Mr. R. H. Gadgil of Bombay in B. H. S. M. Quarterly X-1, in which after describing the copper coins issued by Shivaji, he says that there was a copper coin of $\frac{1}{4}$ Tola, one of $\frac{3}{4}$ Tola and one of 1 Tola. The $\frac{1}{4}$ Tola copper coin was called Rukka and Shivrai was $\frac{3}{4}$ Tola. 192 Rukkas formed a rupee as shown by Mr. Chaphekar. If 48 Rukkas formed a Taka and 12 Takas one hon, we have 596 Rukkas for a hon or 3 rupees. Thus, we have clearly 192 Rukkas to the rupee. A Rukka was thus equal to one pie of modern days.

Mr. Gadgil's idea that 3 Takas went to a rupee would make a hon equal to 4 rupees which is not improbable, as the ratio varied from time to time. But as shown in the beginning, the Moguls changed hons into rupees at the rate of 3 to 1 and hence a Rukka is equal to the modern pie. Who introduced pies and annas and what these words mean by their origin is an interesting subject; for the Moguls had 40 Dams to the rupee, (Dama being derived from old Dramma). But as annas and pies were not known in Shivaji's days, this perplexing subject does not concern us here.

The papers of Shirval Deshpandes, published in Khand XX noted above, deserve to be studied carefully. They contain many figures of Takas and hons and they belong to the time from S'. 1617 to about S'. 1627. The Takas are never converted into hons and they run up to even a thousand. The Takas seem thus to be the usual coin of payment. They again are divided into quarters and further on; thus at page 104 we have a sum of Nakhtayati Takas given as 369'1/4. This sum must be taken to be correct (though Prof. Kale thinks that mistakes are often made in sums). The quarter is correct; but how does the figure 9 come in and how many are to be converted into one quarter cannot easily be determined. The figures and remarks at page 108 will afford us a clue. The total Taka charge on cloth is given as $1\frac{3}{4}+4\frac{1}{2}$; if this is put into figures, taking 48 Rukkas for a Taka, we get $88\frac{1}{2}$ Rukkas and one-tenth of this for the Sardeshmukh would properly be $8\frac{1}{2}$ and one twenty-fifth or Chohotra would be properly $3\frac{1}{2}$ and

कापड मोईन टके
१॥।४॥ ऐन
ऽ८॥ सरदेशमुखी, दाहोत्रा
ऽ३॥ देशमुखी चोहोत्रा
ऽ१॥ सरदेशपांडे दुहोत्रा.

one-fiftieth or Dohotra would be $1\frac{1}{2}$. The remainder is usually neglected. This is my explanation which, I think, is correct. Now if the Taka is to be divided into 48 parts, it can never be a small copper coin. The surmise above made namely that Taka was a silver coin of about 4 annas value and that a hon was equal to 12 Takas seems correct. I have frequently heard the phrase used '*sab ghode bara take*' meaning "every horse cannot be of the highest value."

Prof. Kale lays stress on the word 'Khurda' which is prefixed to Taka often. The word more often prefixed in the above Deshpande papers is Nakhtayati which means cash and hence Taka was a coin. The word 'Khurda' is no doubt interpreted in the Vyavahara-Kosha of Shivaji as copper coin. But that is not its proper meaning. Khurda means small only and not copper.

We have stated above that the authorised coin was hon (divided into Takas and Rukkas). For these alone are mentioned in revenue papers. It may be objected that papers are found mentioning rupees and annas also in this period; *e. g.* No. 14, Rajwade Khand XVIII, (p. 32) which is dated S'. 1589 S'ravana (July 1667) and which gives the revenue of three villages in Tarf-Patas as 524 rupees $15\frac{1}{2}$ annas. But we must remember that this part was in the possession of the Moguls at that time. Indeed, as stated already, since Shaistekhan's occupation in 1660 it was in Mogul possession for six years. And when Shivaji went to Agra after making peace with Jaising, he formally handed this part over to the Moguls. The Moguls used their own currency in their revenue dealings. This paper even bears the Mogul seal. Two other papers Nos. 12 and 13 belonging even to Poona give the Jamabandi in rupees for S'. 1587 and 1588 (1665 and 1666) for the same reason. These papers speak of Perganna Poona as in Sarkar Junnar, Suba Aurangabad. Indeed, if we examine these papers of the Deshpandes of Poona, we find that they belong to the period from S' 1524 to S' 1662 (A. D. 1602 to 1740) and extend over four rules *viz*: Nizamshahi, Shivashahi, Mogulshahi and Shahushahi. In the first two, money mentioned is hon, Taka and Rukka and in the last two, rupees and dams.

It may also be objected that we must see also what coin was used in Bijapur and Govalkonda states. They certainly used hons. Madras letter quoted already shows that Govalkonda had old and new hons. Other papers similarly show that Bijapur used hons. Shivaji paid tribute for territories taken in Mokasa in hons and was paid Chauth also in hons. For dealings with the Moguls, they naturally used rupees; and rupees could be had in their bazaars, as they could be had in Shivaji's.

It is curious to note the following in a Bombay letter, dated 15th December 1673 (PS 1604 ; ER 429, p. 315):— "We hope the trade into Shivaji's country will consume quantities of Europe commodities and particularly be useful for consumption of copper pice and tinnys or tin Budgrooves in great quantities, which will prove of great advantage to your mint and the expense of manufacturing of tin." What were these tin coins? Did the English insist on being paid in English pice and tinnys? Of course in the bazaar any coin is available and it is allowable for any person to ask for payment in the coin he wants. This, however, shows that English pice was much consumed in Shivaji's territory. It is possible that this induced Shivaji to strike his own copper Shivarai to replace English pice or Mahomedan Dhabbu.

IX. Chauth and Sardeshmukhi

Mr. S. N. Sen in his 'Military System of the Marathas' has an interesting article on this subject. He points out first that the idea of exacting Chauth for exemption from plunder is older than Shivaji. It appears from Portuguese papers that some Portuguese villages in Daman territory paid Chauth to the Raja of Ramnagar for this purpose even in 1579 A. D. (p. 34). We must, therefore, hold that Shivaji borrowed the idea of Chauth from the Ramnagar precedent. But we must also concede that Shivaji extended it in a manner entirely his own. He applied it to the whole of the Mogul Deccan as also to the Karnatak territory of Bijapur. It was subsequently applied under the Peshwas to the whole of the Mogul empire.

The idea is natural, however, and may be taken back even to Mediæval times. The idea itself of plundering enemy country is very old, but not older than Mahomedan times in India. Ancient Hindu kingdoms did not, we think, sanction this practice. It was first introduced by Mahmud of Ghazni and the Mahomedans, throughout subsequent history, plundered enemy countries. Malik Kafur surpassed all plunderers when he plundered the whole of Southern India upto Cape Comorin. Mahomedan plundering raids were usual before him in the days of Mahammad Ghori and were carried as far as Benares. To avoid the trouble caused by plundering raids, a tax was imposed in the kingdom of Kanauj and regularly paid to Ghazni. It is noted in inscriptions of the time and is named Turushkadanda. As pointed out in our History of Mediæval Hindu India (Vol. III, p.107), "This tax resembled the Chauth of the Marathas and the Turks kept their officers to realise it as the Marathas did in the Mogul empire." These Turks were subsequently driven away by the powerful Gahadaval kings who, however, continued to realise the tax from the people, though they did not pay it to Ghazni (*Ibid*, p. 201).

Shivaji probably did not know the plundering raids of Mahmud of Ghazni or of Muhammad Ghori; but he took up the idea of plundering enemy countries from the Mahomedans of his time. Indeed, we find it noted in Madras English letter, dated July 1648 (PS 546), that the army of Bijapur regularly maintained 8,000 men for plundering the enemy country. To raise money for maintaining a large army, Shivaji followed this example and regularly plundered enemy country every year. The idea of laying an impost in lieu of plunder was natural and Shivaji adopted and extended this system of demanding Chauth or 1/4 of the revenue for exemption from plunder.

Chauth exaction denoted in a way the subordination of the territory which paid it, but did not involve the dependency of the power which got it. But sometimes a subsidy is paid to a plundering people for refraining from plunder even by a powerful state, just as the British pay subsidies to the Afridi and other Pathan tribes for abstaining from plundering British territory. The payment of a subsidy like this does not indicate the weakness of the paying power, as it is less costly to pay subsidies than to make punitive expeditions. But the Chauth of the Marathas was not a subsidy and was often realised by their officers.

It is not possible that Chauth was paid in addition to the whole amount of revenue; it is nearly certain that the people paid $\frac{3}{4}$ of the revenue to Government and $\frac{1}{4}$ to the Marathas. That Shivaji (and the Marathas generally) respected the covenant and never plundered those who paid Chauth is proved by contemporary records (*e. g.* PS 2224; ER II, 485, dated 24 February 1680. "The towns which pay Chauth, he meddles not with.")

The ideas of plundering enemy country and of imposing a tax in lieu of plunder are old and even natural. But Shivaji applied these ideas on an extensive scale and imposed and realised Chauth towards the close of his career almost over the whole of enemy Maharashtra and on Karnatak. Even Surat paid Chauth (PS 2204) and Khandesh (Chopda, English letter, PS 2224). Hubli governor paid Chauth for Hubli Vilayat, as stated in PS 2038, dated May, 1678, to which the English factors refusing to contribute, their property was seized and sold. Even the Portuguese appear to have paid Chauth not only for Daman, but also for Bassein and other territory (though perhaps not for Goa). PS 2002 refers to Governor of Goa's letters to Annaji Datto, Subedar Prant Konkan, and Moropant Peshwa about the demand for Chauth. PS 2031, a letter from the Governor of Goa to his subordinate, dated 3rd April 1678, mentions payment of *tribute* for two years and more. Of course, it cannot be expected that Chauth was realised every year or that the exact amount was insisted upon.

Going on to Sardeshmukhi, Mr. Sen seems to doubt the statement of Justice Ranade that Shivaji first claimed Sardeshmukhi for the districts of Junnar and Ahmednagar in 1650. He thinks that the demand was first made in 1675 when in a Bombay letter, dated 1st July, we have the mention of a peace, settled between Aurangjeb and Shivaji, by which the latter was made the " Desai of all the country " and the Mogul governor was to move from

Junnar to Kalyan. We find from ER II, 101, that this is given as a rumour only and Shivaji was to be made " the Desai of all the country of Deccan, in return for the latter's delivering all the castles and country he has taken from the Moguls reserving only Saler." This word is wrongly interpreted as Satara, for Satara was not in Mogul territory and Mahuli (p. 67). This is, of course, a clear reference to the demand of Sardeshmukhi (Desai of the whole Deccan). But we have the first reference to Shivaji's asking Deshmukhi of Junnar and Ahmednagar in a letter from Murad to Shivaji, dated Nov. 30th, 1649 (PS 575). This was in reply to Shivaji's proposal made several months before, to enter Mogul service for Shahjahan's interceding in behalf of imprisoned Shahaji, as already stated. Shivaji had just begun his career by seizing Sinhgad and Purandar; he had no difficulty at this time, having revolted from Bijapur, in making this proposal.

The question is " Did Shivaji ask for the Deshmukhi of Junnar and Ahmednagar as a new grant or on the basis of any old claim?" So far as can be seen, there were no old Deshmukhs of prants as yet and this was the small beginning of the larger idea of Sardeshmukhi–a word probably first used by Shivaji. Our surmise is that Shivaji claimed the Deshmukhis of Junnar and Nagar as of right. Shahaji had conquered the setwo districts for the[illegible] themselves before 1633, when they were [illegible]h-khan. Nay, it is possible that wh[illegible] Nizamshah at Pemgiri, he had [illegible] for hi[illegible] Deshmukhis of Junnar and Ahmednagar. But this surmise can only be confirmed if the original letter of Shivaji addressed to Murad be found, so that it may be determined whether Shivaji asked for a new gift or an old claim.

Whatever this may be, it cannot be doubted that this was the origin of the subsequent demand for the 'Desaiship of the Deccan,' in other words, Sardeshmukhi. The office was to carry ten percent of the revenue as emolument. The Deshmukhs of Taluqs or Mahals got four percent and the Deshpandes two percent, as appears from Rajwade Khand XX, p. 108, dated Margashirsha S'. 1617 (December 1695). This was after the death of Shivaji and this also relates to perganna Shirwal which was a part of Shivaji's state since long. There is no proof yet found showing Shivaji's realising Sardeshmukhi in Mogul territory. But he undoubtedly made the proposal which fructified after him in the days of Shahu who got Chauth and Sardeshmukhi by an imperial farman in Mogul dominions.

Ranade states at pp. 223-4 (Rise of the Maratha Power) "In 1668 Bijapur agreed to pay three lakhs of rupees as Chauth and Sardeshmukhi and Govalkonda agreed to pay five lakhs about the same time. In 1671 Chauth and Sardeshmukhi were levied from the Mogul province of Khandesh. In 1674, Portuguese possessions in Konkan paid tribute by way of Chauth and Sardeshmukhi." Sen doubts this and says that "unless the treaties of Bijapur and Govalkonda are before us, we cannot say that the tributes were paid by way of Chauth and Sardeshmukhi." In our opinion Sen is right so far as Sardeshmukhi is concerned; it could not have been levied from any of the southern kingdoms. Ranade seems to have put the two 'Chauth and Sardeshmukhi' together improperly. He bases his statements on Bakhars which jumble matters often. Tribute was, no doubt, paid by Bijapur and Govalkonda as is noted by contemporary English and other papers found. Parṇālākhyāna mentions tribute as paid by the Portuguese and even the Siddi. It was levied from Bednur and Soonda. But it did not mean Chauth; nor certainly Sardeshmukhi which, from these, was out of question.

The idea of Sardeshmukhi might have been borrowed from Sardesais, as Mr. Bendre and Mr. Apte think, the Mavlankar Sardesais being so styled before Shivaji. But as with Chauth, the idea was there and in Konkan. Shivaji took it up and extended it to the Mogul dominions. For there were no Sardeshmukhis then in the Ghat-Matha country nor in Mogul Maharashtra. Even now, there are no Sardeshmukhs in Berar and the Nizam state Maharashtra, nor in Maharashtra proper. Desai is a word derived from Des'apati, a Mediæval word. Sardesais of course arose in Mahomedan times only, as 'sar' shows. The Sardesais are the same as Sardeshmukhs, a word used by Shivaji himself in his Sanad to the Mavalankars of Prabhanvalli; see his sanad in इतिहास and ऐतिहासिक, p. 5. dated Vais'akh 5 1584 (May 1652). But we know that Shivaji had already in 1649 laid claim to Sardeshmukhi in Nagar and Nasik territory and had probably no hesitation to use the word Sardeshmukhi We have shown elsewhere that Deshmukhs were the creations of the Bahamani rule, the word not being used in Mediæval days. We feel sure that there were no Sardeshmukhs in Maharashtra before or in Shivaji's time. Thus, in Shirval papers, Khand XVIII, p. 98, among Kadim (old) Inams, only Deshmukhs are mentioned. They got 4% on the revenue. For the Sardeshmukhi we find 10% assigned in a paper dated S'. 1617 (1695 A. D.). It would be interesting to compare the Sardesai's share with that of Sardeshmukh.

Lastly, Sen also questions the view of Justice Ranade that this idea of Shivaji was taken by the Marquis of

Wellesley in his subsidiary alliances, which deprived the protected states of independence in foreign relations. Here again Sen is right, though partly. Payment of Chauth did not involve dependence of the payer, but Sardeshmukhi indicated the dependence of the Deshmukh, as it involved providing of sufficient force to keep peace and otherwise assist the administration. The Marathas in Shahu's time kept a large force at Delhi for protection. But neither Chauth nor Sardeshmukhi involved the giving up by the protected state of any power of dealing independently with foreign states. This development was no doubt born out of the greater diplomacy of Wellesley. But the Sardeshmukh, though a servant, became the master, because he provided the military power. The nation always falls eventually which seeks the help of a foreign army for protection or any other purpose. The later emperors of Delhi were eaten up by the Marathas and the Marathas in their turn by the English, as the Persians were eaten up by the Turks and the Romans by the Prætorian German guards.

X. ADDITIONAL NOTES

(**Page 12**) :—Kumarila has the following on S'abara Bhashya on the word Raja in the sutra राजा राजसूयेन यजेत of Jaimini जनपदपुररक्षणमकुर्वत्यपि क्षत्रिये राजशब्दमुपयुञ्जन्ते आन्ध्राः which means " A Kshatriya though not following the profession of protecting town and country is called Raja among Andhras. " On this Kumarila adds the gloss दाक्षिणात्यसामान्येन भाष्यकारेण आन्ध्राणामित्युक्तम्। "The Bhashyakara uses the word Andhra generally for the Dakshinatyas."

or Marathas. Kumarila belongs to the 8th century and hence even in his days, ordinary Marathas called themselves Rajas. In Andhra even now Kshatriyas are called Rajas.

(**Page 17**) :—Mr. Y. M. Kale of Buldhana doubts the statement in *Shiva-Bharata* that Maloji died in 1606, because (1) in Khanda 15, No. 460, there is a mention of Maloji and Vithoji granting land in S'. 1531 (A. D. 1609) and (2) a paper found by him in Khedle dated *isane isarin alaf* (1621 A. D.) mentions Maloji Raje. He thinks that Maloji died in 1621 or S'. 1543. But Mr. Kale does not note that in Khanda 15, No. 372, Maloji is mentioned as Marham though his name and that of Vithoji are given together. This is dated S'. 1529, S'ravana (1607 August). The subsequent documents mention Vithoji alone *e. g.* No. 375 of S'. 1533 (1611 A. D.). These two facts make it necessary to hold that No. 400 mentions the gift of Maloji and Vithoji not of that date, but one previously made and (2) that Maloji in the Khedla document of 1621 is another person and not Maloji Bhosle, grand-father of Shivaji and brother of Vithoji. We always find Maloji and Vithoji mentioned together and with Bhosle added.

(**Page 23**) :—Des'agata means the territory over which the Desai enjoyed his rights or exercised his power.

(**Page 48**) :—Shivaji was not styled Maharaj for some time, probably till Shahaji was alive. Thus Shahaji is styled Maharaj and Shivaji simply Raja in PS 662, 655, 650, dated 1653 and 1654.

(**Page 53**) :—That the plan for founding Hindvi Swaraj was formed as early as 1645 A. D. is also proved by PS 503, 504, 506. The first is an order to Dadaji Naras

Prabhu, Deshpande and Kulkarni, Rohidkhede, dated 30th March 1645. It mentions that Shivaji has rebelled and taken possession of a fort in the Khore and called it Rajgad and that collecting men, Dadaji had joined Shivaji. The order calls Dadaji back to obedience and to his vatan. PS 504 is a letter by Shivaji to Dadaji referring to this order from the Vazier of Bijapur. It tells him that the Svayambhu god Rohideshvara (deity of that mountain) has inspired Shivaji to establish *Hindvi Swaraj*; (Dadajipant referred to in this letter is not Dadaji Konddev); and asks him to be firm, assuring him that God wishes that there should be this Rajya. PS 506 is an order from the Diwan again calling upon Dadaji to return to allegiance and assuring him that his vatan would be continued, if recommended by Bandal, Khopde and Jedhe at Shirval.

It must be noted that the fort Rajgad was taken by Shivaji, because it was in his jagir limits, being to the north of the Nira. There was no regular Bijapur force there, for the words are किल्यावरील ठाणें उठवून आपण किल्यांत शिरला. The fort was not in repair also as such forts were under the supervision of the Deshpandes or Deshmukhs. It seems that Shivaji took this fort with the help of Dadaji Naras Prabhu, Deshpande of Rohidkhore and Velavandkhore, who was thus the first to join Shivaji's cause. Shivaji rebuilt and strengthened this fort and called it Rajgad. This was in 1645 and Dadaji Konddev was still alive.

Bandal, Khopde and even Jedhe were at this time against Shivaji and informed Bijapur of these proceedings through the Shirval Thana.

Chakan similarly was not in Shivaji's possession, though it was to the south of the Bhima and in Shahaji's jagir. Shahaji's officer Firangoji Narsala gave possession of Chakan and its fort to Shivaji without any opposition and we have, therefore, shown Chakan as within Shivaji's original fief in the map attached.

(**Page 72**):—Ibrahim Adilshah usually spoke Marathi and accounts were kept in the Bijapur kingdom in Marathi. Even now Kanarese speaking traders in that part keep accounts in Marathi.

(**Page 76**) :—Jijaya tax appears to have been put in force in Khandesh even in Shahjahan's time from 1594 A. D. See Raver Deshmukh's letter. (BISM Quarterly XII)

(**Page 104**) :—Ekangi may refer also to the Yekang method of single sword fighting and wrestling described by Ferishta (Briggs, Vol. III, p. 207).

(**Page 194**) :—Madari Mehter's descendants served as Faras with the Bhosle kings till the last Shahu. Shivaji on his safe return from Agra gave to Madari and his descendants the right to take the coverings of the throne at the time of every coronation. See letter published by Chandorkar (BISM Vol. X).

(**Page 251**) :—PS 2226, ER II 487, p. 299, dated 27th February 1680, states " You should show the *red* paper *i. e.* our articles of peace signed by the Raja and the *white* paper *i. e.* a letter from Annaji Datto." It thus seems that kings signed a red paper embodying articles of a covenant. Does this throw any light on Clive's use of a red and a white paper in connection with Umichand ?

(**Page 252**) :—Vratya means a Brahmin or Kshatriya, or Vais'ya who is devoid of Vedic rites for years or even generations. Vratya ceremony is a sacrifice prescribed for taking such Dvijas into the Vedic fold.

(**Page 283**) :—The following may be quoted from a narrative given by Orme of an unnamed traveller who was an eye-witness to Shivaji's visit to Govalkonda. (ER II 539, p. 349).

" Shivaji was encamped with 12,000 foot and 24,000 horse, three leagues from the town. I saw the departure of this marauder with troops of whose fidelity, especially of his body-guards, he had no doubt.

Shivaji saw the king at the palace. He entered by one door and his attendants, who were permitted, by another. The king came by another. Both then sat down on seats prepared for them and entered into conversation. While they were talking, the palace was surrounded by 6,000 cavalry who approached so silently that even the buzzing of a fly could have been heard. I saw this all from a window. He like a second Masaniello (?) was loved and respected by his subjects. "

XI. CHRONOLOGY

Birth of Shahaji	1601
Death of Maloji	1606
Birth of Ramadas	1608
Shahaji's Marriage with Jijau	1617
Battle of Bhātavadi in which Malik Amber defeated Moguls and Bijapuris combined and Shahaji distinguished himself	Oct. 1624
Death of Malik Amber	May 1626
Shahajahan ascends the throne	April 1628
Ibrahim Adilshah dies	19 April 1629
Lukhaji Jadhav murdered	24 July 1629
Birth of Shivaji	18 Feb. 1630
Fattehkhan released and made minister	18 Jan. 1631
Burhan killed by Fattehkhan	1632

Shahaji places new Nizam on gadi at Pemgiri	Oct. 1632
Shahaji besieged at Mahuli	1633
Shahaji enters Adilshahi service	1636
Shivaji jagirdar of Poona	1645
Shivaji takes Rajgad in his plan of Hindvi Swaraj	1645
Shahaji arrested by Mustafakhan	25 July 1648
Shahaji released	16 May 1649
Shivaji takes Jawali	15 Jan. 1656
Shivaji takes Rairi	May 1656
Muhammad Adilshah dies	Nov.-Dec. 1656
Shivaji plunders Junnar	May 1657
Shivaji marries—daughter of Gaikwad	Feb. 1657
" " " of Jadhav	8 April 1657
" " " of Ingle	May 1657
Shivaji has son Sambhaji	14 May 1657
Shivaji fights with Naushirkhan at Ahmednagar	June 1657
Aurangjeb takes Bedar	4 June 1657
Shivaji takes Kalyan-Bhivandi before Divali day	24 Oct. 1657
Badi Sahebin murders Khan Muhammad	11 Nov. 1657
Aurangjeb goes towards Delhi	Dec. 1657
Fattehkhan poisoned at Bijapur	Dec. 1657
Bahilolkhan also poisoned	July-Aug. 1658
Sonajipant sent to Delhi	30 Oct. 1658
Aurangjeb ascends the throne	5 June 1659
Adilshah orders Deshmukh Jedhe &c. to assist Afzalkhan	April 1659
Shivaji comes to Jawali	10 July 1659
Saibai, Shivaji's first wife, dies	5 Sep. 1659
Afzalkhan sends Krinshnarao Hejib to Shivaji at Pratapgad	Oct.-Nov. 1659

Afzalkhan comes to Pratapgad to meet Shivaji and is killed	10 Nov. 1659
Shivaji takes Panhala	28 Nov. 1659
„ raids Bijapur territory and collects tribute upto Gadag Lakshmeshwar	16 Jan. 1660
Battle near Kolhapur	Jan. 1660
Shivaji asks Kavaji Kondhalkar and Vaghoji Tupe from Jedhe and makes them Hazaris of Hashams	March 1660
Shivaji comes again to Panhala	2 March 1660
„ takes Vasota	June 1660
„ goes from Panhala to Khelna and Baji Prabhu was killed	13 July 1660
Shivaji gives Panhala to Salabatkhan	22 Sep. 1660
Shaistakhan takes Chakan fort	Sep. 1660
Sonopant comes to Rajgad with message from Shaistakhan	Oct.–Nov. 1660
Moropant Pingle is given Majmu	2 Jan. 1661
Shivaji plunders Nizampur (Rajapur), Dabhol and Prabhanvalli	Jan.–Feb. 1661
Kahartalab Khan defeated in Umberkhind	2 Feb. 1661
Shivaji takes Sringarpur	29 April 1661
Narahari Anandrao appointed Peshwa	21 Oct. 1661
Dehrigad besieged by Bulakhi	1661
Siddi Johar fled to Kelosi, is defeated by Ali and dies	1661
Namdarkhan attacked at Pen, Mirya Dongar	1662
Moropant appointed Peshwa and Nilo Sondev Mujumdar	3 April 1662
Anajipant made Surnis	16 Oct. 1662
Surprise attack on Shaistakhan	5 April 1663

Shahaji dies	23 Jan. 1664
Shivaji returns to Rajgad from Konkan	5 Feb. 1664
Khawaskhan attacks Kudal, war declared between Shivaji and Bijapur	Oct.-Nov. 1664
Bajaji Ghorpade killed	„ 1664
Jaswantsing besieges Kondhana	Nov.-Dec. 1664
Khudawantpur plundered	Nov. Dec. 1664
Jijabai weighed against gold at Mahabaleshwar	6 Jan. 1665
Shivaji went to Basnur in ships	Feb. 1665
Sonajipant dies	25 Jan. 1665
Shivaji comes to Purandar to meet Jaising	31 Mar. 1665
Purandar besieged by Dilerkhan	April-May 1665
Peace with Jaising	12 June 1665
Adilshah attacked by the three	Nov.-Dec. 1665
Shivaji starts for Agra with Sambhaji	5 Mar. 1666
Meets Aurangjeb and is confined at Agra	25 May 1666
Escape from Agra in a box	17 August 1666
Trimbakpant and Raghunath Korde arrested at Agra	20 August 1666
Shivaji returns to Rajgad	20 Nov. 1666
Pirkhan and Tajkhan killed	Dec. 1666
Peace with Aurangjeb and मुलखाची बटाई	3 April 1667
Bahilolkhan and Vyankoji besiege Rangna but are driven away	April-May 1667
Peace with Adilshah	8 Oct. 1667
Sambhaji goes to Aurangabad; peace with Moguls	27 Oct. 1667
Meets Jaswant and returns to Rangna	4 Nov. 1667
Prataprao and Niraji went to Aurangabad with army	5 August 1668
Aurangjeb destroys Kashi temple	Sep.-Oct. 1669

Peace broken between Mogul and Shivaji and Prataprao and Anandrao returned with army to Rajgad	Dec.-Jan. 1669
Kondhana taken and Udebhan killed	4 Feb. 1670
Rajaram born at Rajgad	24 Feb. 1670
Nilopant Mujumdar took Purandar	8 Mar. 1670
Junnar besieged. Surat sacked on Divali	4 Oct. 1670
Fight near Dindori with Daudkhan	17 Oct. 1670
Trimbakgad taken by Moropant	Nov. 1670
Ahiwant, Rawla Jawla, Markanda taken	Nov.-Dec. 1670
Saleri taken	Dec.-Jan. 1670
Lohagad taken	13 May 1670
Mahuli taken, Thursday	16 June 1670
Rohida taken	24 June 1670
Mahabatkhan takes back Ahiwant	Apr.-May 1670
Bahdurshah and Diler besiege Saleri	May-Jan. 1671
They raise seige and go to Aurangabad	Sep. 1671
Moropant breaks the siege of Saleri	Jan. 1672
Prataprao and Anandrao seize Bahilolkhan, Mohokamsing and Darkoji Bhosle	Jan. 1672
Moropant takes Jawhar and Ramnagar	June-July 1672
Abdulla Kutubshah dies	21 May 1672
Ali-Adilshah dies, Shikandar placed on throne, Khavaskhan becomes minister, peace broken and Punde returns	Nov.-Dec. 1672
Nirajipant brought 66,000 hons from Bhaganagar	21 May 1672
Panhala taken by Annajipant	6 Mar. 1673
Shivaji goes from Raigad to Panhala	9 Mar. 1673
Prataprao fights and conquers Bahilol	Mar.-Ap. 1673
Parali fort taken	1 April 1673
Satara taken on Sunday	27 July 1673

Shivaji plunders Bankapur on Dasara	10 Oct. 1673
Vithoji Shinde killed in battle with Sarjekhan	Oct.-Nov. 1673
Prataprao killed in battle with Bahilol on Shivaratri day at Nivati	24 Feb. 1674
Shivaji plunders Sampagaon	23 March 1674
Shivaji takes Kelanja	24 April 1674
Shivaji's Munja with Vedic rites	29 May 1674
Shivaji's Coronation	6 June 1674
Shivaji's mother dies at Pachad	17 June 1674
Sambhaji's Munja	4 Feb. 1675
Phonda besieged	6 March 1675
Phonda taken	17 April 1675
Shivaji reviews army at Chiplun and Hambirrao appointed Sarnobat	18 April 1675
Ankola Siweshwar taken	May-June 1675
Satara taken	11 Nov. 1675
Bahilolkhan seizes Khavaskhan	18 Nov. 1675
Sambhaji went to Sringarpur	Nov. 1675
Bahadurkhan and Bahilol fight at Halgi	1 June 1676
Netaji Palkar takes प्रायश्चित्त	19 June 1676
Hussenkhan Maina defeated near Gadag by Waghoji, Sarjakhan and Jedhe died	Dec.-Jan. 1677
Shivaji meets Bhaganagar king	Feb.-Mar. 1677
,, takes Chanji and whole of Karnatak	Mar.-Sep. 1677
,, defeats Sherkhan near Tripati	7 July 1677
Bahadurshah takes Lal Darga at Bijapur	July 1677
,, takes Naldurg from Ranamastkhan	July-Aug. 1677
Shivaji meets Ekoji	11 August 1677
,, takes Vadrachal and his whole Prant and besieges Kolar	11 August 1677
Bahadurkhan replaced by Dilerkhan	Sep.-Oct. 1677

Sarjakhan, Masaudkhan and Bhaganagar fought with Dilerkhan who retired to Naldurga	Sep.-Oct. 1677
Raghunath Narayan Hanmante made Mujumdar and Suba of Jinji	Sep.-Oct. 1677
Shivaji came to Gadag	Oct.-Nov. 1678
Ekoji fights with Hambirrao near Ahir; makes peace with cession of Kolarkot	Oct.-Nov. 1677
Moropant Peshwa plundered Nasik	Nov.-Dec. 1677
Bahilolkhan died, Masaud Karbhari	Dec.-Jan. 1677
Gadag Prant taken; Shivaji comes to Raigad	May-June 1678
Vellore taken by Raghunathpant	22 July 1678
Sambhaji flees to Dilerkhan	Dec. 1678
Earthquake	28 Jan. 1679
Shah Alam viceroy at Aurangabad	25 Feb. 1679
Moropant Peshwa took fort Kopal	3 March 1679
Anandrao takes Balapur	10 March 1679
Dilerkhan takes Bhopalgad (Khed)	2 April 1679
Shamji Naik sent to Bijapur	26 August 1679
Dilerkhan besieges Bijapur	Oct. 1679
Adilshah and Shivaji at peace	Oct.-Nov. 1679
Shivaji plunders Jalna ; fights with Ranamast; returns to Raigad via Patta	,, ,,
Sambhaji returns and meets Shivaji	Nov.-Dec. 1679
Adilshah and Mogul at peace	Jan.-Feb. 1680
Rajaram married	15 March 1680
Shivaji died at Rajgad, Saturday noon	3 April 1680

SUPPLEMENT TO CHRONOLOGY

(Some additions and emendations)

Shivaji's first marriage with Saibai of Nimbalkar family	1640
,, second marriage with Shirke	1644
Shivaji asks for Sardesaiship of Nagar and Nasik	1649
Shivaji's third marriage with Mohite	1653
First sack of Surat	6 Jan. 1664
Shivaji attacks Mudhol and Baji Ghorpade killed	end of Jan. 1664
Shivaji drives away Azizkhan from Kudal	May 1664
Sambhaji leaves Dilerkhan	Dec. 1679
Shivaji meets Sambhaji at Panhala	15 Jan. 1680
Dilerkhan makes peace with Bijapur	end of Jan. 1680

INDEX TO NAMES AND PLACES

SHIVAJI'S KINGDOM (1680)

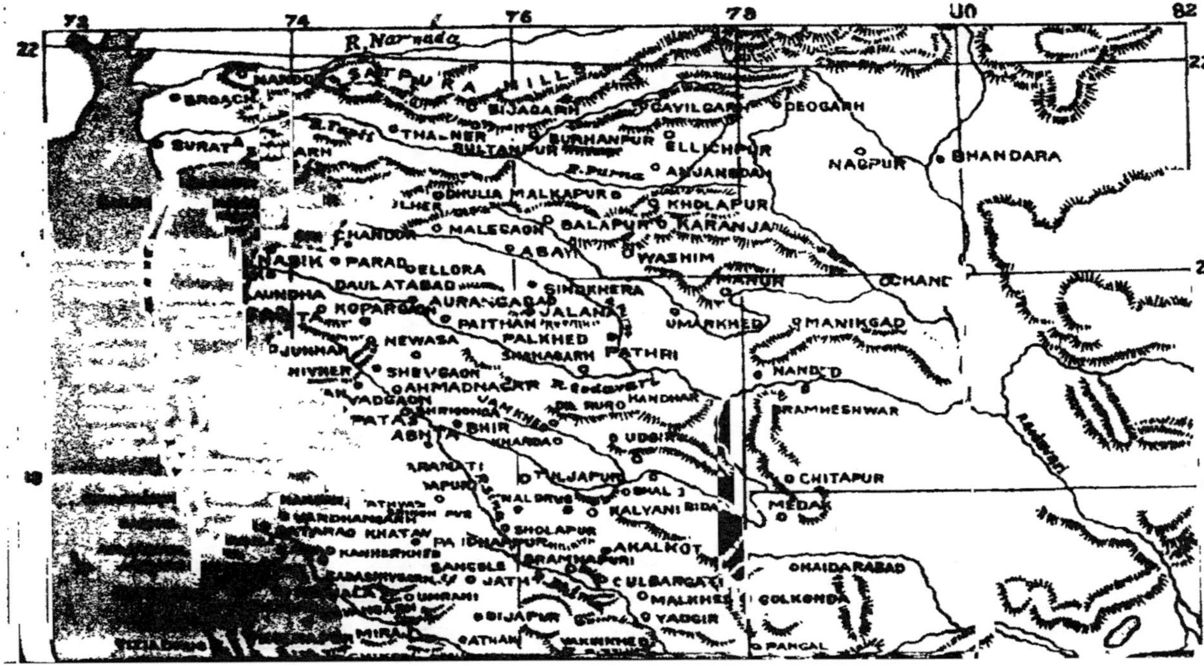

PHOTO-ZINCO, POONA. 2-1931.